THE POLITICS OF REGICIDE IN ENGLAND, 1760–1850

MANCHESTER
UNIVERSITY PRESS

For Janette and Tom,
but also for Neil Maclean, mad man

The politics of regicide in England, 1760–1850

Troublesome subjects

STEVE POOLE

MANCHESTER UNIVERSITY PRESS
Manchester and New York

distributed exclusively in the USA by St. Martin's Press

Published by Manchester University Press
Oxford Road, Manchester M13 9NR, UK
and Room 400, 175 Fifth Avenue, New York, NY 10010, USA
www.manchesteruniversitypress.co.uk

Distributed exclusively in the USA by
Palgrave, 175 Fifth Avenue, New York NY 10010, USA

Distributed exclusively in Canada by
UBC Press, University of British Columbia, 2029 West Mall,
Vancouver, BC, Canada V6T 1Z2

British Library Cataloguing-in-Publication Data
A catalogue record for this book is available from the British Library

Library of Congress Cataloging-in-Publication Data
A catalog record for this book is available from the Library of Congress

ISBN 978 0 7190 5035 0 *hardback*
ISBN 978 0 7190 8746 2 *paperback*

First published by Manchester University Press 2000

First digital paperback edition published 2012

Printed by Lightning Source

Contents

List of illustrations

Acknowledgements

Many people have helped me with advice, conversation and ideas over the last five years whilst this book was being gestated.

I particularly want to thank the British Academy, whose award of a post doctoral fellowship made early research and planning possible; my friends and colleagues at the University of the West of England, Bristol, who gave me a year's teaching-leave to get it finished; and the staff at Manchester University Press for being so patient about overlooked deadlines. My Ph.D. supervisor, John Styles, nurtured my interest in the peculiarities of 'loyalism' and petitioning in late eighteenth-century England. At UWE, the teaching of the late Roger Cranshaw helped me read history as culture, and Mary Gormally helped me apply that to Queen Victoria; and all of my present colleagues have kept me going with scholarly encouragement, personal good humour and a constant supply of cheap instant coffee. Getting immersed in a monograph has occasionally done terrible things to my enthusiasm for the subject. At various times and in various places, a number of people have made positive noises about my work and made me realise there was 'something in it' after all. They might have forgotten, but I have not (!): Dorothy Thompson, Greg Claeys, Roger Wells, John Barrell, John Money, Malcolm Chase, Stephen White, Hannah Barker, Nick Rogers, Jim Sack, and Flora Fraser. I have also received generous help from the staff of the Public Record Office and the British Library, and from Edwina Ehrman at the Museum of London, Patricia Allderidge at the Bethlem Archive, and Sheila de Bellaigue at the Royal Archive. I acknowledge the gracious permission of Her Majesty the Queen to make use of material stored there.

Professional debts are one thing; personal debts are another. Geoffrey Poole spent long hours expertly pouring over his Bible in pursuit of intercessionary women, and Roger, Fiona, Charley and Alex Kiff, who preside over the most convivial free floor-space in London, have often fed me to excess and plied me with drink. But my biggest debts are to Janette Kerr who put up with all kinds of nonsense, surrounded me with love and gave me the mental and physical space to single-mindedly finish the work, and to Tom Poole-Kerr, who now equates the social role of the historian with the prevention of computer gaming.

1

Introduction: monarchy, contractualism and history

Monarchy and the historical imagination

At the Temple of Reason and Humanity in Wych Street, London, in the autumn of 1795, a radical orator, John Gale Jones, delivered an extraordinary address about the consequences of a recent attack on the King's coach. Government's proposed legislation to muzzle the English freedoms of speech and assembly was an over-reaction, he argued, for the situation was anything but unique.

> Is this the first time that the King has been insulted or attacked? Has not a knife been directed against his life by Margaret Nicholson? Was not the King alarmed by Stone? And by the pistol fired by Sutherland, the unfortunate suicide? Did we then hear anything about a Convention Bill? No.[1]

Jones was not only displaying an impressive knowledge of obscure past events here, but assuming a familiarity with them on the part of his audience. The names may mean nothing to us. Yet Margaret Nicholson was assigned to an asylum in 1786 after attempting to stab George III outside St James's Palace. She had petitioned him for assistance more than twenty times without a single reply. A year later, Thomas Stone was sent to join her after persistently trying to gain access to the palace and believing himself in love with the Princesses. The third figure, James Sutherland, did not try to kill the King or marry his daughters, but presented a pistol to his own breast in front of the royal coach in 1791. He too had been a frequent but frustrated petitioner of the Crown. Jones's invocation of these now largely forgotten men and women gives the lie to their obscurity. What unites them is a shared belief in the close and reciprocal relationship between monarch and subject. Their apparent inability to understand the *limits* of that relationship has been the reason for their marginalisation, their dismissal as lunatics and their historical obscurity. But I begin here with the premises that their 'madness' was not unique or even unusual in Hanoverian England, and that, while their reality may not be ours, it nevertheless deserves investigation.

The discourse of royal reciprocity is not one with which we are familiar. Contemporary commentators were sometimes similarly puzzled when confronted by its most unacceptable aspect, the practice of assaulting the monarch The seemingly unprovoked outrages of even the best-known assailants – Nicholson, Frith, Hadfield, Collins, Oxford, Francis and Bean – were shocking and memorable, but rarely understood. When John Francis shot at Queen Victoria in 1842, the political diarist Charles Greville, for one, could not explain it:

> There is no semblance of insanity in the Assassin and no apparent motive or reason for the crime. This young Queen, who is an object of interest, and has made no enemies, has twice had attempts made on her life within two years. George III, a very popular King, was exposed to similar attempts, but in his case the perpetrators were really insane; while George IV, a man neither beloved nor respected, and at different times very odious and unpopular, was never attacked by anyone.[2]

If relative levels of unpopularity are not a useful index to the incidence of assault, and if we are not going take refuge in the levelling and language of undiscriminating madness, how are we to understand it? The argument of the following pages is both constitutional and contractual, and its starting-point is the custom and practice of petition, remonstrance and resistance. I am not concerned with the fashionable exposure of myths about the monarchy, but I am concerned with some of the mythologies of the Constitution – their popular reading, and the consequences of that reading on the functional stability of the State. While it is easy to argue that the British monarchy never really had a tangibly contractual basis, there is no more point in doing so than in pointing out that there is no such thing as the English Constitution. What matters is whether people believed in it, and whether contractualism influenced the behaviour of either the monarch or the monarch's subjects. Historiographically, my interest lies somewhere between that of Marilyn Morris and Linda Colley in the 'apotheosis' of royalty, and that of their critics who stress the insurrectionary disloyalty of the masses.[3] My inspiration, on the other hand, comes from the urging of James Epstein and John Belchem that we take constitutionalism seriously without thereby oversimplifying it.[4]

Practical Hanoverian contractualism, it is argued here, was played out within the boundaries of an imagined distance between monarch and subject, governing the degree to which a given monarch, at any given time, was understood to be accessible to his or her subjects. Royal space was (and is) purely imaginary, but its contraction and expansion were apparent nevertheless, usually as a function of the warp and weft of radical and loyalist politics. The basis of contractualism lay in the 'Glorious Revolution' of 1688,[5] a mythical event in itself, and the protection offered by the Bill of Rights in 1689 to the right of petition. The custom and practice of approaching the throne, in person, with petitions of right (that is, petitions from individuals seeking the resolution of a personal problem, often related to disputed property or remuneration from the state for services rendered), or with collective petitions of grievance (usually political), were believed inviolable. It was understood that the King welcomed personal contact with his subjects and owed them his care and intercession as a contractual condition of their allegiance. This book considers the shifting boundaries of royal space as the flexible arena in which petitioning took place. It begins with the creation of a myth of accessibility and 'ordinariness' around the monarchy of George III in the 1780s, a response to both the French Revolution and the King's domestic unpopularity during the first twenty years of his reign. And it ends with a retreat from the myth of accessibility under Victoria through a rescripting of 'ordinariness' in which privacy and respectability count for more than the hearty boisterousness of the Georgian John Bull.

Historiographical interest in the monarchy is limited in its conceptual scope. Most studies focus on the enduring popularity and survival of the Crown, either with reference to its mythologies and 'invented traditions'[6] or to the institutional conservatism of plebeian English patriotism. Petitioning is seen as increasingly inclusive and popular, facilitated by a developing public sphere and the mass platform, and associated with collectivity rather than individuality.[7] Petitions of right are often overlooked and little distinction is noted between petitions to Parliament and petitions to the Crown.[8] Historiographical approaches to troublesome subjects like Nicholson commonly accommodate eighteenth-century agendas of unquestioning madness,[9] or else deploy twentieth-century terminologies like 'terrorism'. Franklin L. Ford has charted the classical roots of 'legitimate' tyrannicide from the ancient Greeks to the Red Army Faction, but has difficulty in accommodating the apparent ineptitude of English would-be assassins like Nicholson. In finding answers to the question of why so few European monarchs were assassinated in the 'age of Enlightenment', Ford discovers nothing about the motivation of the men and women who harassed and irritated George III, but perhaps never meant to kill him. Nicholson's attempt, he tells us, was not only ineffectual but 'trivial'; whereas the attempt of Hadley (Hadfield) in 1800 was 'much more dangerous' because it involved a shot from a gun that could have killed the King if only the 'demented' assailant's aim had been better.[10] Ford has simply misunderstood what was going on.

While the anthropological meanings of royal rituals around the world have received attention from a growing number of sociologically inclined scholars,[11] the *nature* of the relationship between monarchs and subjects has not. Under the influence of E. P. Thompson, left-leaning English social histories have either ignored the Crown or seen it as an obstructing or occasionally supporting factor in collective popular struggles against 'Old Corruption' and towards institutional democracy. John Cannon once detected 'almost a conspiracy' of indifference about the survival of the monarchy, for 'neglect is too mild a word'. Yet Cannon too confined himself to an institutional explanation for continuity.[12] As Jeremy Black has pointed out, this rather impersonal emphasis is partly the legacy of concerns that occupied nineteenth-century Whig historians.[13] If the traditional Left has never seemed much interested in the false consciousness of monarchism, the Right has rarely shown an interest in the social dimension. Conservative historians have asked few questions about reception and audience, and remain prone to glib statements of self-congratulation. John S. Moore recently stated the case for the integrity of monarchy by contrasting it with Bolshevism, and castigating those British intellectuals and historians, from the Webbs to Bertrand Russell, E. H. Carr and Eric Hobsbawm, who once had the 'effrontery' to turn their backs on 1,500 years of tradition and embrace the Soviet republican experiment. But he offered a no more profound vision of constitutional history. In Moore's England, monarchical continuity has simply bequeathed a nation of happy, well-clothed, ale-tipplers in well-kept cottages secure from the European indignities of brown bread and eviction at the hands of unenlightened tyrants.[14] For John Derry, 'the greatest shift of political feeling in the 1790s was the eruption of patriotic loyalism, staunchly opposed to anything savouring of French ideas',[15] but there is no suggestion that any of this 'loyalism' was qualified by contract theory or complicated by Epstein and Belchem's notion of a radical constitutionalism.

On the cultural side, Hobsbawm and Ranger's *Invention of Tradition* collection of 1983 still casts a long shadow over the academy. David Cannadine's influential contribution argued that British society was stabilized and its institutional politics preserved in the nineteenth century through the manipulative 'invention' of 'ancient' monarchical pageants, ceremonies and rituals, the function of which was to keep the industrial masses in order through the lavish pantomime of royal spectacle. But royal ceremonials were shambolic until the 1867 Reform Act enfranchised the working class and kick-started the elite into a defence of tradition.[16] Cannadine's principal concern was with the exposure of mythology in the name of liberal and meritocratic rationality. The equally impacting later work of his partner Linda Colley on the cultural and social *construction* of George III's 'apotheosis' is a logical outcome of the 'invention' thesis. Colley's work continues the drift away from belief in the binary oppositions of 'loyalism' and 'radicalism', but the unqualified loyal enthusiasm of Georgian Britons, expressed in such phenomena as 'Volunteering' against the French, is not significantly questioned.[17] Scholarly interest in a more contested idea of loyalism has coincided with spreading uncertainty about structural theory and a consequent loss of faith in the paradigm of social class and its attendant ideologies. Notwithstanding the ease with which James Sack accommodates the anachronistic phrase 'right-wing' in his study of Toryism in the long eighteenth century,[18] radicalism, patriotism and loyalism, once common shorthand for 'proto-left' and 'proto-right', have now become categories often without clear ideological boundaries or neat lines of trajectory to the politics of modernity. Interest in monarchy from these perspectives has been shown in two specific areas, other than that of the popularity of George III: the 'Queen' Caroline affair of 1820; and the monarchy of Queen Victoria. Fresh cultural and feminist approaches to the Caroline affair have substantially revised our view of both popular radicalism and the activities of women in the public sphere; while the reign of Victoria has provoked scholars of a more literary and cultural bent to re-appraise representations of gender, power, politics and domesticity.[19]

From the 1990s, some significant challenges to Cannadine's 'invented tradition' thesis should also be noted. William Kuhn's examination of the later Victorian monarchy rejects what he sees as Cannadine's misreading of Geertzian cultural anthropology and urges a more sympathetic understanding of the importance and value of myth-making in history. Cannadine's work, complains Kuhn, has too easily been appropriated by republican polemicists like Tom Nairn and Christopher Hitchens who believe 'myths have no place in a manly, rational, forward-looking and enlightened society'.[20] Cannadine has also been tackled more empirically by Walter Arnstein. The idea that successful pageantry began in 1867 is nonsense, he argues, and cites evidence of widespread popular enthusiasm for Queen Victoria's State Openings of Parliament throughout the 1840s; for her coronation and marriage, and for her trips to the industrial provinces with her dutorious Consort.[21]

Other challenges have arrived in more hagiographic mode. Frank Prochaska's detailed account of the role of the Crown in welfare provision conjures unbroken lines of charitable royal largesse from George III to Elizabeth II. The book is packed with apocryphal tales of kindness to the poor from one monarch or another and is generally disapproving of contemporary radical critiques of royal idleness and narcissism; such complainants 'rarely seeing beneath the surface'. Prochaska's work actually fills an important gap in royalist scholarship, but his wholesale acceptance of bounty as *welfare* seriously compromises his critical distance so that, for example, the hugely unpopular Queen Adelaide is eulogised as the perfect queen on the strength of her charitable generosity. The point Prochaska repeatedly misses with all his impressive spadework in the Royal Archive, however, is that while it may be true that successive monarchs secured their institutional safety and personal popularity through almsgiving and charitable endowments, their fundamentally *contractual* status persuaded many Britons that such tender mercies were as much a constitutional *right* as a privilege. Increased expectation and demand were often as much in evidence as were awe-struck gratitude, and the practical inability of the Crown to alleviate poverty and misfortune on a national scale sometimes made even well-intentioned kings more vulnerable than adored.[22]

Traditional studies of *opposition* to monarchy have largely confined themselves to an assessment of republicanism. Like Norbert Gossman, most scholars concentrate on the movement's brief emergence from marginality during the second half of the nineteenth century and set about trying to explain its failure in the face of continued popular support for the Crown. Constitutional arguments about resistance and contract are not employed; instead the phenomenon is located within the rubric of meritocratic liberalism and as a function of Victorian bourgeois ideology and the 'march of mind'.[23] There has also been a revival of interest in republicanism among scholars who fear that the fashionable rehabilitation of Crown and constitution-centred history now 'precludes any discussion at all of plebeian criticism of monarchy when it occurred, and closes off the very conception of a "republican"-style movement *per se*'.[24] Antony Taylor's insights are, however, conceptually contained by a polarising discourse in which popular culture either supports or opposes monarchy as an institution. Significance is found in Chartist disruptions of civic meetings to congratulate Victoria on her escape from the regicide Edward Oxford in 1840.[25] But this is an oversimplification. By and large, Chartists were not republicans. They sought to use meetings like these for their own constitutional ends, certainly, but their disrespect was generally reserved for bourgeois civic elites, and not extended to the virgin Queen in the capital.

The loud and lewd declamatory critique of monarchy unearthed to such effect by Ian McCalman[26] in late Hanoverian Britain tells us rather more about the strength of Rowlandsonian constitutionalism than about support for a republican alternative. Equally, the scandal surrounding the resignation of the Duke of York from his post as Commander in Chief of the army in the middle of the Napoleonic War reminds us that public toleration of moral laxity in the Royal Family was not unqualified.[27] Such incidents do not amount to evidence of anti-monarchism, but of popular belief in contractual accountability. Taylor prefers the term 'anti-monarchism' because it was not the English way to present a positive republican blueprint for overhauling the Constitution. The English preferred instead to emphasise the essential problems of monarchy, that it was 'irredeemably flawed by the sloth, intrigue and dissoluteness of a leisured and pampered lifestyle'. Chartist newspapers, he says, often contrasted the glitter and expense of royal extravagance with the poverty of those who manufactured it. Radicals also made much of royal scandals and profligacy to show how dissolute the lifestyle made them. But, although Taylor makes as much as he can of anti-monarchical rhetoric in the nineteenth-century radical press, he remains too willing to read dissatisfaction with expense or over a particular monarch's poor performance as opposition to the Crown as an institution.[28]

The historiography of monarchy has become bogged down by questions about the strength, nature and character of its institutional popularity; about the political character and number of its supporters and detractors, about the role it played in the prevention of revolution, and with the exposure of inauthentic rituals and mythologies. Monarchy *is* about performance, but its theatre is directed as much by the expectation and demands of the audience as of the players.

Constitutional contract theory and the Whig tradition in eighteenth- and early nineteenth-century England

> Rouse, my countrymen! rouse! lay your grievances at the foot of the Throne. You have a King who is the Father of his People, who only wants to *know* in order to *redress* your complaints.[29]

It is a contention of this book that assaults against the monarch are most usefully understood within the cultural discourse of petitioning. Many assailants nursed private frustrations over the failure of petitions already sent to the King and the resort to physical pressure, however desperate its expression, was not without a legitimising rationale. While this mode of explanation may be applied with some justification to countries other than Britain, the constitutional Settlement of 1688–89 substantially re-defined the relationship between Crown and people in ways that were unique to the British Isles. Drawing on the inspiration of John Locke, the resulting constitutional 'contract' placed theoretical limits on the king's role in government by shaping power relationships into an equilateral triangle between Crown, Lords and Commons. For Locke, power originated with the people and was deputed by them to their governors on 'trust'. Any serious betrayal of trust might legitimately be resisted by the people, in which case they were answerable to God alone for their actions. In a sense then, while divine right was denied to the contractual king, it survived as the ultimate sanction for popular sovereignty.[30]

In practice, of course, although it remained the business of Parliament to make law, it was, as a number of Tory pamphleteers pointed out, the king's job to choose the ministers who would do so, and this was understandably the source of some of the most bitter political arguments of the eighteenth century. The ambiguous boundaries of the royal prerogative became, indeed, the principal motivator of radicalism before 1832, just as bourgeois and parliamentary 'betrayal' fuelled its fire in the years *after* the Reform Act. The theoretical vitality of the Glorious Revolution should not be underestimated. The reorganisation of constitutional power into three equal and mutually dependent parts, Commons, Lords and Crown, was a crucial step in the desacralisation of monarchy. As John Thelwall understood it more than a century later:

> It is not the man who is sacred, it is, in reality the office. I do not mean that you have a right to assault the magistrate at any time; but I mean to say that the veneration that you owe to the magistrate is attached to him only while he is discharging the duties of his office: at all other times you ought only to regard him as a man and an equal.[31]

Halevy thought the monarchy had been reduced to a debased and 'harmless fetish' by the start of the nineteenth century, but he oversimplified. If judgement was reserved over the worth of individuals, the institution of monarchy was widely revered.[32] The Walpolean Whigs went to extraordinary lengths to associate the founding of the Hanoverian dynasty under George I in 1714 with the libertarian gains of the Glorious Revolution.[33] While the Riot Act of 1714 and the Septennial Act of 1716 theoretically curtailed the direct influence of both the unenfranchised and the enfranchised, George I's readiness to redress grievances was loudly eulogised. When discontent over excise schemes was raised in 1727, for instance, 'the complaints and cries of the People (which were now grown almost universal) reached the Court and pierced the ears of a most indulgent Prince'.[34]

In formulating his *Idea of a Patriot King* in the 1730s, Walpole's great rival Bolingbroke carefully avoided any repudiation of contract theory, professing, on the contrary, to strengthen it by positioning his ideal monarch above faction and party, a true representative of the nation rather than a tool of the Whigs. Bolingbroke's aim was to sever the cosy relationship between the King and his Whig ministers, bestowing the monarch with an independent and almost divine understanding of popular concerns. 'He will distinguish the voice of his people from the clamour of a faction and will hearken to it. He will redress grievances, correct errors, and reform or punish ministers.' But the patriot king's admiring subjects are jarringly absent from the Bolingbroke blueprint, and the means by which they will treat with him is far from clear. Few Tories were overtly opposed to contractualism, but they were reticent about public approaches to the throne. Although the *idea* gained wide currency, Bolingbroke's patriot king was little more than a device for undermining the hegemony of Walpole and the text never achieved the influence or popularity he had hoped for.[35]

By the time of his own succession in 1760, George III's adherence to the contractual Settlement was taken for granted. He nevertheless strained at the boundaries of the Settlement by clashing with Parliament in the early years of his reign over the limits of the prerogative. George II, it has been suggested, did not challenge Walpole's supremacy in government as often as he might have liked because he was conscious of the requirements of national unity (or Whiggish consensus against Tory opportunism) to counter the threat of Jacobitism. It was, as Jeremy Black has noted, an important stage in the continuing 'education of monarchs'.[36] In the favoured narrative of Whig historians, George III's education had to be completed in the school of hard knocks at the hands of the mobility, whose discontent over the King's preferment of the authoritarian Tory Lord Bute did not endear him to them. 'Saturated with the ideas of an autocrat', as Jephson saw it, the King's attempt to present himself as a patriot king who 'glories in the name of Briton' counted for nothing unless he acted under the tutelage of public opinion. From this perspective, the maintenance of Whig consensus in government was the only way of safeguarding the Settlement against the schemes of divine-right Tory, Jacobite or Catholic wreckers. The consequence of the King's attempts to exceed the limits of his own contract was popular clamour. Its constitutional character was petitionary, and its name was John Wilkes.[37]

The Bill of Rights was generally understood to have overturned the Stuart statutes of 1661 which made the 'tumultuous petitioning' of 'lewd persons' and beggars seditious and placed a limit on numbers. The intention of these statutes had been to protect the monarch from mobbing, either physically or through an 'overwhelming' accumulation of signatures. Although it did not allude directly to the statutes, the Bill of Rights guaranteed protection for petitioners in principle and ensured 'all prosecutions for such petitioning are illegal'.[38] It also forced the removal of a clause in the Oath of Allegiance declaring it unlawful 'upon any pretense whatever' to take up arms against the king. Through a process of omission, this attempt to retrospectively confirm the legitimacy of the Civil War created three areas of constitutional uncertainty: whether rules could still be applied to govern the method of presenting petitions (singly or en masse); whether petitioners had any right to present petitions to the king in person; and in what circumstances it might be legitimate to take up arms against the king.[39] The language of 1688 did not, however, impress all eighteenth-century radicals. For John Gale Jones, Magna Carta was a far more authoritative basis for constitutional liberty, whereas the Bill of Rights had 'given us nothing. It was merely an acknowledgement of those rights which we before enjoyed'.[40] Tom Paine, who saw all petitioning as an acceptance of the master–slave relationship, cared for neither charter, for 'whatever the rights of the people are, they have a right to them, and none have a right either to withhold them or to grant them'.[41] Thelwall was kinder. The Bill of Rights was severely flawed, he accepted, but nevertheless it provided a more modern framework for the limitation of royal prerogative and the notion that 'an oppressed and injured people had rights to choose their own Government and elect their own chief magistrate'.[42]

Because of its endorsement in both Magna Carta and the Bill of Rights, petitioning remained sacrosanct without any reference to its effectiveness. For Cobbett in 1817, the petition was the English commonalty's 'only safeguard against being as much slaves as the negroes are', for without it 'the rich and powerful may knock the brains out of the poor with impunity'.[43] Opponents of radicalism did not disagree, but they sang from a different hymnsheet. Thanks to the right of petition, a loyalist tract put it in 1792, 'every man is, not *virtually*, but *individually*, represented in parliament', making it 'immaterial how members are elected'.[44] Multiply signed reform petitions, argued Lord Brougham in 1817, were a 'natural preventive against violence'.[45]

English contract theory had no direct parallel in pre-revolutionary France, as all Englishmen were fond of reminding themselves. French constitutionalists found it difficult to identify any precise limits to royal power, although the Enlightenment had introduced notions of popular sovereignty to political discourse. The word 'treason' was not in general use. Anything that tended to undermine the power and dignity of the king was referred to as *lèse-majesté*, and the punishment was quartering, but in Diderot's opinion legal definitions were so vague as to encourage 'despotism'. French kings, says Arlette Farge, often adopted the sort of impersonal and unapproachable style that actively discouraged their subjects from seeking redress for personal grievances. The explicit assumption of unassailable divinity did not keep them safe, however, for their distressed and unhappy subjects sometimes sought redemptive martyrdom by seeking to kill that which could not, in any case, be killed. Consequently, assassination attempts were not uncommon. Similar themes of redemptive magic in the first half of the eighteenth century occupied the courts in a number of autocratic Italian provinces, where regicide became associated with witchcraft, prosecution with malicious denunciation, and punishment was similarly barbarous.[46]

Why was the right to petition the monarch considered so important in Britain? Unlike Parliament, the Crown was presumed to be free from factional control, above the venality of politics and genuinely concerned with the welfare of the people. Individuals were equally free to petition Parliament of course, but most Britons enjoyed only virtual representation on its benches and so wielded no real influence over it. Members of Parliament were understood to fall too easily under self- or factional interest, and were rarely expected to be swayed by a petition, even if 'instructed' by their constituents.[47] Then there was the issue of Parliament's status as a petitioning body itself. Although the Glorious Revolution had supposedly expunged its ancient role as a body whose primary purpose was to 'petition' the king on behalf of the people,[48] radicals still sporadically referred to the Commons as a house of 'middle men', and not all could see the point of petitioning mere petitioners. Direct appeals to the king made more sense. Moreover, Parliament's powers were strictly legislative. Subjects with personal problems and grievances craved personal and unconditional adjudication. From the 1770s, Parliament was nevertheless petitioned with apparent enthusiasm and without tangible success by huge numbers of social and political reformers. Petitions were presented by a sympathetic MP and read by the clerk, sometimes in a 'barely audible voice' and often amid 'coughing and clamour'. Reform petitions were rejected in 1817 on the ground that they had insulted the dignity of the House by calling it 'unrepresentative'. Lord Cochrane admonished ministers for 'cavilling nicely' over mere language, and insisted they should 'receive the Petitions of the People, as thus only could the sense of the Country be known', but his advice was not taken.[49] Frustrated petitioners took the view that rejection simply proved the justice of their case and the deafness of Parliament to the will of the people. There was, then, a very real reason to petition the king; not just to protest corruption, but to demand the replacement of ministers, a prerogative of the Crown alone.

Some historians question the extent to which ordinary people understood the principles of contract theory.[50] Yet the issues were often in the public domain, discussed in newsprint or haggled over in debating clubs. In 1780 for example, a London society debated the question 'Is not a king of Great Britain bound by his Coronation Oath to redress the grievances of his subjects when they appeal to him?'[51] As we will see, many Britons thought that he was. Take, for example, the anonymous ex-lieutenant who 'grabbed' the reigns of the King's horse at a review on Wimbledon Common in the 1780s 'and demanded his grievances be attended to'.[52] Joseph Williams, whose petitions to the King were met with 'silence and contempt', conceived it a crime against the 'Great Charter of the Subject', deserving prosecution 'in any court of Westminster Hall'.[53] In the following century, English crowds were constantly reminded of their contractual rights by orators at platform meetings. In 1817, John Bagulay maintained that the Regent had forty days to respond to a petition, in default of which he could be legitimately imprisoned by the people.[54] In 1838, R. J. Richardson reminded a crowd of 15,000 that the Queen was effectively elected in exchange for a promise to protect British liberties.[55] Beliefs like these suggest a theoretical justification for demanding redress from the throne, rather than just the right of supplication.

These ideas were far from new at the accession of George III. Whig polemic in the 1720s, for example, particularly in the *Cato's Letters* of John Trenchard and Thomas Gordon, had argued that the right of petition was only meaningful if reciprocated by a duty of redress. It was not a question of justice alone but of security from discontent. For Trenchard and Gordon, 'Our Kings have always accepted so powerful an application ... It has indeed been always thought highly imprudent, not to say dangerous, to resist the general moans and entreaties of the people, uttered in this manner.' Invoking the civic humanism of the Roman Republic, they concluded:

> Titus and Trajan, conscious of their own virtuous administration, and worthy purposes, courted Addresses and Informations of this kind from their subjects: They wisely knew; that if the *Roman* People had free leave to speak, they would not take leave to act; and that whilst they could have redress, they would not seek revenge.[56]

The end of the Jacobite challenge in 1745 permitted a relaxation in the Protestant consensus around Hanoverian government so that, by the time of George III's accession, the assertive rhetoric of resistance was fast becoming a commonplace in opposition literature. An influential populariser of these themes in the 1770s was the Rev. James Murray, who rose to prominence as a critic of John Wesley's stentorian assertion that the resistance of the American colonists was unchristian. On the contrary, he retorted, the rights and liberties of the people were bestowed by God, and their defence was a Christian duty. He stopped short of advocating resistance at home, however, for the King would surely redress all grievances if properly presented by petition. 'Let the oppressed ask orderly and they shall receive', he counselled.[57] John Baxter, a militant member of the plebeian London Corresponding Society (LCS) in 1795, had fewer qualms. Pitt's repressive Gagging Act was provocation enough, for 'any Act which is totally subversive of the Constitution is a just ground of Resistance'.[58]

In most circumstances, physical resistance to monarchs was not to be resorted to without a constitutional 'written warning' or remonstrance. In practice, a remonstrance was nothing more than a 'strongly worded address' and was actually no more dangerous a weapon than a petition (except in its ability to cause affront to the recipient). Yet it remained a powerful exercise in semantics. Parliament might refuse to accept any document presented without a formal 'prayer', but the Chartist Convention of 1838–39 overcame many rank and file objections to its proposal for a first great National Petition by filling the text with 'demands'. Lancastrians, it was claimed, 'would not have signed it, had it only prayed, they signed it because it demanded'. It was not rejected outright, but fourteen formal Chartist remonstrances were ruled inadmissible in 1842.[59]

Although the right of resistance was traceable to Magna Carta, in 1215, justifications for it were theoretically compromised before 1688 by the contradictory claims of divine right.[60] Whigs and radicals alike reserved a special place in their hearts for the 'patriotic' martyrs who fell in the struggle for the Settlement, and none more than the 'martyred' resistance theorist Algernon Sidney, whose *Discourses Concerning Government* (1683) formed part of the Crown's evidence of his treason.[61] Thomas Hardy, secretary of the London Corresponding Society in 1792, wanted only to 'take his stand by the side' of Sidney, for he was one of those who had resisted the 'ruffian arm of arbitrary power, and dyed the field and the scaffold with their pure and precious blood, for the liberties of their country'.[62] Whether attracted to Sidney or appalled by him, all English constitutionalists understood the need to confront the events of the Civil War and Interregnum. Radicals like Hardy familiarised themselves with seventeenth-century justifications for resistance because they provided precedents through which the ambiguous language of the 1688 oath of allegiance could be interpreted. As Robert Zaller has shown, for propagandists of the Protectorate like Henry Parker, tyranny did not require precise definition because, since all royal authority was derived from the people, kings might be removed 'merely by the libertie and right of free born men to be govern'd as seems to them best'.[63] Unsurprisingly, there was a general blossoming of resistance tracts under Cromwell. John Milton's *Eikonoklastes*, his two *Defences of the People of England*, and James Harrington's utopian *Oceana* were well known, but the most celebrated in Hardy's day was Silas Titus and Edward Sexby's much re-published *Killing No Murder*, a book offering comprehensive guidance on the identification of tyranny. 'By the law of nature, when no justice can be had, every man may be his own magistrate and do justice for himself'.[64] The precedents of the 1640s were generally taken as justification for resistance and regicide, but not necessarily for republicanism. The greatest tyrant in *Killing No Murder* is Cromwell, and radicals were usually ready to accept the Restoration provided the constraints of 1688 were acknowledged as necessary. Mainstream radical attitudes during the 1790s are perhaps best illustrated by the conditional loyalty of an unidentified young reformer in 1795: 'That our present Sovereign may long reign over a happy and loyal people is only the second sentiment of my heart; the first sentiment next my heart is that the people shall be free'.[65]

In practice, the right to bear arms, supposedly guaranteeing self-defence in the absence of a standing army, was legally limited by the poaching laws, but rhetorically it remained an important weapon against royal 'tyranny'. In its popular conception, writes James Epstein, the bearing of arms was not just a right but 'a duty, the true badge of citizenship'. Indeed, resistance was upheld in Parliament by the liberal MP Ralph Bernal Osborne as late as 1848.[66] As a radical orator of some influence, John Thelwall's position on physical resistance in 1794–95 is worth examining more closely. For Thelwall, violence was a complex issue. Although in principle he opposed both 'the idea of civil discord' (or collective insurrection) and 'the energies of the dagger – the logic of assassination' (individual *attentat*); he reserved the right to 'uplift the arm of violence' in defence of either life or liberty, as a 'last extremity'.[67] The 'tyranny' of George III was suggested by the King's indifference to domestic starvation and famine and contrasted unfavourably with George II's 'glorious and magnificent conduct' in permitting the relief of the French famine with English grain in the 1750s.[68] George III, argued Thelwall, was more like the Old Testament King Jehu, a man whose notoriety was firmly embedded in the despotic bloodletting of his reign,[69] or King Chanticleer, 'a strutting and greedy cockerel tamed only by the farmer's punishing knife'.[70] Thelwall drew historical lessons from the Anglo-Saxons, who regularly replaced any king who was not sufficiently 'konning', or wise. George III claimed legitimacy through the hereditary principle alone, he noted, but the monarchy was 'only hereditary under certain restrictions: that is to say, upon condition of a strict compliance, on the part of the House of Brunswick, with the compact and terms under which the crown was granted'.[71]

There is an implicit acceptance in Thelwall's language that regicide served no purpose beyond the replacement of an unacceptable monarch with a better one. Its legitimacy under law had nothing to do with republicanism, as a contemporary *Constitutional Catechism* explained:

> *Q*: Does the King ever die?
>
> *A*: Politically speaking, he does not. The law only speaks of his demise; which means rather a transfer of property: That, on the disunion of the monarch's natural from his political body, the Kingdom is instantly (without the smallest interval of time) transferred or demised to his successor.[72]

A similar understanding of the Constitution lay behind Henry Hunt's attitude to resistance. As radicals considered their response to Peterloo, Hunt looked to the 1640s for precedents and found a 'coincidence of the events of the present time with those which occurred in the reign of Charles the First', for it was then that 'resistance became a duty'. He did not confuse resistance with republicanism, however, and even from his post-Peterloo prison cell, continued to defend the democratically elected mixed government espoused by his early mentor Henry Clifford.[73]

Hunt was steadfast in his belief in the efficacy of petitioning the throne. 'I suggested that it was in vain to petition the corrupt knaves in the House to reform themselves', he said in 1811, 'but that, as the Prince Regent was entering upon his regal office, I thought it would be a good opportunity to address him on that subject'.[74] Like most radicals of his day, he was affronted by the pomp and spectacle of monarchy; but he had no wish for its abolition and was uncomfortable with the disrespect advocated in Spencean circles. When the younger Watson proposed to march on Carlton House in 1816 to demand redress from the Regent, Hunt thought it 'quite preposterous, as well as unjust and unreasonable. As a private gentleman, I myself would not submit to be intruded upon in such a manner, and it was very unreasonable to expect that it would be endured by the chief magistrate of the country'.[75] In Hunt's *Memoirs*, two monarchical themes stand out; the profligacy and social injustice of the civil list, and its consequence – the steady decline of the King's sense of constitutional duty. In charting the progress of this decline as a linear trajectory marked by pivotal moments of betrayal, Hunt effectively inverted the whiggish constitutional meta-narrative of libertarian advance. He must have known that his agreement to deliver a remonstrance to the Regent in 1817 was not, as he claimed it to be, 'the first time a public remonstrance to the throne was ever agreed to by the people', but his purpose was to qualify the remonstrance as a benchmark on the long road to slavery.[76] Hunt's narrative of constitutional decline was capped by a redemptive suggestion that the 'bloody reign of George III', in which all of these misfortunes fell, finally attracted the sublime judgement of the Almighty, who punished his representative on earth with insanity.[77]

Notwithstanding crowd attacks on the coaches of George III and George IV in 1795 and 1817, and the possibility that Colonel Despard genuinely intended to blow up the King with cannon or landmines, in 1802, British radicals rarely turned the rhetoric of collective physical resistance to the monarch into action. Elsewhere in Europe matters could be different. Nineteenth-century Frenchmen for instance, opposed their kings with a far greater fervour than did their English counterparts, particularly during the 1830s. Louis Phillipe survived at least eight attempts on his life during the eighteen years of his reign. Republicans were blamed for (and acquitted of) a shooting attempt in 1833, but the most celebrated assassin was the Bonapartist Joseph Fieschi, who rigged together twenty-five gun barrels into an 'infernal machine' and volleyed them into a royal parade from an overlooking window, killing several onlookers but missing his target. He and three others were guillotined. Each new outrage brought fresh conspiracy theories, internment and repressive legislation, but some regicides appear to have been settling personal grievances. Alibaud, who tried to shoot the King in 1836, held him responsible for the economic ruin of his family, likened himself to Brutus, and boldly told his prosecutors: 'Regicide is the right of all men who are debarred from any justice but that which they take into their own hands.' He too was guillotined. Yet serious revolutionaries were actually as wary of practical tyrannicide as were most British reformers. As the socialist Louis Blanc put it, 'by sweeping away the man, the personification is not destroyed – it is renewed. Caesar, assassinated, sprang to more terrible life in the person of Octavius'.[78]

Some other European monarchs, like Ferdinand of Spain who was sent three parcel bombs in 1831, had lucky escapes. But not every target was so fortunate. Capo D'Istrias, President of Greece, was assassinated in Napoli later in the same year. The British radical press, cautious to a fault when it came to judging attempts on British monarchs, allowed itself full reign on foreign affairs and relished the discomfort such outrages must be causing to William IV as he tried to stall the Reform Bill. Regicide may be an unsophisticated form of politics, thought Hetherington, but 'how are we to get rid of them in any other way?' It was justifiable to despatch a tyrant like 'a tiger or wild beast', and although it was reasonable to warn them first with a firm remonstrance, that would not always be possible. If Sir Charles Wetherall had been assassinated as soon as he made his infamous anti-reform speech in Parliament, the greater evil of the Bristol riots might have been avoided.[79]

But Tory political culture had never accommodated the right of resistance. Objections were founded on the writings of the seventeenth-century absolutist Robert Filmer, whose *Patriarcha* (1680) challenged the oxymoronic notion of an accountable king. Tory intransigence achieved its widest public notice with the trial of Dr Sacheverell in 1710. Sacheverell was indicted by Whig ministers for libelling the Bill of Rights in a sermon proclaiming the constitutional illegality of resistance to kings. Although convicted, Sacheverell's trial begged disturbing questions about the Whigs' denial of his own rights of free speech and 'resistance'. The Sacheverell position resurfaced in mid-century as John Shebbeare's *Letters to the English People*, which sought to rehabilitate Britain's last divine right-monarch, James II, and Timothy Brecknock's proscribed *Droit le Roi* (1764) and then again in the 1790s when the arch-loyalist John Reeves was successfully prosecuted for over-asserting the primacy of the monarchy.[80] Tory challenges to resistance theory often inspired an extraordinary vitality in radical counter-argument. In 1795 John Baxter, whose commitment to physical force is often taken to have been unequivocal, railed against loyalist misrepresentations of 'resistance' as 'rebellion'. From a constitutional point of view, the distinction was important, and some radicals took solace in the clearer term 'self-defence', with its evocation of common-law solutions to the petty 'oppressions' of assault and robbery. This was a term, moreover, that was far more accommodating to *individual* rather than purely collective or 'national' acts of resistance.[81] Some radicals tried to justify the crowd attack on the King's coach in 1795 as an act of resistance, but were unsettled by the claims of their opponents that it was simple 'rebellion' and were well aware that moderate opinion in the country regarded it as an outrage. The test, according to one LCS member, was whether or not the man who broke the coach windows was an 'enemy of tyranny'. Richard Hodgson disagreed, 'for a man might be an enemy of tyrants only because he wished to be a tyrant himself'. The question was, rather, was he a friend of liberty? Since none of those arrested were members of a reform society, Hodgson decided the answer was no, and gratefully washed his hands of the problem.[82]

According to the Tory view of the constitution, the punishment of kings was the business of God alone; the role of the subject was one of passive obedience. While many Whigs interpreted the old adage 'The king can do no wrong' as confirmation of the king's accountability in law, and radicals saw in it a reason to blame his ministers for everything, Tories generally took it as a statement of infallibility.[83] The controversy was ultimately unresolvable. Even Blackstone was ambivalent. The learned judge held the king to be beyond the reach of the law, except under certain undefined circumstances of 'oppression ... which a fertile imagination may furnish'. Salvation lay in 'the exertion of those inherent (though latent) powers of society, which no climate, no time, no constitution, no contract can ever destroy or diminish'. Historical precedent, he said, revealed times when 'the nation has very justifiably risen as one man to vindicate the original contract between the King and his people'.[84] This right or duty was restricted to the 'national interest', but Blackstone did not clearly define it or distinguish the interests of the individual from those of the *collective* nation. For the purposes of this study, at least, such a distinction is critically important. But the Tory position was practicable as well as intellectual. The idea that the regicide Despard had acted under legitimate theories of resistance in 1802, for example, was rejected because the grievances of which Despard complained were not in the king's gift to redress. Of course, 'the wretched and aggrieved have access to his Royal person; he listens to the *individual's* complaint; redresses his wrong and relieves the sufferer', but it was 'not in the power of any ruler to relieve the *numbers* who suffer in poverty or want' (emphasis added), however much he might patronise charities and support his well-intentioned Parliament. 'When the ignorant or misguided imagine that the welfare and happiness of the laborious classes solely depend upon their sovereign, they grossly deceive themselves; and injure our best and most beloved monarch, who is ever attentive to everything dependent on his limited power for their relief.'[85]

Notes

1 Public Record Office (hereafter PRO), London, HO 42/37: Informer's report, 16 November 1795.

2 ed. L. Strachey and R. Fulford, *The Greville Memoirs, 1814–60*, (London 1938), vol. 5, p. 24.

3 L. Colley, 'The apotheosis of George III: loyalty, royalty and the British nation, 1760–1821', *Past and Present*, 102 (1984), 94–129; L. Colley, *Britons: Forging the Nation, 1707–1837* (New Haven, CT, 1992), ch. 5: 'Majesty'; M. Morris, *The British Monarchy and the French Revolution* (New Haven, CT, 1998); R. Wells, *Insurrection: The British Experience, 1795–1803* (Gloucester, 1986). Disagreement about the nature of British polities, especially during the 1790s, has degenetated into a dialogue of the deaf in recent years. For a glimpse into the yawning chasm between protagonists on either side, see Wells's unforgiving review of Morris's book in the *Canadian Journal of History*, 33 (1988), 468–70.

4 J. Epstein, *Radical Expression: Political Language, Ritual and Symbol in England, 1790–1850* (Oxford, 1994); J. Belchem, 'Republicanism, popular constitutionalism and the radical platform in early nineteenth-century England', *Social History*, 6 (1981), 1–32; J. Belchem, *'Orator' Hunt: Henry Hunt and Working Class Radicalism* (Oxford, 1985); J. Belchem, *Popular Radicalism in Nineteenth-century Britain* (London, 1996).

5 On the relevance of 1688 to the Hanoverians, see J. R. Jones (ed.), *Liberty Secured? Britain Before and After 1688* (Stanford, CA, 1992); H. T. Dickinson, 'The eighteenth-century debate on the Glorious Revolution', *History*, 61 (1976), 28–45; K. Wilson, 'Inventing revolution: 1688 and eighteenth-century popular politics', *Journal of British Studies*, 28 (1989), pp. 349–86.

6 D. Cannadine, 'The context, performance and meaning of ritual: the British monarchy and the invention of tradition, c. 1820–1977', in E. Hobsbawm and T. Ranger (eds), *The Invention of Tradition* (Cambridge, 1983), pp. 101–65.

7 For petitioning, see C. Leys, 'Petitioning in the nineteenth and twentieth centuries', *Political Studies*, 3:1 (1955), 45–64; E. N. Williams, *The Eighteenth-Century Constitution, 1688–1815* (Cambridge, 1960); P. Fraser, 'Public petitioning and Parliament before 1832', *History*, 46 (1961), 195–211; J. E. Bradley, *Popular Politics and the American Revolution in England: Petitions, the Crown and Public Opinion* (Macon, 1986); M. Knights, 'Petitoning and the political theorists: John Locke, Algernon Sidney and London's monster petition of 1680', *Past and Present*, 138 (1993), 94–111; S. Drescher, 'Whose abolition? Popular pressure and the ending of the British slave trade', *Past and Present*, 143 (1994), 136–66; C. Tilly, *Popular Contention in Great Britain, 1758–1834* (Cambridge, MA, 1995); D. L. Smith, 'The root and branch petition and the Great Remonstrance: from petition to remonstrance', in D. L. Smith, R. Strier and D. Bevington (eds), *The Theatrical City: Culture, Theatre and Politics in London, 1576–1649* (Cambridge, 1995), pp. 209–23.

8 An interesting exception is V. A. C. Gatrell, *The Hanging Tree: Execution and the English People, 1770–1868* (Oxford, 1994), which offers extensive analysis of petitions to the King for mercy.

9 I. Macalpine and R. Hunter, *George III and the Mad Business* (London, 1969), pp. 310–18. This serious study of the royal malady does not hesitate to marginalise

all of the assailants of George III as insane. Similar unsubstantiated judgements may be found in V. Carretta, *George III and the Satirists from Hogarth to Byron* (Athens, GA, 1990), pp. 166, 275, 313; Morris, *British Monarchy*, p. 37; and I. McCalman, 'Mad Lord George and Madame La Motte: riot and sexuality in the genesis of Burke's *Reflections on the Revolution in France*', *Journal of British Studies*, 35 (1996), in which Nicholson is described as a 'deranged enthusiast' (p. 359).

10 F. L. Ford, *Political Murder: From Tyrannicide to Terrorism* (Cambridge, MA, 1985), pp. 194–9, 207.

11 For example, E. Shils and M. Young, 'The meaning of the coronation', *Sociological Review*, I (1953); I. Hayden, *Symbol and Privilege: The Ritual Context of British Royalty* (Tucson, AZ, 1987); D. Cannadine and S. Price, *Rituals of Royalty: Power and Ceremonial in Traditional Societies* (Cambridge, 1987); O. Gulbrandsen, 'The King is king by the grace of the people: the exercise and control of power in subject–ruler relations'; and D. Streckfuss, 'Kings in the age of nations: the paradox of lèse-majesté as political crime in Thailand', *Comparative Studies in Society and History*, 37:3 (1995), 415–44, 445–74.

12 J. Cannon, 'The survival of the British monarchy', *Transactions of the Royal Historical Society*, fifth series, 36 (1986), p. 143.

13 J. Black, 'The British monarchy, 1714–1837', in R. Smith and J. S. Moore (eds), *The Monarchy: Fifteen Hundred Years of British Tradition* (London, 1998), pp. 210–12.

14 John S. Moore, 'Introduction', in Smith and Moore, *The Monarchy*, pp. 6, 27.

15 J. W. Derry, *Politics in the Age of Fox, Pitt and Liverpool: Continuity and Transformation* (London, 1990), p. 85. Similarly credulous and simplistic approaches to the polarised positions of treasonable 'revolutionaries' and popular loyalists can be found in I. R. Christie, *Stress and Stability in Late Eighteenth-century Britain: Reflections on the British Avoidance of Revolution* (Oxford, 1984), pp. 49–53.

16 Cannadine, 'Invention'.

17 In addition to works already cited, see H. Cunningham, 'The language of patriotism, 1750–1914', *History Workshop Journal*, 12 (1981), 8–33; G. Newman, *The Rise of English Nationalism: A Cultural History, 1740–1830* (London, 1987), J. Dinwiddy, 'England', in O. Dann and J. Dinwiddy (eds), *Nationalism in the Age of the French Revolution* (London, 1988), pp. 53–70; D. Eastwood, 'Patriotism and the English State in the 1790s', in M. Philp (ed.), *The French Revolution and British Popular Politics* (Cambridge, 1991), pp. 146–68.

18 J. J. Sack, *From Jacobite to Conservative: Reaction and Orthodoxy in Britain, c. 1760–1832* (Cambridge, 1993). The term is used, says Sack, to avoid the 'horrendous gaucherie' of applying some more contemporary term, like 'Jacobite' or 'Ultra' to the whole period (p. 1).

19 On Caroline, see T. Laqueur, 'The Queen Caroline affair: politics as art in the reign of George IV', *Journal of Modern History*, 54 (1982), 417–66; A. Clark, 'Queen Caroline and the sexual politics of popular culture in London, 1820', *Representations*, 31 (1990), 47–68; T. Hunt, 'Morality and monarchy in the Queen Caroline affair', *Albion*, 23 (1991), 697–722; D. Wahrman, 'Middle-class domesticity goes public: gender, class and politics from Queen Caroline to Queen Victoria', *Journal of British Studies*, 32 (1993), 402–19; J. Fulcher, 'The loyalist response to the Queen Caroline agitation', *Journal of British Studies*, 34 (1995),

481–502; a useful historiographical essay on Caroline is R. McWilliam, *Popular Politics in Nineteenth-century England* (London, 1998), pp. 7–13. For Victoria, see D. Thompson, *Queen Victoria: The Woman, the Monarchy and the People* (New York, 1990); A. Munich, *Queen Victoria's Secrets* (New York, 1996); M. Homans and A. Munich (eds), *Remaking Queen Victoria* (Cambridge, 1997); M. Homans, *Royal Representations: Queen Victoria and British Culture, 1837–1876* (Chicago, IL, 1998).

20 W. M. Kuhn, *Democratic Royalism: The Transformation of the British Monarchy, 1861–1914* (London, 1996).

21 W. L. Arnstein, 'Queen Victoria opens parliament: the disinvention of tradition', *Historical Research*, 63 (1990), 178–94.

22 F. Prochaska, *Royal Bounty: The Making of a Welfare Monarchy* (New Haven, CT, 1995), chs 1–3. For references to Queen Adelaide, see pp. 56–7. For similarly credulous remarks about Queen Charlotte's thriftful economy, see pp. 17–20. Charlotte's flirtation with retrenchment in the Royal Household was widely lampooned in the public sphere. For a lively critique on this theme, see M. Pointon, 'Intrigue, jewellery and economics: court culture and display in England and France in the 1780s', in M. North and D. Ormrod (eds), *Art Markets in Europe, 1400–1800* (Aldershot, 1998), pp. 201–19.

23 N. J. Gossman, 'Republicanism in nineteenth-century England', *International Review of Social History*, 7 (1962), 47–60. See also F. D'Arcy, 'Charles Bradlaugh and the English republican movement, 1868–1878', *Historical Journal*, 25 (1982), 367–83.

24 A. Taylor, 'Republicanism reappraised: anti-monarchism and the English radical tradition, 1850–1872', in J. Vernon (ed.), *Re-Reading the Constitution: New Narratives in the Political History of England's Long Nineteenth Century* (Cambridge, 1996), p. 154.

25 A. Taylor, 'Reynolds's Newspaper, opposition to monarchy and the radical anti-Jubilee: Britain's anti-monarchist tradition reconsidered', *Historical Research*, 68:167 (1995), 321.

26 I. McCalman, *Radical Underworld: Prophets, Revolutionaries and Pornographers in London, 1795–1840* (Oxford, 1993).

27 P. Harling, 'The Duke of York affair (1809) and the complexities of war-time patriotism', *Historical Journal*, 39:4 (1996), 963–84.

28 Taylor, 'Republicanism', pp. 155–62.

29 *Felix Farley's Bristol Journal*, Letter from 'Atticus', 25 March 1769.

30 Locke's contractualism was published as the *Two Treatises on Government* (1690). For the origins of contract theory and some of the debates surrounding it, see H. T. Dickinson, *Liberty and Property: Political Ideology in Eighteenth-century Britain* (London, 1977), especially pp. 65–79.

31 J. Thelwall, 'A warning voice to the violent of all parties; with reflections on the events of the first day of the present session of Parliament', in G. Claeys (ed.), *The Politics of English Jacobinism: Writings of John Thelwall* (Pennsylvania, 1995), pp. 314–27.

32 E. Halevy, *England in 1815* (London, 1924), p. 5. For an examination of the depth of criticism about the immorality of such prominent royals as the Prince Regent (later George IV), the Duke of York and the Duke of Clarence (later William IV), see Sack, *Jacobite to Conservative*, pp. 136–45. Sack uses this evidence to question

Colley's assertions about the monarchy's 'apotheosis' under George III. See also P. Langford, *A Polite and Commercial People: England, 1727–1783* (Oxford, 1992), pp. 578–81.

33 K. Wilson, *The Sense of the People: Politics, Culture and Imperialism in England, 1715–1785* (Cambridge, 1995), pp. 87–96.

34 From *The Craftsman*, quoted in J. Black, *Robert Walpole and the Nature of Politics in Early Eighteenth-century Britain* (London, 1990), p. 83.

35 H. St. John, Viscount Bolingbroke, *The Idea of a Patriot King*, ed. S. W. Jackman ([1749], Indianapolis, 1965), p. 50.

36 Black, *Walpole*, pp. 56–60; F. O'Gorman, *The Long Eighteenth Century: British Political and Social History, 1688–1832* (London, 1997), p. 130.

37 H. Jephson, *The Platform: Its Rise and Progress, vol. 1* (London, 1892), 1, pp. 25–41.

38 W. A. Speck, *Reluctant Revolutionaries: Englishmen and the Revolution of 1688* (Oxford, 1988), pp. 142–3, 232–3.

39 The alteration to the oath of allegiance was for instance cited specifically in defence of armed resistance by LCS militant John Baxter in 1795; J. Baxter, *Resistance to Oppression: The Constitutional Right of Britons Asserted in a Lecture Delivered before Section Two of the Society of the Friends of Liberty on Monday November 9 1795* (London, 1795).

40 PRO, HO 42/37: Informer's report, 25 November 1795.

41 T. Paine, *A Letter Addressed to the Addressers* (London, 1792). Or, as one modern scholar has put it, 'petitions, by their very nature, acknowledge the power of the rulers and the dependence of the aggrieved' (R. Bogin, 'Petitioning and the new moral economy of post-revolutionary America', *William and Mary Quarterly*, third series, 45, (1988), 20–1).

42 PRO, HO 42/37: Report of a lecture by John Thelwall, 25 October 1795.

43 *Political Register*, 11 January 1817.

44 PRO, HO 42/22: Dalrymple to Nepean, 17 November 1792, with enclosure.

45 Jephson, *Platform*, vol. 1, pp. 571–5; *Hansard*, vol. 35, col. 84 (London, 1817), 29 January 1817.

46 G. A. Kelly, 'From lèse-majesté to lèse-nation: treason in eighteenth-century France', *Journal of the History of Ideas*, 42:3 (1981), 273–7; A. Farge, *Subversive Words: Public Opinion in Eighteenth-century France* (Oxford, 1994), pp. 132–95; S. Loriga, 'A secret to kill the king: magic and protection in Piedmont in the eighteenth century', in E. Muir and G. Ruggiero (eds), *History from Crime* (Baltimore, MD, 1994), pp. 88–90. See also J. W. Merrick, *The Desacralisation of the French Monarchy in the Eighteenth Century* (Baton Rouge, LA, 1990).

47 For the constitutional debate over the status and legality of 'instructions' to MPs, see Wilson, *Sense of the People*, pp. 133–4.

48 Brecknock's *Droit le Roi* of 1764 claimed that Parliament's law making was no more than a 'right of privilege', and that the Lords and Commons were 'not to be partners in the legislature, but petitioners'; quoted in J. C. D. Clark, *English Society 1688–1832: Ideology, Social Structure and Political Practice during the Ancien Régime* (Cambridge, 1985), p. 203.

49 For a very full and critical account, see *Hone's Reformists' Register*, 1 February 1817.

50 Of the reigns of the first two Georges, for example, O'Gorman has stated: 'The

idea that authority might derive from a contract between governors and governed was confined to a small minority of Whig and radical writers' (*Long Eighteenth Century*, p. 131).

51 Noted by D. T. Andrew, 'Popular culture and public debate: London 1780', *Historical Journal*, 39:2 (1996), 414.

52 *The Times*, 7 August 1786.

53 PRO, HO 42/18: J. Williams to E. Nepean, n.d. (1791). Williams punished the King by swearing allegiance to the Prince of Wales and dedicating a pamphlet to him.

54 PRO, HO 42/158: Information of Peter Campbell and Samuel Fleming, 28 January 1817.

55 Francis Place Papers, British Library (hereafter BL) Additional MS 27820, fols 202–19: 'Account of the meeting in Palace Yard, Westminster, on the 17 September'.

56 *Cato's Letters* no. 24, 8 April 1721, 'Of the natural honesty of the people and their reasonable demands. How important it is to every government to consult their affections and interest', in D. L. Jacobson (ed.), *The English Libertarian Heritage* (San Francisco, CA, 1965), pp. 66–7.

57 Rev. J. Murray, *Sermons to Asses* (London, 1817), pp. 4–5, 14, 15, 30; *New Sermons to Asses* (London, 1818).

58 Baxter, *Resistance to Oppression*. The London Corresponding Society, established in 1792, was the first body with an open membership to actively campaign for universal manhood suffrage in England.

59 Francis Place Papers, BL Additional MS. 27820, fols 202–19. For rank and file reluctance, see D. Thompson, *The Chartists* (London, 1984), 57–60; and for the full text of the first National Petition, see R. G. Gammage, *History of the Chartist Movement, 1837–1854* (facsimile reprint of 1894 edition, London, 1969), pp. 87–90. The six points of the Charter are 'demanded', and these demands make up its overall 'prayer'; *Hansard*, vol. 62, cols 1223–7 (London, 1842), 7 April–2 May 1842.

60 See Morris (*British Monarchy*, ch. 1: 'History and legitimacy') for a useful and concise account of contemporary controversies around contested theories of divine right and resistance.

61 A. C. Houston, *Algernon Sidney and the Republican Heritage in England and America* (Princeton, NJ, 1991), pp. 62–3.

62 *Memoir of Thomas Hardy ... Written by Himself* (London, 1832), in D. Vincent (ed.), *Testaments of Radicalism: Memoirs of Working Class Politicians, 1790–1885* (London, 1977), p. 51. Hardy, like most English radicals of his day, was (at least publicly) far more attracted to Sidney's image as a martyr to liberty than to the reality of his uncompromising republicanism. Sidney did not believe that a workable compact between monarch and public was either possible or desirable, and would not have been impressed by the rhetoric of the 1688 Bill of Rights.

63 R. Zaller, 'The figure of the tyrant in English revolutionary thought', *Journal of the History of Ideas*, 54:4 (1993), 585–610.

64 J. Cannon, 'Survival of British monarchy', p. 145; S. Titus and E. Sexby, *Killing No Murder* (new edition with an anonymous Preface, London, [1657] 1792). The 1792 edition was dedicated to three modern monarchical despots, Gustavus III of Sweden, Leopold II of Germany and Catharine II of Russia. For the quotation, p. 39.

65 PRO, HO 42/37: Informer's report of a debate at Wych Street, 16 November 1795.

66 Epstein, *Radical Expression*, p. 13. During a Commons' debate on the 1848 Crown and Government Security Bill, Osborne said: 'Circumstances might arise in this country which would make it the duty of every man to make war on the sovereign (cries of 'oh, oh' from several members, and 'hear, hear' from Mr Hume)'; *Northern Star*, 15 April 1848.

67 Claeys, *Thelwall*, pp. 72–3, 101.

68 *Ibid.*, p. 173.

69 *Ibid.*, p. 72. The story of Jehu can be traced in 2 Kings 9 and 10. The King fights a holy war against the worshippers of Baal, but in slaughtering every last one of them he is judged no better than they.

70 Quoted in Epstein, *Radical Expression*, p. 116.

71 For these arguments, see Thelwall's Beaufort Buildings' lecture of 9 September 1795, 'Report on the state of popular opinion and the causes of the rapid diffusion of democratic principles, part the second', also published in the *Tribune:* Claeys, *Thelwall*, pp. 209–17.

72 J. Rose, *A Constitutional Catechism, adapted to all ranks and capacities, illustrated with copious notes: principally extracted from the commentaries of the late Judge Blackstone* (Bristol, 1795), pp. 22–4. See also M. Walzer, *Regicide and Revolution: Speeches at the Trial of Louis XVI* (Cambridge, 1974), pp. 2–3, where Walzer discusses the theoretical distinction between the regicide as the slaying of monarchs and as the destruction of monarchy: the difference in effect between the execution of Louis XVI and the assasination of Williiam Rufus.

73 *Memoirs of Henry Hunt, Esq.; Written by Himself, in His Majesty's Jail at Ilchester, in the County of Somerset* (London, 1820–22), vol. 1, pp. xix, and 21.

74 *Ibid.*, vol. 2, p. 435.

75 *Ibid.*, vol. 3, pp. 201, 332–3.

76 *Ibid.*, vol. 3, pp. 515–16.

77 *Ibid.*, vol. 3, p. 199.

78 L. Blanc, *The History of Ten Years, 1830–40, or France Under Louis Philippe*, (Philadelphia, 1848), vol. 2, pp. 96–101, 366–77, 412–20; *The Times*, 31 July 1835; R. Tombs, *France 1814–1914* (London, 1996), pp. 265, 270. See also comments on the case of Gallois, a republican acquitted in 1831 for threatening to butcher the 'citizen' King if he failed to impress, in the Owenite American *Free Inquirer*, 27 August 1831.

79 *Voice of the People*, 30 July 1831; *Poor Man's Guardian*, 12 November 1831.

80 Sack, *Jacobite to Conservative*, pp. 116–29. Brecknock's pamphlet was publicly burned by order of Parliament, and its author ended his life on the gallows in 1786; see also Clark, *English Society*, pp. 201–16. Clark's portrait of an *ancien régime* England in which divine-right doctrines retained wide circulation makes little distiniction between text and reception. Obscure sermons and other tracts of dubious influence are bestowed with an importance somewhat at variance with the probable size of their readership. For a detailed analysis of the Reeves case, see D. Eastwood, 'John Reeves and the contested idea of the Constitution', *British Journal of Eighteenth-Century Studies*, 16:2 (1993), 197–212.

81 Baxter, *Resistance to Oppression*. The 'self-defence' argument is strongly presented in C. Condren, *The Language of Politics in Seventeenth-century England* (London, 1994), pp. 115–39. For a lively nineteenth-century radical/loyalist

argument covering much of the same ground, see the debate between the then-future Bishop of Calcutta, Daniel Wilson, and the publisher William Hone in 1817: Rev. D. Wilson, *The Duty of Contentment Under Present Circumstances* (London, 1817); *Hone's Reformists' Register*, 26 April and 3 May 1817.

82 PRO, HO 42/37: Informer's report of a debate at Wych Street, 16 November 1795.

83 For a thorough discussion of the ambiguity of the maxim, see J. L. Malcolm, 'Doing no wrong: law, liberty and the constraint of Kings', *Journal of British Studies*, 38 (1999), 161–86. The Whig position was sometimes supported by reference to seventeenth-century cases in which judges had indeed ruled the king's actions unlawful and void. As late as 1840, the Chartist *Northern Star* 25 January 1840 believed that 'The Sovereign, indeed, can do no wrong, but the Sovereign's advisers are responsible for the sins of their advising'. For the Kantian view of resistance as a self-contradictory doctrine, see Michael Lobban, *The Common Law and English Jurisprudence, 1760–1850* (Oxford, 1991), 248–9.

84 As quoted in Rose, *Constitutional Catechism*, pp. 22, 55.

85 Amicus Patriae, *British Liberty; or Sketches Critical and Demonstrative of the State of English Subjects* (London, 1803)

2

The Crown and the secular magic of petition

Historiographical interest in 'loyalism', whether radical or conservative, has tended to reduce the problem of agency to a debate over whether patriotism was organic or imposed from above. Because the *mentalités* of the loyal have not been rediscovered beyond this point, little notice has been taken of the sheer forwardness and self-assertiveness of many subjects in their dealings with the throne. What was it, for example, that permitted even lower-class women to address the monarch with a confidence they might never have displayed before a parliament of fellow subjects? To what extent did the 'divinity' of the monarch survive the secularising influence of Protestantism and Enlightenment?

Jon Mee, John Barrell and others have investigated the interplay of millenarian prophecy and political radicalism at the end of the eighteenth century. The importance of the king to the seditious imaginations of such key millenarian seers and publishers as Richard Brothers and 'citizen' Richard Lee, has been noted,[1] but active scriptural prophesying was not limited to the articulate and well-read few. In the days following Prime Minister Spencer Perceval's assassination in May 1812, the Regent was deluged with unsolicited biblical counsel. A semi-literate and 'pour feable weak-sited woman' sent a courteous letter recommending methods by which he might save the poor from 'oppression'. It was perhaps not her place to advise monarchs, she admitted, and she 'never saw your Royal person, and never shall yet', but she drew comfort from scriptural precedent:

> I see good has ben done by women plading with Kings for ester pladed with ashanierus and saved her own life and the life of mordecia her unkel and the hole nation of jews and how ebergal prevailed when Daved determon to slay nabel and all his house and Daved praised God that she prevented him.[2]

The woman was making reference to two Old Testament stories of female intercession with a king. In the first, Esther risks courting royal displeasure by appearing before her King without being summoned and opening his eyes to injustices engineered by a scheming and duplicitous courtier. In the second, Abigail skilfully solicits mercy from King David after her brusque husband jeopardises the security of their family by offering insults to the King.[3] One is struck not only by this semi-literate woman's knowledge of Old Testament tales and by her ability to deploy scripture as legitimisation, but by the coupling of the two stories as parables of contemporary political concerns. Poor women may have been excluded from conventional politics, but the spiritual nature of the monarchy facilitated dialogue just as nonconformity permitted active worship. The effrontery of Margaret Nicholson and the forthright language in which she addressed George III finds something of a parallel here.

Neither was it the first time that month that the Prince had been exhorted to consult scripture by one of his lowlier subjects. After all, monarchs ran a far greater risk of contravening the received wisdom of scripture than politicians because scripture makes far more reference to the moral behaviour and duties of monarchs. 'Show our beloved King [ch.] 14 Proverbs, [v.] 28' suggested one anonymous scribbler on the Prince's coronation in 1820: 'In the multitude of people is the king's honour: but in the want of people is the destruction of the prince'.[4] If the Regent heeded scripture and reduced the suffering of his people, reasoned John Duncan, fear of assassination by lunatics need never trouble him. But, as Ecclesiastes 7:7 plainly puts it, 'Surely, oppression maketh a wise man mad.'[5] Another quoted Isaiah in a denunciation of vice, luxury and immorality, exhorting the Prince to lead the whole nation in repentance, else all would perish. 'How has every attempt at the life of your Venerable Father been averted, and why? Because he has regarded the word of the King of Kings and Lord of Lords.'[6] As we will see, George III's deliverance from Margaret Nicholson in 1786 and James Hadfield in 1800 had been rhetorically moulded as a case of divine intervention, and the King's own words and body-language fashioned into signs of his divine nature. The divine side of monarchy had once found full expression in the 'the royal touch', the practice of curing scrofula by the laying on of royal hands. Theoretically, the touch had been abandoned by the secular Hanoverians. In fact, however, the practice survived through the process of petitioning for redress.

Petition and the secular divinity of 'the touch'

Belief in the touch as a cure for scrofula had been actively promoted by the restored Stuarts in the 1640s. James II once touched nearly 4,500 sufferers in nine months, a symbolic reminder both of the distance between the King and his people, and of the magical possibilities of direct contact. But, aside from a temporary revival under Queen Anne, the Protestant constitutional Settlement of William III had no use for such autocratic magic. As David Hume put it, the touch 'could no longer give amazement to the populace, and was attended with ridicule in the eyes of all men of understanding'.[7] The 1689 Bill of Rights replaced the superstitious intercession of the touch with the 'rational' intercession of the *petition*. In its popularly understood form as a right to approach the body of the king in person, the petition, and the readiness of the king to respond, became the royal touch of the secular proto-modern state.

The effectiveness of the 'cure' may be measured in the Royal Family's dispersal of bounty to needy petitioners or in the endowment of charities. It has been the making, as Frank Prochaska would have it, of a 'welfare monarchy'. George III gave £14,000 per annum to charity and bestowed financial relief on poor families, not only on his Windsor estates but during tours of the provinces. William IV enjoyed a reputation for finding petitioners hard to resist, leading to an equally 'heavy charge' on the privy purse, and Victoria dealt with more than 800 personal petitions and begging letters in 1854 alone. Many applicants were relieved with payments of £1–2.[8] The monarchy was not deified simply because of its generous acts of kindness, however. Contractual kings were expected not just to accept the petitions of their subjects but to respond to them. People were not entirely impractical about this. Margaret Nicholson's friends had warned her many times that the King could not be expected to help all of his people simply on demand, but they did not try to dissuade her from carrying on the correspondence.[9] What petitioners did expect was to be taken seriously and to receive a reply. If, as it was said, George III laughed openly at one of John Wilkes's petitions, or if he failed to acknowledge any of Margaret Nicholson's appeals for assistance, these were serious constitutional offences. The King was petitioned, informally and without reference to the formal procedures of the levee, persistently and often. The crowd that regularly gathered around the garden gate at St James's to hand petitions to the King every time his carriage swept in was 'sometimes so great as almost to obstruct his entrance to the royal apartments'.[10] In the autumn of 1787, George III admitted he had been 'so often deceived' by petitioners that he had come to view the whole exercise with cynicism. Two French women who approached him in October were turned down simply because he had decided 'never to look' at petitions from foreigners.[11]

The symbolic survival of the touch linked the themes of petition and divinity. Ferdinand Smith Stuart, a war veteran, petitioned the throne in 1812 for the restoration of his pension. When, after being rebuffed by Prime Minister Perceval, he discovered that 'the Prince Regent has not read one line of my memorial', he realised he had only the Almighty left to turn to. Although sorry when his prayers for divine intervention were answered by Perceval's assassination, Stuart was convinced the Regent's negligence was the cause.[12]

Belief in the divinity of the monarchy survived the Act of Settlement in other ways. Divine intervention appeared to preserve the lives of kings and queens alike from the guns, rocks and knives of plebeian assailants, and the patient forbearance with which they endured their suffering, no less than their kindness in forgiving the miscreants, consistently evinced Christ-like qualities. When George III showed himself to the doubting Thomases of the levee room after being stabbed by Nicholson, 'even those who were best acquainted with his constitutional fearlessness were astonished at his admirable imperturbability'. And, in 1795, he rode dutoriously and 'fearlessly' through the middle of a violent and hostile mob after reminding his Lord of the Bedchamber that 'there is One above us all who disposes of everything on whom alone we depend'.[13] The audience at Drury Lane were incredulous at the King's decision to stay and watch the play after James Hadfield shot at him from the pit in 1800. 'A man on such an occasion should immediately feel what is his duty', he remarked to Sheridan.[14]

If the laudable dignity of George III helped launch his 'apotheosis', it was jarringly contrasted with the behaviour of his son in similar situations. Under attack by an unfriendly crowd in 1817, the Prince of Wales was criticised for appearing frightened, uninterested or aloof in the back of his carriage. While George III had spoken words of compassion and profundity to ensure Margaret Nicholson's safety, the very undivine William IV rather indecorously cried 'God, I'm hit!' and fell off his chair when Dennis Collins hit him on the head with a stone in 1832. Re-engagement with divinity did not occur until the accession of Victoria, who 'bravely' continued her evening carriage rides in 1840 and 1842 despite three separate attempts to shoot at her as she did so. In the opinion of the radical *Poor Man's Guardian*, the terrible English treason laws had been invented only to overawe the people. In the rationalist and secular republic of America, it pointed out, there were no such laws, but our own statutes were 'for nothing else but to establish and guard monarchy by terror and to impress the minds of ignorant people with the sentiment that the King is something more than a man ... which is all done for stage effect'.[15]

Finally, secularisation could not deny reliquary. Just as Nicholson's knife became a fetish-ised object, claimed and exhibited like a piece of the true cross, and pieces of George III's coach window, shattered by a hostile crowd in 1795, were sold as 'sacrilegious' souvenirs, so the pathetic personal effects of Dennis Collins, assailant of William IV, acquired symbolic value. Collins after his arrest gave his wooden leg and his ragged clothes to an enthralled French woman, and she, 'for the sake of possessing these relics, gave Collins new clothes for old ones'.[16]

Petitioning the throne in custom and practice

I saw him fall; the victim of distress,
To rolling royalty, had bent the knee:
But mis'ry, in the garb of merit's dress,
Pomp pass'd, with scorn, and grandeur would not see.[17]

The theoretical readiness of the Hanoverian monarchy to receive petitions was celebrated during the reigns of the first two Georges, although there is little evidence that either King was enthusiastic in practice. 'It were to be wished the King had more affability', sighed the Earl of Egmont after watching an enemy of Walpole slighted by George II in 1734; 'there are conjunctions of time when Kings should take some pains to please'.[18] Yet, despite Colley's conclusion that there was no popular 'cult of monarchy' before the reign of George III, a scattering of apocrypha survives.[19] John Bacon, an undertaker, was admitted to the Royal Chapel during Communion in 1728 so that he could present a letter to George II. Bacon placed a sealed infant-sized coffin beside the altar and left. The casket turned out to contain only 'insignificant' papers which the King kindly ordered to be returned to Bacon if he called for them. This he could not do, however, because the Bishop of London, who took umbrage at his interruption, had him committed to an asylum.[20] There was no suggestion that Bacon's intrusion had endangered the King. On another occasion, George II was prepared to spend a considerable time listening to the grievances of a man, dressed as a woman, who accosted him in Kensington Gardens in 1738, then presented him with a sealed petition and ran off. The content is unrecorded, but it does not appear to have pleased the King who sent a party of guards after the man and ordered night patrols in the gardens.[21]

Isolated though these two instances are, they do indicate that, although there were correct and formal procedures for presenting grievances to the throne, informal approaches were also tolerated. The correct form was by application to a civil servant at the palace. As we have seen, however, daily crowds of petitioners were allowed to wait for the King at St James's Gate until at least 1786. The Prince of Wales was a good deal less indulgent, and made perfectly plain his refusal to read unsolicited letters left for him at Carlton House. His equerries sent all letters back unanswered but took stronger action if the occasion demanded it. Nathaniel Jefferys, who believed the Prince owed him money, wrote repeatedly for attention but found 'all private remonstrances in vain'. When he threatened to publicise the debt, the equerry Colonel McMahon had him arrested and charged with the capital crime of extortion.[22] By the time of his coronation, George's inaccessibility had become well known. Some found it frustrating. Charles Emery told the Home Secretary that if his private letter to the King was to be opened and read by civil servants, he would rather have it returned instead. Sidmouth duly sent it back to him, unopened.[23]

If petitioners enjoyed sufficient influence at court, or were themselves important institutional bodies, the King might be prepared to receive their prayer 'on the throne'. Although this was comparatively rare, it did at least guarantee an immediate and formal response. The incumbent Bishop of London and the current Dean and Chapter of St Pauls jointly and successfully addressed the throne ten times between 1701 and 1795. Four were loyal addresses on accession, but there were anti-Jacobite addresses in 1716 and 1745, congratulations to George III on his escape from Margaret Nicholson and illness and an address supporting the proclamation against sedition in 1792. On all but one of these occasions, the address had been received on the throne and an answer given. The exception had been presented at the levee 'by mistake'. To deliver a loyal address in 1795, twenty-five 'principal' London clergymen were admitted to the palace and the address was 'received on the Throne in the Great Council Chamber. The King gave a written answer and we all kissed his hand'.[24] Institutions which fell out of royal favour risked losing such special dispensation. In Henry Hunt's opinion, the 'first time' George III 'refused to receive a petition from the Common Hall of the City of London upon the throne', in 1797, was commensurate with the decline of its political influence. The liverymen's acquiescence in the denial of their 'ancient right' to do so was unforgivable. When Common Hall petitioned the King in 1810, therefore, they were instructed to present their address via the Secretary of State, making this the 'first instance of a petition agreed to at a Common Hall being refused to be received in person by the King'.[25]

Cobbett tried in vain to obtain a personal audience with his King in September 1830, but was frustrated by the palace's insistence that the Home Secretary was the 'proper channel for petitions to his majesty'. When a small delegation of operative button-makers was permitted to approach the throne later that year, Cobbett believed it to be the first time 'the working people' had been so indulged since 1786.[26] It was certainly true that government interference became increasingly obstructive during the final years of the 'Old Corruption'. Ministers would not allow Hunt to present a radical address from Common Hall to William IV on his coronation in July 1830, and he complained bitterly about the unconstitutional behaviour of the new King's 'secret counsellors'.[27]

Alternatively, with the secretary of state's approval, petitions and letters could be presented to the King at the levee. For most private petitioners, this was the best channel of communication they could hope for, but replies were rarely given. This was rarely done in person however. More often, the task was performed by the home secretary himself, an aristocratic MP, or by a member of the court after the formal business of the levee was concluded. But the alienating etiquette of the levee was rarely to the taste of popular constitutionalists, who discouraged compliance with its forms. For the republican Richard Lee, the pretensions of the levee were an insult to the reciprocity of contract. Individuals who prostrated themselves before the King with an address so that they might be permitted to 'kiss his great red hand' were more like madmen than citizens, although they might rationalise their self-abasement as loyalism. 'Pitiful sorry wretch!', snorted Lee. 'Loyal thou may'st be; a man thou can'st never pretend to be!' [28]

Until the accession of William IV, the rules governing the presentation of addresses and petitions to the King at the levee were actually far from clear. It was not until the 'May Days' of 1832, when petitions praying for reform began to arrive by the cartload, that orders were issued from the Lord Chamberlain's Office to speed up and regulate presentation. Noblemen charged with presenting petitions were to write a brief account of the subject matter on a small card for the benefit of one of the lords in waiting, who would then quickly read it to the King while the petition was handed over.[29] Presentation was always accomplished in strict silence. After submitting a number of petitions via the Secretary of State without result, an impoverished cleric named Nathaniel Highmore attended George IV at a levee in 1821 but made the mistake of addressing the King on the 'fruitlessness' of his previous efforts. 'Push him', commanded the King, as soon as Highmore began to speak, and he was led out of the room. Highmore was affronted and declared the action unconstitutional: for how could a contractual King 'push from his feet a wronged and justly complaining subject'? Highmore's subsequent attempts to have his pension restored were doomed, and he took to writing rude notes to the King charging him with 'breach of covenant'. He was eventually arrested, charged with seditious language and locked in the bridewell.[30]

Correct and formal language was no guarantee of notice, as the tragic suicide of James Sutherland would reveal in 1791. Sutherland had been forced out of a well-paid job with the British Admiralty on the Mediterranean island of Minorca after a personal feud with the governor. He returned to London in 1785 to clear his name and claim compensation. He was advised he would not be noticed at the levee, so he arranged for a courtier to present four petitions to the King on his behalf between April and July 1785. They were not answered. Someone suggested that he might make more of an impression if he attended the Queen's Drawing Room, but it was the King he wanted to communicate with. The next three petitions, between 1786 and 1790, he himself pressed into the King's hand after following him to Windsor and Weymouth. But by this time frustration and poverty had overtaken Sutherland, who lost his home and family and fell prey to violent 'convulsions in my head'. All he wanted was a reply. When Parliament had turned him down, 'its sentiments were therefore made known; but, to this hour, I have not had the means of acquiring those of His Majesty'. A law should be passed, he wrote, 'to assure the communication of the Royal will by His Majesty's ministers to every subject who may in future present such a petition to the King'.[31]

Sutherland's next attempt to attract the King's attention was his last. In August 1791, with a loaded pistol in one hand and a final letter to the King in the other, he waited for the King's carriage in St James's Park, stepped forwards, dropped on one knee and shot himself dead. The note in his hand read:

> TO THE KING
> Sire ...
> ... With spirited and dutiful appeals and humiliating supplications, I have addressed you and your ministers; allegiance and protection are constitutionally reciprocal, and as the former never was forsaken by me, I had a right to expect that you would afford the latter ... When my hard case shall be published, how will the world be shuddered to hear that humanity had deprived me of every recourse but DEATH.[32]

Ministers frequently threw obstacles in the path of petitions they did not wish the monarch to receive. A loyal address to the King from an east Midlands' committee of dissenters was submitted to Under Secretary Evan Nepean shortly before Parliament debated the repeal of the Test and Corporation Acts in 1790 by a Mr Cooper, who also wanted to know whether the language and approach were correct. Nepean at first ignored the note, but Cooper presented himself at the Home Office to say that he needed a reply quickly as he wanted the King to receive the address before Fox introduced his motion for repeal the following day. The King was not in town, said Nepean, and 'it is not usual to present petitions of any sort to His Majesty on any other days than Wednesdays and Fridays', after the levee. Moreover, the form of Cooper's petition was 'not sufficiently regular to authorize its being laid before the King', and George III was never troubled by it.[33] Henry Hunt had enormous difficulty presenting the Spa Fields' petition to the throne in 1816. He could either hand it over at the levee in three weeks time, he was told, or, if he wanted an earlier response, he could submit it via Home Secretary Sidmouth immediately. When Hunt asked Sidmouth when he could expect a reply, he was told it was not the practice of the Regent to reply to petitions. If it required action, ministers would act upon it swiftly, making the answer perfectly clear.[34] A more cynical form of obstruction occurred in 1837 when Lord John Russell informed the London Working Men's Association that the

Queen might receive their loyal address in person at the levee provided they presented it wearing full court dress. This forced the LWMA to withdraw the application, but William Lovett was indignant at the 'gothic ignorance' that made 'such absurdities as dress swords, coats and wigs' necessary apparel for 'letting the sovereign hear of the addresses and petitions of the people'.[35]

Since neither social class nor good connections were any guarantee of Royal indulgence, petitioners often resorted to the purplest of prose to catch the king's ear. 'Most Glorious Sovereign!' began Warren Fitzroy, estranged fourth son of Lord Southampton, from a debtor's cell in 1791, 'It is with the greatest Humility, Respect and Obedience that I prostrate myself at your Majesty's feet, to implore the Gracious assistance of the most Humane, Just, Generous and Benevolent Sovereign in the Universe ...' (or so he hoped).[36] But Fitzroy was no more in need of a solicitous and forgiving father-figure than was Elizabeth Cook, a poor woman from Colne, Lancashire, who believed she had been cheated out of an inheritance. Cook admitted an inability to command fine phrases, but was certain 'your Majesty's wisdom will weigh my meaning more than the manner of performing'. She addressed him in plain language, therefore, 'knowing of your Fatherly care and tender affection which you show to all your great and numerous famely at large as a preserver of Wrights and liberty to all your Subjects'.[37] The faith of the poor in royal intercession knew no boundaries. Catherine Roberts, who thought the Prince of Wales owed her a property, hoped the King would call on her at home 'to Bring the afair to a Conclusion', and was disappointed when he did not come. She had seen the King in his carriage more than once, so knew what he looked like; but she could not speak to him because she was of a 'Bashful disposition amongst strangers' and lacked the 'curage to aproch so Great a Personage as you ... I nowd I had no Plase to Acomodate your Majesty nor the Prince of Wales neather'.[38]

Perhaps the most frequently employed form of petitioning, however, was the appeal for clemency from sentence of execution.[39] The institutionalisation of this aspect of the royal prerogative was effective, both as a brake on the sheer number of public executions (but not on the deterrent effect of a liberally applied bloody code) and as a regular demonstration of the king's concern for even the lowliest and most dysfunctional of his subjects. William Blackstone was not the only legal theorist to perceive the wider social benefits of these 'repeated acts of goodness coming immediately from his own hand'. The grand jury of the Isle of Ely considered the prerogative 'the brightest jewel in the British crown, and the most precious of the rights of the people'.[40]

Early murmurs of discontent: popular resistance to George III from Wilkes to Sayre

The first two decades of the reign of George III were marked by two popular causes productive of large-scale petitioning before the throne: the parliamentary ambition of John Wilkes; and support for the American rebels.

Wilkes's rise to the status of popular hero was meteoric. While MP for Aylesbury in 1763 he was jailed in the Tower for using his journal, *The North Briton*, to publish criticisms of the King's self-congratulatory speech to Parliament at the conclusion of the Seven Years' War.[41] Expelled from Parliament on his release, Wilkes left the country an outlaw, but returned to popular acclaim in 1768 to request a pardon and contest a parliamentary seat for Middlesex. He won, but was debarred from taking his seat. In the riotous scenes of protest that followed, Wilkes assumed the mantle of a popular defender of constitutional liberties against the arbitrary influence of the Crown. By casting himself as a friend of liberty and the defender of contract; Wilkes was instrumental in popularising theoretical concerns about the accountability of the king, the protection of the right to approach the throne and the greater exercise of communication by petition. Tory opinion was affronted at the inevitable vulgarisation of the Constitution and railed at the indignity of a king being told how to govern by 'every cobbler, tinker, porter and hackney-coachman'.[42] The vigour with which these campaigns were fought in the face of concerted opposition from the King and his ministers, made the revival of seventeenth-century arguments about legitimate resistance to oppression almost inevitable. By this means, Wilkes became the re-embodiment of Sidney, Hampden and Russell.[43] While constitutional questions like these were certainly expressed most audibly in the 1760s and 1770s through the medium of radical mass politics, we should not be surprised to find the consequences taking root in everyday life – in the personal and imaginary relationship between king and subject. The contractual basis of the discourse, in other words, did not confine its expression to issues of parliamentary reform.

The Wilkesite disturbances had an immediate impact upon the Crown. In 1768, the King was presented with petitions on the one hand appealing for intercession from striking sailors and on the other from supporters of Wilkes demanding the removal of ministers. These came not just from London, where one petition carried over 5,000 signatures, but from all over the country. Fifteen counties presented petitions to the throne: 1,200 people signed in Wiltshire, 1,800 in Berkshire, 2,000 in Gloucestershire and a remarkable 11,000 in Yorkshire. The total was claimed to be 60,000.[44] As Jephson saw it, Wilkes's petitions were remarkable both for their number, and for their language, which was 'far less deferential than usual', a clear sign that the public now saw

Parliament as 'venal and corrupt'.[45] George, who made no secret of his irritation with Wilkes and had openly urged ministers to have him removed from the House, did not hide his disdain. A year later, while Wilkes himself was again serving time in prison, a procession of loyalist merchants bearing an address to St James's, congratulating the King on his Government's resolute refusal to admit Wilkes to the Commons, was ambushed and pelted as it approached the palace. Wilkes's crowd proved so ferocious, in fact, that despite the arrival of sabre-wielding cavalry the merchant's procession was all but routed in a pitched but one-sided battle right outside the gates. The King and his ministers were almost 'besieged' in their own palace, and 'many of the mob cried Wilkes and no King, which is shocking to think on'. Popular disapproval of the King's inattentiveness to the supplications of Wilkes and his supporters grew rapidly. His coach was surrounded by protesting crowds as it went to and from the House of Lords in April, and further insults were hurled when he tried to escape to the races at Epsom in May. 'The behaviour of the people was as offensive as it could be without actual tumult', thought Walpole.[46]

Incidents like these made the King appear isolated and out of touch with popular opinion. The City of London, indignant at his refusal to answer their petition of protest in 1769, despatched a strongly worded remonstrance to the palace in response, comparing the King to the autocratic Stuarts. 'To a Remonstrance', wrote James Sedgwick, 'an answer must be given. If not, force and arms are the only remedies. May heaven prevent the use of such remedies.' But no such remedies were proposed. George received the remonstrance reluctantly and read the City a prepared answer castigating their efforts as 'disrespectful to his Majesty, injurious to his Parliament, and irreconcilable to the principles of the Constitution'. When he had finished he 'instantly turned round to his courtiers and burst out laughing'.[47] The affronted City agreed an even more forceful remonstrance in 1773, bemoaning the 'neglect and disregard' afforded to their previous efforts, and so strongly worded that the mayor was loathe to present it. Wilkes declined to accompany his fellow aldermen to St James with his handiwork because he was 'obnoxious to the King' and didn't wish to 'force himself into the Royal presence'. When the mayor finally presented it on 29 March, 'the King in his answer treated it as not serious, and as if the remonstrants could not expect any other response'.[48]

Whatever the merit of Wilkes's claim, the King's attitude to his petitioners was far from placatory and lent only added poignancy to the formation of the overtly Wilkesite Society of Supporters of the Bill of Rights. The SSBR, whose extravagant enthusiasm for petitioning knew few bounds, pioneered extra-parliamentary campaigning in defence of the 'true principles of the constitution' and paved the way for the mass platform politics of the *fin de siècle*. By referring the country back eighty years to the drafting of that Bill, the Society reminded the King and his ministers of their 'obligation' to respect public opinion in the form of petitions and the contractual consequences of arbitrary measures. In denying Wilkes and his electors their constitutional rights of just representation, claimed Sir George Saville, ministers had not only acted 'illegally' but 'betrayed their country'.[49]

George III's public profile continued in a perilous state during the Second Parliament of 1771. Ministers were pushed, insulted and jostled en route to the Commons, the royal coach was 'excessively hissed' and an apple thrown at the King as he made his way to the Lords. One man was taken up for shouting 'No Lord Mayor, no King!'; he defended his right to do so because he conceived himself a 'citizen' of London. The opposition blamed Government for destroying loyalty to the throne and alienating the King from public opinion. The Queen, it was said, had urged the King to stop the coach and 'ask his people what they wanted, what they complained of. You will have the truth told to you without disguise, said she, and hear what they clamour at'. Pitt declared the scale of disaffection completely without precedent and invoked the concord of the previous reign, when 'No petitions, much less remonstrances for redress of grievances, were carried up to the throne; nor were hired mobs necessary to keep the sovereign in countenance by their venal shouts'.[50] George II's cultivated indulgence of public opinion during the Jacobite years was, as already noted, a feature of Hanoverian constitutional mythology. When that monarch was surrounded by crowds in 1739 after the celebrated Captain Jenkins had portentiously lost his ear to the commander of a marauding Spanish privateer, it was recalled, he had listened to their complaints and acted upon them. The incident had 'so irritated the populace that they surrounded the parliament house, stopped several of the members and called repeatedly for War! War!, and on the late King's return to St James, addressed him in the same terms, which they constantly echoed whenever he appeared in public til the declaration of hostilities was made'.[51]

The contractual crimes of George III were further explored in popular satires and prints. He was the first British monarch to be caricatured in ways that rendered his personal character, personality and physicality instantly recognisable to the public. This is important because it identified the failings of the man rather than the institution, helping to clarify the demarcation between the human and divine spheres of royalty in the public mind. Graphic prints like *The Effects of Petitions and Remonstrances* and *The Fate of City Remonstrances* (1770) expressed outrage at the King's disregard for public grievances, not because he was quintessentially ill-disposed but because he was the feckless puppet of designing ministers. The fate of the city remonstrance, it was suggested, was to be fashioned into a kite for the young Prince of Wales to play with. But 'Junius', in a series of celebrated letters to the *Public Advertiser* considered the King more personally culpable. That 'dictum of the law, that the King can do no wrong', he suggested in 1771, was clearly an instance 'where theory is at variance with practice'.[52]

Other interest groups besides the Wilkesites sought to capitalise on George III's constitutional unpopularity during the early 1770s. Popular Jacobitism, no longer a significant insurrectionary threat, nevertheless retained a capacity to disturb and destabilise the Protestant State through occasional plots and conspiracies. The execution at Bristol of the English soldier Jonathan Britain for forgery, in 1772, exposed one such minor conspiracy. According to Britain's own eve-of-execution confession, supported by his posthumous autobiography, in 1769 he had become acquainted with a group of disaffected Irishmen and Frenchmen pledged to 'retard the progress' of the 'heretics who have overrun the greater part of Europe and America'. With four accomplices, Britain claimed complicity in the firing of British shipping in the naval dockyard at Portsmouth in 1770, a programme of inducing catholic soldiers to desert and join the French and a plot to assassinate the King in 1771.

According to Britain, he and three French accomplices first intended to shoot the King during a review on Wimbledon Common, but the plan was dropped at the last minute in favour of a nocturnal ambush in St James's Park on 6 June. If the story is true, George III, who had passed Britain in his sedan protected only by two Yeomen, owed his life that night to the assassin's faulty pistol. Britain stepped out from cover with his gun but, 'luckily examining the pan, found the priming gone'. He withdrew quickly and escaped. Britain was familiar with the argument that regicide was a pointless enterprise, but his French contacts had persuaded him otherwise. Wilkes' agitation had severely divided English public opinion,

> and if it was not for his Majesty (who is in the way), the patriots would be actually in open rebellion. Now if his Majesty was dead, a Regency must be appointed (as the heir is a minor) which would entirely consist of those noblemen who are at present unpopular in the public eye, and whose proceedings would never be relished by the opposite party, which would soon produce such intestine broils as would tear the constitution to pieces and at length bring on a civil war; and as several noblemen in this kingdom are more attached to the Stuart line than the House of Brunswick, he did not doubt that the true religion of Christ might once more flourish in this kingdom, tho' at this time nearly extirpated by the cursed heretics.

Fearing arrest, Britain decided to inform against his French comrades and spent several days trailing the King around London, holding treasonable letters as proof of his complicity in the Portsmouth plot. 'I never meant to shout at or hurt the person of his Majesty', he explained. 'True, I had a loaded pistol in my pocket at the time of following him, which my fears dictated as a guard to me and for no other purpose.' The whole plot, he wrote, had been nothing but a 'plain demonstration to what excesses men (by a mistaken zeal for religion) may be driven to'.[53] Another lone Jacobite, Edward Cavendish, wrote to Secretary of State Lord Rochford in 1772 to solicit his help in removing George III 'from the face of the earth and send him to hell'. Rochford ought to help, reasoned Cavendish, because he was 'secretly connected to the Stewart family'.[54]

If Lord North's administration had learned nothing else from their trouble with Wilkes, they had at least learned something of the symbolic power of public opinion. North's attempt to make the Platform an element in loyalist discourse at the outset of hostilities between Britain and the American colonies was dutifully supported by the King, although he was prophetically fearful of the consequences. 'As you seem desirous that this spirit should be encouraged', he assured North on being presented with a fawning address from Manchester in 1775, 'I will certainly not object to it, though by fatal experience I am aware that they will occasion counter-petitions.'[55] While loyalist and ministerial addresses to the throne were far more effectively co-ordinated (and carefully disseminated for publication in sympathetic newspapers) in these years than in the previous decade,[56] oppositionist petitioning ran into the usual difficulties of obstruction and ineffectuality. The King announced in 1775 that addresses to the throne, with the exception of those drawn up and presented by corporate bodies, would in future be received only at the levee,[57] and his ministers established a 'committee of oblivion' into which petitions protesting the war were allowed to drop out of sight, undiscussed.[58] At the same time, public petitioning steadily adopted more inclusive forms. Some 50,000 Britons between 1775 and 1778 signed their names to petitions or addresses either in support or opposition to the war. The widening chasm between the practices of presentation and reception was a source of further discontent and remonstrance before the throne.[59]

By the spring of 1775, the American newspaper press was suggesting that English radicals were now ready and willing to rise against the British Government. In March, two London liverymen, Arthur and William Lee, were the suspected authors of a tract urging British troops embarking for America to refuse to fire on the rebels. They were certainly the authors of a Common Hall address, a remonstrance and petition to the throne which accused the British State of exercising 'arbitrary power' in the colonies. Wilkes presented it to the King who declined to accept it on the grounds that it was unrepresentative. Livery petitions like this would in future be accepted only at the levee. The liverymen challenged these rules in June with another petition, but since the King reiterated his earlier decision with a reminder that 'I am ever ready to receive addresses and petitions, but I am the judge where', the contest remained unresolved.[60] Matters were brought to a head by the appearance of the 4 February edition of an opposition paper, *The Crisis*, which, in an essay entitled 'To the King' exposed every detail of George III's 'shameful and inglorious reign' and warned him unequivocally of impending insurrection:

> We are called upon, by the necessity of the times ... to point out to you, Sir, your own critical and DANGEROUS situation ... [no-one] can protect you from the People's Rage, when drove by your Oppressions, and till now unheard of cruelties, to a State of Desperation ... Be assured Sir, your Danger is great amidst all this *fancied* Security; and it will be impossible for them to preserve YOU from the just Resentment of an enraged, long abused, and much injured Nation ... Whenever the State is convulsed by civil Commotions, and the Constitution totters to its Centre, the Throne of *England* must shake with it; a Crown will then be no SECURITY, and at one Stroke, all the gaudy Trappings of Royalty may be laid in the Dust ... the Rights of mankind will be the only Objects in View; while the King and the Peasant must share one and the same Fate, and perhaps fall undistinguished together.[61]

In an attempt to stem such immoderately republican language, the House of Lords prosecuted the publisher, Samuel Axtell, for a seditious and treasonable libel against the King, but success in the courts did not calm the popular mood. When the paper was publicly burned by order of the court, there were disturbances on the streets of the capital as radical crowds tried to extinguish the flames.[62]

The Government saved its most decisive move until the autumn. In October, Stephen Sayre, a wealthy American recently elected a sheriff of London, and a friend of Wilkes, was arrested and thrown into the Tower for complicity in an alleged plot to kill the King. The principal witness for the prosecution was an American loyalist, Francis Richardson, an officer in the guards whose responsibilities included the defence of the Tower. According to Richardson, Sayre told him that since ministers had now lost faith in their own American policy the only real obstacle to peace was George III. If Richardson could persuade or bribe the soldiers in the Tower to neglect their duty, anti-war radicals 'in disguise' would take control of the building, kidnap the King as he went to open Parliament, confine him there briefly, then exile him to his German dominions and establish a British republic under Lord Mayor Wilkes and his sheriffs. 'Tearing Lord Mansfield, Lord North and Lord Bute to pieces would be of no material consequence', Sayre is supposed to have said 'We must strike at the fountainhead.'[63]

Many, including Walpole, thought the entire affair a ministerial invention to conjure an 'air of vigour' against popular opposition, intimidate leading radicals like Wilkes and Sawbridge, or to distract attention from unpopular colonial policies. Sayre's reported plans were so absurd, thought Walpole, that ministers would have put him in Bethlem if they thought he really believed in them, not taken him seriously by confining him in the Tower. In fact, Sayre did not appear to believe in the plans at all, and went to jail protesting his innocence. Government nevertheless seized the opportunity to arrest and question a large number of 'suspects', including several dissenting clerics and a smattering of disaffected guardsmen. Something, they believed, was definitely projected to disrupt the State Opening of Parliament. 'Thousands of incendiary papers' inciting a popular uprising were in circulation, and one had been shown to the King who ordered a doubling of his guard but would not cancel the procession. 'I know what my duty to my country makes me undertake and Threats cannot prevent me from doing that to the fullest extent', he declared.[64] There was no disturbance. Two days later, Sayre was finally granted bail and released. All charges were dropped by the end of the year and Sayre successfully prosecuted Lord Rochford the following summer for false imprisonment.[65]

Historians have been inclined to take the Sayre affair surprisingly seriously. Both John Sainsbury's study of London radicalism at the time of the American war and Bridget Hill's biography of Catherine Macaulay treat it as 'a genuine, albeit risible attempt at domestic insurrection', and draw heavily on the ministerial version of events in the Treasury Solicitor's Papers. Yet the prevailing opinion among contemporary commentators was sceptical. Sainsbury is reluctant to see ministerial intrigue behind the affair, despite acknowledging that Richardson was often in debt and certainly in receipt of secret service payments for his testimony. Richardson had also made himself conspicuous two months before Sayre's arrest by agitating for the American cause among striking shipwrights at Chatham. His loyalist credentials were not outstanding and he later admitted that he had formerly been an enthusiast in principle for American 'liberty'.[66] Richardson was critical of the ministry for its failure to convict Sayre. He was still living with the 'ridicule' heaped upon his testimony in the public prints more than a decade afterwards, and it niggled him that he had received no preferment from Government. He was still expressing his full belief in the plot in 1787, telling Evan Nepean that Sayre had been arrested too early by an impatient Secretary of State and against his own advice.[67] An even less plausible conspiracy was 'discovered' in 1777 when a confidence trickster and fraud, David Brown Dignam, tried to implicate the Duke of Richmond and Lord Shelburne in a new assassination plot. Dignam was imprisoned for fraud in April and died in Newgate in 1780.[68]

The universal acceptance of mass or inclusive petitioning by both radical and loyalist pressure groups was temporarily derailed in 1780 when the so-called Gordon Riots prompted a rethink of the whole notion of participatory politics. In Lord Loughborough's opinion, at least, the five days of destructive rioting in London that followed Parliament's rejection of the Protestant Association's enormous petition against Catholic relief had been caused by the attempt to present it *en masse* and in an intimidatory manner.[69] The scale and unexpectedness of the destruction, and the length of the disturbance, no less than the huge death toll, were quite without precedent in England and confirmed many people's worst fear that 'popular sovereignty' was but another name for mob rule. Apprehension about the unpredictability of large crowds therefore complicated the planning of the great Constitution Jubilee celebrations of 1788 marking the first centenary of the Glorious Revolution. In many provincial towns, crowds were marshalled and controlled at meticulously managed pageants but not encouraged to actively participate. In Bath, where the only Gordon rioting outside of London had broken out, there was no celebration at all; but the success with which a heavily structured itinerary imposed 'the utmost regularity and decorum' on the unpoliced market town of Devizes in Wiltshire[70] generated both relief and approval. In the years between the Constitution Jubilee and the degeneration of the French Revolution into terror and war, extra-parliamentary campaigning was fully revived in Britain by the renewal of popular agitation against the slave trade in the two inclusive petitioning campaigns of 1788 and 1792.[71]

At the same time, George III's public image was steadily rejuvenated. Beginning with his dismissal of the Fox–North coalition in 1783, 'joining the people on so important an occasion, against his ministers and against the parliament', as Samuel Romilly would later put it,[72] George was transformed from malignant autocrat to constitutional guardian in the space of twelve short months. The King's arbitrary appointment of Pitt to the post of First Minister trumpeted the Crown's clear independence of the legislature, casting the usually contentious prerogative in a suddenly favourable light, and giving future radicals cause for hope when entreating the King to dismiss unpopular regimes. By inviting the enfranchised to approve his decision by ejecting as many coalition members as possible in the 1784 election, the King further cemented his compact with public opinion.[73] All George's past faults, exclaimed Nathaniel Wraxall, were forgotten overnight:

> The same prince who, in March 1782, laboured under a load of prejudice and unpopularity, was considered in March 1784 as the Guardian of the Constitution, worthy of the warmest testimonies of affection, gratitude and respect. They poured in on him from all quarters, acknowledging the

blessings of his paternal government and approving the recent interference of his prerogative ... a new order of events and a new era seemed to commence from this auspicious date.[74]

From the middle of the 1780s, then, George III became an object of fascination for the English public. He seemed able to temper his natural aristocratic detachment with a disarmingly normal family life in which morality, economy and fatherly wisdom were well to the fore. At the same time, he patronised the arts and sciences, enjoyed the theatre and took a personal interest in the agricultural improvement of his own estates. 'Farmer' George, it appeared, was as much at home mucking out the pigs with his Windsor labourers, playing cards with the Queen, or ticking off his profligate son for wasteful expenditure, as he was in receiving foreign dignitaries at St James's or overseeing the nation's survival against Napoleon. By 1832, even the sternest critics of royalty looked back on his reign with fondness and allowed that, despite some early errors of judgement, his intentions had always been thoroughly patriotic. Lady Anne Hamilton's irreverent *Secret History* regarded the death of George IV as a 'providential release' but absolved George III from any 'intentional tyranny' whatsoever. Fault, if fault there was, was laid at the door of politicians and foreigners. Indeed, 'many a time has this monarch advocated the cause of the productive classes and as frequently have his ministers, urged on by the *Queen*, defeated his most sanguine wishes until he found himself a mere cipher in the affairs of state'. But for becoming the Queen's 'perfect slave' and the unwitting dupe of other 'crafty and designing persons', the old King would have become 'the real father of his subjects' and heeded all of their petitions.[75]

Notes

1 J. Barrell, 'Imagining the King's death: the arrest of Richard Brothers', *History Workshop Journal*, 37 (1994), 1–33; for Lee, see J. Mee, 'Apocalypse and ambivalence: the politics of millenarianism in the 1790s', *South Atlantic Quarterly*, 95:3 (1996), 672–97.
2 PRO, HO 42/123: Anon. to Prince Regent, 30 May 1812.
3 Esther 2:8; I Samuel 25.
4 PRO, HO 44/3: Anon. to Sidmouth, 23 October 1820.
5 PRO, HO 42/123: J. Duncan to the Prince Regent, 31 May 1812.
6 PRO, HO 42/123: Anon. to Prince Regent, 21 May 1812. The references were to Isaiah 1:16–18 and 55:6–23.
7 M. Bloch, *The Royal Touch: Sacred Monarchy and Scrofula in England and France* (London, 1973), pp. 11–12, 21–7, 219–23. Paul Kleber Monod argues that the abandonment of the touch had more to do with politics than with rationality, however. It was perfectly logical for the Hanoverian kings to scoff at a practice that only helped to legitimise the claims of the Jacobite opposition. See

P. K. Monod, *Jacobitism and the English People, 1688–1788* (Cambridge, 1989), pp. 127–32. The touch is not altogether dead, as anyone who remembers Princess Diana touching victims of leprosy or hugging aids patients will be aware.

8 Prochaska, *Royal Bounty*, pp. 12–16, 53–7, 94–6.

9 *Authentic Memoirs of Margaret Nicholson who Attempted to Stab his Most Gracious Majesty with a Knife as he was Alighting from his Carriage* (London, 1786).

10 Historical Manuscripts Commission, *Rutland Manuscripts*, vol. 3 (London, 1894), p. 329, Thomas Orde to the Duke of Rutland, 4 August 1786.

11 *The Times*, 17 October 1787.

12 PRO, HO 42/123: Ferdinand Smith Stuart to Richard Ryder, 22 May 1812.

13 J. H. Jesse, *Memoirs of the Life and Reign of King George III*, vol. 2 (London, 1866), p. 533; vol. 3, p. 214.

14 *Morning Chronicle*, 23 May 1800.

15 *Poor Man's Guardian*, 28 February 1835.

16 *Examiner*, 26 August 1832.

17 Eunohoo, *Elegy on the Death of James Sutherland Esq.* (London, 1791).

18 Historical Manuscripts Commission, *Manuscripts of the Earl of Egmont: Diary of the First Earl of Egmont (Viscount Percival)*, vol. 2: *1734–1738* (London, 1923), pp. 34–5.

19 Colley, *Britons*, p. 202.

20 *Felix Farley's Bristol Journal*, 12 and 19 October 1728.

21 *Egmont Diary*, p. 508.

22 J. H. Prince, *A Vindication of Mr Jefferys and his Pamphlet Against the Prince of Wales* (London, 1807). Jefferys was not prosecuted.

23 PRO, HO 44/2: Charles Kingsley Emery to Lord Sidmouth, 30 May 1820; Sidmouth to Emery, 9 June 1820.

24 PRO, HO 42/37: Bishop of London to Duke of Portland, with enclosures, 4 December 1795.

25 *Memoirs of Henry Hunt*, vol. 1, pp. 333 and 467; vol. 2, pp. 387–8.

26 *Political Register*, 11 September and 6 November 1830.

27 Belchem, *'Orator' Hunt*, pp. 181–2.

28 R. Lee, *The Rights of Kings: Number One of a Political Dictionary* (London, 1795).

29 *Figaro in London*, 17 March 1832.

30 Highmore addressed his letters variously to 'The Promise-breaking King', 'The Covenant-breaking King' and 'The Untruth-telling King'. The final message, sent to the King's private secretary, ran: 'Sir, King George the fourth is a liar and a cheat.' PRO, TS11/80/249: Papers for the prosecution of Nathaniel Highmore, 1821; N. Highmore, *A Letter etc. etc. to his Most Excellent Majesty the King* (London, 1819); N. Highmore, *A Petition Humbly Praying His Majesty (then Prince Regent) to Dismiss From His Ministry the Earl of Liverpool; Presented at the Levee* (London, 1820).

31 J. Sutherland, *A Letter to the Electors of Great Britain by James Sutherland Esq., Late Judge of the Admiralty at Minorca* (London, 1791).

32 *The Times*, 18 and 19 August, 1791.

33 PRO, HO 42/16: Nepean to Grenville, 1 March 1790, enclosing copy of the address.

34 *Memoirs of Henry Hunt*, vol. 3, pp. 357–62.

35 Birmingham Public Library, Lovett Papers, 'The Queen and her Ministers', fol. 110.
36 PRO, HO 42/19: Petition of Warren Fitzroy to the King, 30 October 1791.
37 PRO, HO 42/18: Petition of Elizabeth Cook to the King, 9 January 1791.
38 PRO, HO 42/18: Petition of Catherine Roberts to the King, January 1791.
39 For a comprehensive discussion of the mercy petitions preserved in HO 47, see Gatrell, *Hanging Tree*, pp. 197–221, see also P. King, 'Decision-makers and decision-making in the English criminal law, 1750–1800', *Historical Journal*, 26:1 (1984), 26–58; and, for an overview: C. Emsley, *Crime and Society in England, 1750–1900* 2nd edn, (London, 1996), pp. 253–5; R. Hughes, *The Fatal Shore: A History of the Transportation of Convicts to Australia, 1787–1868* (London, 1986), pp. 35–6; and Leon Radzinowicz, *A History of English Criminal Law and its Administration from 1750* (London, 1948), vol. 1, p. 190.
40 Both quotations from Gatrell, *Hanging Tree*, pp. 200, 203.
41 The best sources for Wilkes are still G. Rude, *Wilkes and Liberty* (London, 1962) and J. Brewer, *Party Ideology and Popular Politics at the Accession of George III* (Cambridge, 1976); but I have found the following helpful: Colley, *Britons*, pp. 105–17; Tilly, *Popular Contention*, pp. 150–75.
42 John Wesley quoted in Clark, *English Society*, p. 237.
43 Wilson, *Sense of the People*, pp. 212–28.
44 Rude, *Wilkes and Liberty*, pp. 116–22.
45 Jephson, *The Platform*, vol. 1, pp. 48, 53.
46 Rude, *Wilkes and Liberty*, pp. 63–5, 71. See also letters from Walpole to Horace Mann, 23 March and 11 May 1769, in W. S. Lewis, W. H. Smith and G. L. Lam (eds), *Horace Walpole's Correspondence with Horace Mann* (London, 1967), pp. 98–9, 115.
47 G. Thomas (ed.), *Memoirs of the Marquis of Rockingham and his Contemporaries*, (London, n.d.), vol. 2, pp. 173–4. For Sedgwick, see Jephson, *The Platform*, vol. 1, p. 69.
48 D. Doran (ed.), *Horace Walpole's Journal of the Reign of King George III, 1771–1783* (London, 1858), pp. 188–93.
49 Thomas, *Rockingham*, p. 173.
50 W. S. Taylor and Capt. J. H. Pringle (eds), *Correspondence of William Pitt, Earl of Chatham* (London, 1839), vol. 4, pp. 171–2. See also the letter from Walpole to Mann, 30 March 1771, in Lewis, Smith and Lam, *Correspondence*, p. 291; *Newcastle Journal*, 30 March – 6 April 1771, 6 April – 13 April 1771.
51 *Felix Farley's Bristol Journal*, 9 November 1771.
52 Carretta, *George III and the Satirists*, pp. 119–122, 129, 138–9, 146–53.
53 J. Britain, *History of the Life of Jonathan Britain* (London, 1771); *Some Particulars of the Life and Death of Jonathan Britain who was Executed at Bristol for Forgery, by a Gentleman who Attended him* (Bristol, 1772).
54 PRO, SP 37/9: Anthony Todd to Sir Stanier Porton, with enclosures, 20 October 1772.
55 Jephson, *The Platform*, pp. 71, 94-5.
56 Bradley, *Popular Politics*, pp. 53–4, 189–91.
57 *Ibid.*, p. 45.
58 *Ibid.*, pp. 24-5.
59 Tilly, *Popular Contention*, p. 173. These inclusive forms of collection were im-

portant because they signalled a move away from the principle of virtual representation by local elites in the petitioning process, and its replacement of the maxim of 'quality' with one of quantity.

60 J. Sainsbury, *Disaffected Patriots: London Supporters of Revolutionary America, 1769–1782* (Gloucester, 1987), pp. 84–92.

61 PRO, TS11/209/884: Notes for the prosecution of the *The Crisis*, 1775, and the *The Crisis*, 3 and 4 February 1775.

62 J. B. Saunders, '*The Crisis* of London and American revolutionary propaganda, 1775–1776', *Social Studies*, 58 (1967).

63 Sainsbury, *Disaffected Patriots*, p. 100; PRO, TS11/542/1758, Information of Francis Richardson, 20 October, 1775.

64 Doran, *Walpole's Journal*, pp. 506–9; Letters from Walpole to William Mason, 25 and 27 October 1775, cited in C. Bennett, G. Cronin Jr and W. S. Lewis (eds), *Horace Walpole's Correspondence with William Mason*, vol. I (London, 1955), pp. 227, 229; *Annual Register*, Appendix to Chronicle, 1775, pp. 239–43; J. Fortescue (ed.), *Correspondence of George III, 1760–1783*, vol. 3: July 1773– December 1777 (London, 1928), p. 274: Lord Rochford to George III, 25 October, 1775; Sainsbury, *Disaffected Patriots, pp. 100–1.*

65 See *The Trial of the Cause on an Action brought by Stephen Sayre Esq. against the Right Honourable William Henry, Earl of Rochford ... for False Imprisonment* (London, 1776).

66 Sainsbury, *Disaffected Patriots*, pp. 100, 102 and 104–5; B. Hill, *The Republican Virago: The Life and Times of Catherine Macaulay, Historian* (Oxford, 1992), p. 194.

67 PRO, HO 42/12, Francis Richardson to Evan Nepean, 30 July 1787.

68 See letters of Walpole to Mason, 13 March 1777, in Bennett, Cronin and Lewis, *Walpole's Correspondence with Mason*, pp. 288–9; and of Edmund Burke to D. B. Dignam, 25 September 1779, in J. A. Woods (ed.), *Correspondence of Edmund Burke*, vol. 4 (Cambridge, 1963), pp. 134–5.

69 N. Rogers, 'Crowd and people in the Gordon Riots', in E. Hellmuth (ed.), *The Transformation of Political Culture: England and Germany in the Late Eighteenth Century* (Oxford, 1990), pp. 48–50.

70 *Bath Chronicle*, 6 November 1788; *Salisbury Journal*, 10 November 1788.

71 S. Drescher, *Capitalism and Anti-Slavery* (London, 1986), p. 74.

72 Quoted in Colley, *Britons*, p. 208.

73 J. Gifford, *History of the Political Life of William Pitt* (London, 1809), vol. 1, p. 163.

74 Jephson, *The Platform*, vol. 1, pp. 152–5, 164-5.

75 Lady Anne Hamilton, *Secret History of the Court of England from the Accession of George III to the Death of George IV* (London, 1832), vol. 1, pp. 43, 59, vol. 2, p. 233

3

Monarchy and the policing of insanity

'It is remarkable', observed the *Morning Chronicle* in 1786, 'that most of the miscreants who either murdered or attempted to murder their monarchs were insane'.[1] Regicide, it was often suggested in the eighteenth century, could be a product only of insanity, for who but a lunatic would compass the death of the king? But the casual association of regicide with madness is not confined to the ill-considered judgements of contemporary polemic. 'Most would-be assassins are mentally ill' was Nigel Walker's considered twentieth-century judgement. 'Even a constitutional monarch seems to capture the imagination of the mentally disordered more easily than the most charismatic of politicians'.[2]

While the theory of the eighteenth-century Constitution placed the king as an equal partner in a tripartite and secular separation of powers, the treason laws protected him as they had done since the reign of Edward III. The king's earthly body remained central to the cosmology of the State for, 'he is the Sun of the System, communicating life, light, motion and energy to every part and maintaining the whole in order, harmony and cohesion'.[3]

The Treason Act of 1351 defined high treason in a number of ways, beginning with the 'compassing and imagining' of the death of the king, the queen, or the prince of Wales. The deliberately vague language of the Act was intended to cover the commission of any 'overt act' that might cause the king to lose either his title or his life. Since he was bound by the coronation oath to defend a Constitution comprising King, Lords and Commons, any threat to the institution of monarchy might also endanger his life. The treason law thereby protected each of the king's 'two bodies' at one and the same time. By clarifying amendments passed in 1796 and 1817, it became explicitly treasonable to compass or imagine *any* harm to *any* member of the Royal Family, and implicitly treasonable to publicly advocate republicanism or any other political ideas that might result in the death of the king.

In theory, the prosecution had to demonstrate the accused's *intention*, but it was always arguable that, since any sane man should have considered the consequences of his actions, whether *expressly* intended to kill the king or not, he must certainly have 'compassed and imagined' the outcome.[4] The latitude of the law was much discussed and was occasionally the source of wry humour. Two 'shabby' London fortune-seekers alleged a fictitious plot to kill George II with a wind-gun in 1756. Instead of the reward money they had anticipated for their 'loyalism' however, they were thrown into jail by the Earl of Holderness, 'it being High Treason to imagine the death of the King'.[5]

Such levity notwithstanding, treason defendants enjoyed a number of special privileges, so that they were, in Erskine's words, 'covered all over with the armour of the law'. By far the most inconvenient of these from the government's point of view, was the right, granted by an act of William III, to retain the most eminent defence counsel in the land at public expense. This not only guaranteed the case further publicity but made securing a conviction doubly difficult – especially if the accused was defended by an advocate as able as Erskine – and the treason complained of somewhat doubtful. A treason defendant was also entitled to the addresses of all the jurors and witnesses and a copy of the indictment ten days before the start of the trial. Government was understandably reticent about bringing to court treason cases where the overt act of the accused was either trifling or insane. It is true that the wilful conflation of all regicide with insanity was more a matter of colloquial usage than of law, but defendants were aware that if they could prove themselves *non compos mentis*, they would be judged incapable of compassing or imagining anything very much at all.

Such was the fear that genuine traitors might secure acquittal by affecting madness that the law was amended during the reign of Henry VIII to prevent a defence of insanity resting on the behaviour of the accused *after* the act was committed, but these clauses were subsequently repealed. The relationship between an insanity defence and the treason statutes was refined several times by case law during the eighteenth century, however, the most often-cited cases being generally obstructive ones. In 1723, Lord Onslow was shot and wounded, and a threat made against the King's life, too, by a servant known as 'Mad Ned Arnold'. The defendant was not mad enough to impress the judge, however, who ruled that if he was able to buy a gun and fire it at his intended victim, he could not be entirely deprived of reason. Arnold's insanity defence was therefore inadmissible. In 1760, Lord Ferrers murdered his own steward and stood trial before his peers in the House of Lords. His attempt to establish his own insanity was unsuccessful because it required him to demonstrate an ability to reason, an unattainable quality for anyone truly insane.[6]

In June 1788, on the eve of the French Revolution, George III suffered the first attack of an illness which, over the years, would slowly incapacitate him, deprive him of his sight and leave him 'raving' like a lunatic. After 1810, he became incapable of effectively performing his duties, so that a Regency Bill conferring those responsibilities on the Prince of Wales was reluctantly conceded the following year. Believed at the time to be a form of nervous madness, the King's complaint has since been diagnosed as porphyria.[7] In effect, the precise nature of the illness mattered very little. Its importance was that, in the 'Age of Reason', George's own ability to reason and make decisions on matters of State was severely compromised; negating, indeed, his contractual qualification to be king. According to Locke, if a king lost his authority, 'there he is no King', and if he clung to power he might become a just cause of resistance. Locke's hypothesis referred to a king who lost his authority by exceeding it, a constitutional error rarely levelled at George III in the late 1780s, but it was nevertheless a pertinent observation on the consequences of royal insanity.[8] Although his great dignity under affliction did George immense credit, his derangement and official incapacity played some part in the construction of a secular, fallible and essentially ordinary monarchy. The suffering George, with his delicately wavering personal and institutional authority, was the first British monarch to invite both sympathetic approachability and unruffled voyeurism among his subjects.

That the King's illness should have struck him at a time when political 'madness' was threatening to sweep monarchs from their thrones the length and breadth of Europe only made matters more grave. In classical literature, kings had long been driven to Lear-like madness by their own narcissism and the neglect of their public responsibilities. Public belief in the madness of George III would not only have been politically devastating for Pitt's ministry, but constitutionally devastating at a time when the radical critique of power – the alleged neglect of the people and their petitions – and the promotion of such innovative abstractions as the 'rights of man' threatened to undermine the whole basis of tripartite government. Radical and Whig politicians alike found in the King's apparently degenerating mental state all the proof they needed for their assertions that personal ambition and corrupt connivance with the aristocracy had undermined *his* constitution as surely as it had undermined the nation's. Accordingly they demanded a regency for the unpopular Prince of Wales for no better reason than that he could be relied upon to remove Pitt from office. As Nicholas Rogers has pointed out, the 'quite genuine' relief felt by many Britons at the King's temporary recovery in 1789 had as much to do with popular opposition to a Foxite Regency as it did with love for the King.[9]

The poignancy of that first illness was all the greater because it came just two years after George had so impressively stamped his own wisdom, reason and humanity on the course of the Margaret Nicholson affair. Nicholson's outrage had affected wider public attitudes to insanity, for it offered incontrovertible proof that mental instability posed a threat to the realm. It requires no wholesale endorsement of Foucault's 'great confinement' thesis to acknowledge that at this time English attitudes to the 'dangerously mad' became increasingly sympathetic to their confinement.[10] And the systematic confinement of men and women who became 'troublesome' to the King was far more readily accepted after the summer of 1786 than it had been before. As the Earl of Guildford put it a few days after the Nicholson outrage,

> Our laws are, in my opinion, very deficient in not taking care of the confinement of persons insane. I meet two frequently in my garden whom the people who ought to confine them at home let them go about where they please – They appear at present very inoffensive. – But when the senses are disordered, nobody can tell what a sudden phrensy may put into their heads.[11]

The presence and possible danger of madmen around the Royal Family suddenly became more noticeable. As the author of *Sketches in Bedlam* noted in a comment about the unsuccessful regicide Urban Metcalf, he was 'one of the class of lunatic visitants who, some years since ... were so assiduous and troublesome in their visits to Buckingham House, and their endeavours to gain admission there'.[12] Nicholson's detention eased the process by which the dangerously mad might be neutralised through confinement in asylums. Some were a nuisance but were hardly dangerous. In 1788, for instance, Thomas Smith Murray was committed by order of Grenville and Nepean. Claiming to be an illegitimate son of the deceased former heir to the throne Prince Frederick, Murray was incensed at the King's refusal to acknowledge his petitions for recognition and believed George's illness was a form of divine punishment. 'His Majesty will never enjoy health while I am thus unjustly persecuted', he told ministers, but Nepean judged him a 'scoundrel' and he was committed for lunacy.[13]

Two men who imagined themselves in love with the King's daughters were confined to asylums on Home Office instructions. Thomas Stone, a lawyer with 'somewhat encumbered estates', in 1787 begged the Queen to let him marry the Princess Augusta Matilda. To stop his frequent appearances at the palace gates, Stone was taken up and put first in the bridewell, and then, with the complicity of the mad-doctor Thomas Monro, admitted to Bethlem. As Georgiana Townshend noted, Stone was not the first 'mad lover' the Princess had endured and the *The Times* thought it 'singular that a profession of love for the Princess Royal should be considered as a crime equal to the attempt of assassinating the King'. Stone seemed rather surprised himself, and said he 'would never have entered on the business if he had imagined such a rout would have been made of it'. In Bethlem, visitors remarked about Stone's 'steady, rational' conversation and apparent soundness of mind. He could understand the King's desire to have him incarcerated, he is reported to have said, but (indicating the deranged inmates all around him) 'Are these ... fit companions for a man not desperately mad? To be obliged to live in such a place is of itself sufficient to create distraction. Oh! I could scarcely have committed an offence that deserved such a punishment.'[14] He was followed, in 1788, by a hairdresser called Spang who supposed himself in love with the Princess Elizabeth. Arrested for wandering about in Windsor Castle 'boldly as he ought, like a man', Spang was sent as a vagrant back to his parish where parish officers secured him in a private asylum.[15] Stone and Spang may well have been harmless. Ministers were not so sure about a man from Leeds who wrote to the King in 1791 giving him a month to offer the hand of Augusta Sophia on pain of 'Treason and Death if my request be not granted ... I have both friends and money and a large army that will assist me in gaining the object of my heart'. But the man could not be traced.[16]

Cases like these point to associations between the themes of madness, love and regicide. As Arlette Fargé has observed, 'King loving and King killing were the same attitude seen from a different angle and generated by the very principles of sovereignty.'[17] This sometimes produced unexpected results. In 1820, a man who first fantasised about his membership of a secret conspiracy to kill George IV suddenly had a 'religious vision' in which God ordered him not to kill the King but to save him instead. He accordingly the following day supplied the Home Office with a list of fantasy conspirators.[18] For lovers of the Royal Family, the conceptual boundaries of royal space were a good deal harder to read within the rules of constitutional and contractual monarchy than they had ever been under divine right. Where, for example, did approachability end and intrusiveness begin? Under the reciprocity of contract, what limits could be placed upon the mutual love of monarch and subject? And if the king was less divine than human, more open to sensibility, emotion and feeling than purely spiritual *agape*, how were the sacred and the profane to be distinguished?

Most subjects read the parameters of royal space conventionally and without causing offence. For the troublesome, however, boundaries were there to be negotiated. The sexual mystique of the monarch was associated at root with the mythology of the royal touch. A desire for physical contact, most commonly to kiss the royal hand, frequently inspired ordinary people to travel immense distances in the hope of indulgence. Apocryphal tales of occasional successes only encouraged the practice. In 1717, for instance, the *Weekly Journal* carried the story of a poor country woman who presented herself at the gates of St James's and informed the porter she had just travelled 150 miles in the hope of kissing the Prince of Wales's hand. When news of her mission reached the Prince, he did not pronounce her mad, but admitted her to an ante-room where he 'graciously granted her request', presented her with five guineas and sent her down to the kitchens for a free lunch.[19]

We will meet a large number of deluded royal lovers on the following pages, mostly men, and often those who made an appearance early on in the reign of the young, virginal and eligible Queen Victoria. It is a theme which frequently expressed itself in the subversive symbolism of penetration fantasies; the 'irrational' desires of the mad to illicitly force their way into the most private recesses of royalty, and the inquisitive journalism of the respectable press that gave them nourishment. One can also read these interests in the representative politics of scurrilous radicalism in the Regency years. As Iain McCalman has found, disreputable radicalism revelled in making scandalous connections between royalty, depravity and immorality. Jacobin infiltration of the court was equally enticing.[20] Popular enjoyment of the scandal that arose over the murder of Sellis, the Duke of Cumberland's valet, in 1810 was rooted in rumours of sexual indiscretion, but rumours also surfaced that Sellis was a secret Jacobin, intimate with a French cook who had obtained work in the Royal household (and who was therefore in a position to poison the entire Royal family); a frequent passer of seditious remarks, and even 'the man who threw the stone at the King in going to the House of Commons' in 1795.[21]

Nicholson's madness was believed to have been the result of melancholia over a lost lover; a condition which developed into an irrational love–hate relationship with her King. Eighteenth-century women were believed especially susceptible to this sort of Ophelia-like distraction.[22] Similarly, Elizabeth Davenport, a royal servant who had to be dragged screaming from the Queen's bedroom in 1813, was thought to be suffering from an unrequited passion for a clergyman.[23]

Alternatively, troublesome subjects might fall prey to what the mad-doctor William Perfect in 1787 defined as 'arrogant insanity'. Caused by an excess of pride, the most typical manifestation of mental arrogance was a deluded belief in one's own superior claim to the Crown (and occasionally to divinity).[24] John Goode, committed in 1837 for shouting obscenities at Queen Victoria, is a good example. Goode thought he was King John II, the second son of George IV and Queen Caroline. Sometimes, noted his keepers, he thought he was God. In the same period, James Stevenson thought he had a better claim on the Crown than Victoria because of a private seventeenth-century Act of Parliament in his favour, and John Darby Shelly thought he was the Duke of Australia. All three were committed to Bethlem by order of the secretary of state.[25] But relatively few individuals who suffered delusions of this kind ever became directly troublesome to the Royal Family and so remained beyond the notice of Whitehall. Many were nevertheless committed privately to asylums by worried relatives. In 1849 William South thought Victoria wanted to marry him, Thomas Rex believed he was heir to the throne by direct descent from William III and Raimond Gibouin considered himself not only the rightful ruler of France and England but actually 'Emperor of the Universe' as well. All three were privately committed to Hanwell asylum, Middlesex.[26]

Bow Street and the security of the monarch

The pride taken by freeborn Englishmen in the low-cost amateurism of the nation's policing has become something of a mainstay in historical accounts of crime and social control in the eighteenth century. In stark contrast to the centralised, overbearing and intrusive policing endured by the French, a strong libertarian mythology effectively obstructed the introduction of a professionally organised force in England until after the passing of the Great Reform Act in 1832.[27] Consequently, while the security of the French King was watched over by a legion of spies, informers and uniformed officers, all under the direct control of government, the personal safety of his British counterpart was largely dependent on social compact, consensual politics and good luck.

The royal palaces were guarded during the eighteenth century by an intentionally unobtrusive complement of guards, equipped with muskets and live ball. The military's unpopularity with civilians was, however, occasionally problematic. In 1791, for instance, a roofer was shot by a sentry at St James's for carelessly dropping a brick-bat too close to the latter's foot.[28] The guards, who also formed a colourful mounted escort for the King whenever he travelled, were rarely called upon to deal with any trouble, and their main function was ceremonial rather than practical. Since 1773, the royal parks surrounding the palaces had been out of bounds to horses and private carriages without tickets. This was intended to preserve patrician privileges from the democratising threat of 'throwing open the Park Gates to every shopkeeper in London', and to enhance the security of the monarch. Guards had lists of all those granted entitlement, but by the end of the century there were 550 names to keep track of and 'every day numbers pass without leave or under wrong names'.[29] Protection from hostile and over-enthusiastic subjects was left to the Bow Street magistrates' office. Headed by a chief magistrate who was answerable, after 1782, only to the newly created Home Office, Bow Street was generously funded from the civil list, enjoyed city-wide jurisdiction and exerted a degree of informal influence in the provinces as well. The office therefore set its own agenda during the 1780s under Sir Sampson Wright and William Clark.[30] and kept an eye on known troublemakers and stalkers around the palaces. In the absence of a significant number of trained constables, however, security operations remained low-key.

Improvements were first made after the Nicholson incident in 1786 for, according to one officer, the 1780s and 1790s were years in which 'the King and the Royal Family were frequently teased with lunatics'.[31] Some time before 1796, two reliable Bow Street officers were made permanent constables to the Royal Court. 'The palaces were afterwards frequently infested with mad people', it was recalled in the *Court Journal*, 'one of whom actually got into the Queen's palace and found his way into the private apartments of the princess of Homberg. Three of the porters were in consequence discharged and [John] Townsend and [Patrick] Macmanus were appointed to attend the court'.[32] Their duties, which involved both protection and detective work, were not confined to the capital. Macmanus was sent to Weymouth with another officer, Anthony, in July 1796 to attend the King throughout his stay there.[33] In 1788, Sampson Wright sent him to Somerset in pursuit of a man suspected of making a nuisance of himself at St James's. The Reverend Henry Norman had made threats against the King and tried to gain admittance to his birthday ball; Norman had then visited his family in Somerset and stabbed his brother with a breadknife. Macmanus, who believed Norman's whole family had a 'rooted aversion to the Royal Family, which they never scrupled to express in the most public manner', was ordered to find and detain him.[34] Lunatics continued to find their way into the palaces, however. In 1796, a woman calling herself Charlotte Guelph and claiming to be an illegitimate daughter of the Queen was found wandering the corridors of the palace and demanding family papers. She would 'have her majesty's head off and trample it under her feet', Guelph told the guards who arrested her. 'Lunacy has been amazingly prevalent of late', observed a pamphleteer who saw the problem as a contagion spreading from those 'eminently conspicuous first rate lunatics' Nicholson and Brothers.[35]

Townsend and Macmanus were not appointed solely to police lunacy: there was concern among ministers about the ideological threat posed to the King by emissaries of the French Revolution, especially after the outbreak of war in 1793. Lord Grenville had information from various sources, including a double-agent of his own, that the Jacobin Convention intended sending assassins to England to murder George III. The King did not appear to take these threats seriously, either in London or during tours of the provinces. He felt safe enough behind the walls of his palace to attribute the number of 'dangerous weapons' discovered in his garden in 1799 to the zealous efficiency of the police chasing 'dangerous persons' around the city and forcing them to throw incriminating materials over his wall. When he visited Weymouth to take the waters, he grew irritated with his military escort and saw no need to tolerate them while he exercised his legs on the cliffs. During the excursion of 1794, responsibility for the King's safety fell to the Marquis of Buckingham, an incorrigible alarmist who was convinced his charge would be carried away by a nocturnal raiding-party of French smugglers and loudly complained about the inadequacy of the military forces at his disposal. He had a thirty-two gun warship 'whose captain is never sober', two frigates (which accidentally exchanged shots with one another during a false alarm in September) and 150 foot soldiers, but still thought the King 'most insecure'.[36]

After the cathartic shock of the crowd attack on George III's state coach in 1795, the policing of the processional route between St James's and Parliament was slowly improved. The coach itself was strengthened with copper panels instead of the usual plate glass on either side of the central window,[37] and additional soldiers and constables drafted in to escort the King in and out of the palace.[38] At the Opening of Parliament in May 1796, magistrates and constables were ordered to be 'particularly careful that no person whatever be permitted to get into the trees in that part of the Mall through which His Majesty will pass', magistrates instructed to sit through the night, and thirty additional life guards assigned to the coach.[39] When Richard Ford became chief magistrate in 1800, the system was further improved. Stipendiaries from each of the seven police offices were now told not only to take responsibility for designated stretches of the routes but to marshal a total of 350 Bow Street and Westminster constables. All officers were to be in place an hour before the King left the Palace. Ford told them 'to be particularly careful in preventing any ill-disposed persons from creating any Disturbance', and to remain on duty until late in the evening.

Ford, already well aquainted with secret service work through his previous post as private secretary to the Duke of Portland and through his links to William Wickham and the Alien Office, took his responsibilities towards the Royal Family extremely seriously, filing occasional reports to Evan Nepean at the Home Office. By 1802, Ford had reorganised and enlarged the royal protection squad to five with three officers drawn from the 'most active, intelligent and decent officers' on the payroll, and assigned them to permanent duty in each of the palaces. The old hands, Macmanus and Townsend were joined by John Sayers to cover St James's Palace and Buckingham House, Henry Edwards was assigned to Windsor and Thomas Dowsett to Kew. Two of them would also be sent with the King to Weymouth whenever he went there, and the squad's remit was to 'prevent improper people from approaching His Majesty or committing depredations on the persons of those who go to court'. Ford already considered them to have been 'of great use' in the past, but their role as royal police was now made fully institutional.[40]

The gradual modernisation and enlargement of the capital's police during the first quarter of the nineteenth century made the prevention of trouble around royal premises considerably easier. Ford established a large and innovatory force of mounted police at the Bow Street office in 1805, and these men were available to be despatched at short notice to the Regent's palace at Carlton House – in 1811, for instance, simply because magistrates thought there was a possibility of a hostile gathering beside the garden wall.[41] Closer Home Office control of Bow Street was steadily formalised under Sidmouth through the appointment of government placemen as supervisory officers.[42] Moreover, the general growth of the force effectively relieved Townsend and Sayer of any other police work, so that by 1816, they were accompanying the Regent virtually everywhere he went. As Sayer put it: 'We attend at Carlton House and follow all the movements of the Royal Family; therefore wherever the Royal Family go, we go; on public occasions we attend them. We are not suffered to go into the country; we must not go into the country; we never go into the country at all, without it is when the Royal Family go.' For these responsibilities, he and Townsend received an annual salary of £200 each.[43]

As the management of planned royal spectacles made increasing demands on manpower, large squads of officers from the new police became indispensable. William IV was attended by a large force of Bow Street men on visits to the races at Epsom and the chief London magistrate enjoyed complete autonomy over their deployment, despite it being far from his jurisdiction. After the establishment of the Metropolitan Police in 1829, however, Bow Street's role began to be questioned. As Secretary of State at the death of William IV in 1837, Lord John Russell requested 100 Metropolitan officers to help regulate the dead King's lying in state at Windsor, 'to prevent the entrance of known improper or suspicious characters' and to ensure 'proper decorum'. But Russell's insistence that the men take orders from the Bow Street magistrates was enormously humiliating to the Metropolitan Commissioners, whose sole authority over their own men had been guaranteed in 1831. There was tension and a lack of co-operation between the two squads.[44]

In 1839, the Home Office assumed formal control of the Bow Street force and incorporated it, along with the Thames River Police, into the Metropolitan Police. At the same time, a small police station was established close to Buckingham Palace, in Gardiner's Lane, in an effort to professionalize the protection of the building, and to afford immediate assistance to the military guards who patrolled the grounds each night. Inspector Russell, placed in charge of a small body of regular uniformed constables at Gardiners' Lane, therefore became the Royal Family's first full-time police inspector.[45] The attitude of the State towards the young and 'vulnerable' Victoria was palpably protective from the moment of her accession; but particularly after the discovery of incorrigible intruders like the Boy Jones and the apprehension of

Oxford, Francis and Bean for attempting to shoot at her. In 1838, police officers were introduced to the interior of Buckingham Palace for the first time and a house temporarily converted into a station for them in Stafford Row.[46]

But the newspaper press demanded more effective security for the Queen's public appearances as well. According to an unidentified nobleman who attended Victoria for more than ten years, 'never did Her Majesty proceed to open or to prorogue parliament without my receiving, in the morning, two or three letters warning me that an attempt would be made on our dear Sovereign's life!' Some of the thoroughfares she had to pass down were feared as potential ambush sites, so narrow were they. Constitution Hill should be closed to the public on state occasions and a guard of honour instructed to hold crowds back from the palace gates. It was even argued that Victoria should 'withdraw for a time to Claremont or to the Home Park at Windsor, aloof from public contact in the streets and high roads until the regicidal mania no longer absorbs public attention'.

These suggestions were unrealistic. When the Queen held her first Drawing Room of the new season, in June 1843, police tinkered with the crowd that gathered in the park to watch her arrival at St James's by preventing elevated views from the rear on tables, makeshift platforms or chairs, just as they had done for the royal wedding three years earlier, but the spectacle of the British monarchy was not to be obscured by armed guards or spirited away to private residences. Victoria's journey to prorogue Parliament in August 1843, for instance, took place with the usual public ceremony before large and friendly crowds. The *Illustrated London News* engraved the event for the front page; mounted guards took their places in front of and behind the Queen's coach but no-one rode alongside it in order not to obstruct the view.[47] Although it remained unthinkable in England to interfere with the spectacle of monarchy, the active removal of suspected lunatics from the vicinity of the palaces was, as we shall see, approached by the Metropolitan Police with an assiduity that was quite foreign to the essentially reactive practice pioneered at Bow Street in the eighteenth century.

Prosecuting troublesome subjects

The law governing the forcible confinement of lunatics in the eighteenth century did not make Bow Street's task of policing the royal palaces especially easy. Traditionally, establishing criminal guilt depended on the demonstration of intention, or the *mens rea*. According to Blackstone, if a defendant's understanding was defective either when he committed the offence, or at the time of his trial, he was no more culpable than a child, and if he had no will of his own (because he was adjudged an idiot) he was no more culpable than a beast, 'no, not even for treason itself'. Lunatics were therefore not to be held responsible for their actions. The policing of the mad was dependent upon the Vagrancy Acts. The basic legislation, passed in 1714 and amended in 1744, enabled any two justices to jointly order the confinement of anyone they believed dangerously mad for as long it appeared necessary. They should be 'kept, maintained and cured', either at their family's expense or else at the cost of their home parish. This was the legislation under which the Privy Council removed Nicholson to Bethlem. However, magistrates were generally reluctant to burden either parishes or parishioners with the costs of maintenance unless absolutely necessary, and families and local authorities were disinclined to keep their charges confined for any longer than they could help. 'Dangerousness' lay not only in the eye of the beholder, but in the depth of the purse. Many mad people, although known to the authorities, were therefore cared for at home under varying degrees of supervision.[48]

In London, most detainees were confined at Tothill Fields, the Westminster bridewell. As a 'house of correction', the building's purpose was theoretically to moderate the behaviour of beggars and vagrants whose defective morality cast them beyond the pale of civic polity. From the beginning of the eighteenth century, however, Tothill Fields served as a gaol for convicted felons and prisoners awaiting trial, forcing the mixing of criminals, lunatics and indigent paupers under one roof. The prison reformer John Howard considered the chances of effecting cures for the insane in the prison extremely poor. 'Where they are not kept separate', he wrote in 1777, 'they disturb and terrify other prisoners. No care is taken of them although it is probable that by medicines and proper regimen some of them might be restored to their senses and to usefulness in life.'[49] Families with the means to do so might prefer to place their mad relatives in private asylums, of which there were a growing number by the 1780s. In larger urban areas there was a scattering of asylums financed by a mixture of fees and charitable subscriptions, and the best-known of these was London's Bethlem Hospital. New charitable asylums for the poor blossomed during the 1790s, reflecting some of the social instability felt in an age of revolutions, but often offering minimal levels of care. An 1807 select committee report led to the County Asylums Act, an attempt to regulate the growing asylum trade, enable the setting up of county institutions and prevent abuses. Yet, thanks largely to the objections of rate-payers, local authorities were not compelled to provide them until 1845.[50]

Before the confinement of Margaret Nicholson, the legal obstruction of troublesome subjects was piecemeal, and particularly difficult to implement outside of the capital's orbit of jurisdiction. The inefficiency of the law was well illustrated in 1763 by the case of John Painter of Ipswich. Although assumed in Whitehall to be mad, Painter was not initially detained over the deranged letters he sent to the King. But when he began recommending his own execution – because 'there may be danger with respect to your Majesty or the Queen and I think it right to do it' – and alluding to 'divine power', Under-Secretary Weston decided that 'it does not seem consistent with prudence to leave such a person at liberty'. Ministers asked the Attorney General if Painter could be legally confined to an asylum. He told them they could not order it themselves, but that his family or his parish certainly could, provided they shared Weston's belief that Painter was dangerously mad. The mayor of Ipswich, he suggested, could be asked to organise it. Weston successfully persuaded the mayor to arrest Painter under the Vagrancy Act, and his family agreed to pay for confinement at Bethlem. But when the asylum sent two men to Ipswich to fetch him, another magistrate objected that Painter had been illegally imprisoned. He was neither a vagrant nor insane, he said, and threatened to prosecute the mayor for exceeding his authority. The mayor compromised. He had been correct in confining Painter, he thought, but not to assist in his 'capture' and removal by outsiders, so he sent the Bethlem men back empty-handed. He would keep Painter in the lock-up at Ipswich, he informed Weston, but could not impose the financial burden on the parish for long. The Attorney General pointed out to Weston that the only way to guarantee his long-term confinement now would be for Painter's family to petition the Lord Chancellor for a commission of lunacy. The outcome is unrecorded.[51]

Further difficulties were endured in 1788 when Sampson Wright sent Patrick Macmanus to Somerset after the mad cleric Henry Norman. Norman's family had already sent him to a private madhouse in Dorset, so Macmanus went there to assess security. 'I did not want to see the King', Norman told him 'I wanted to have him cut off from the face of the earth ... for the Thirty-Nine Articles and the American War'. Macmanus had no doubt that Norman posed a danger to the realm but he was unhappy about leaving him at the asylum in case his family stopped paying the bill. On dubious authority therefore, he instructed the keeper 'that he should not suffer him to be taken away till he heard further', and paid him five shillings for his co-operation.[52] It can be seen, then, that even after the precedent set by Nicholson's permanent detention at Bethlem in 1786, government had no sure means of controlling men and women who posed a potential threat to the safety of the monarch, but whose 'crimes' were either unrealised or unworthy of arraignment for high treason. The relative autonomy of the provinces sometimes reduced ministers to an advisory role, although a measure of control was at least possible in London. In 1778, Rebecca O'Hara broke the window of George III's sedan with a knife as he climbed out at St James's. The King asked her what she wanted but she gave only an 'impudent answer' and insisted her name was Queen Beck. Ministers had her removed, first to the bridewell and then to an asylum.[53]

In the post-Nicholson shakedown, lunatics who might otherwise have been disregarded were more actively sought for confinement. Anne Withers was par for the course. Withers had made threats against the lives of the King and his ministers in letters to the Home Office earlier in the summer of 1786, but was not taken into custody. After Nicholson's arrest, however, Home Secretary Sydney advised Pitt: 'I should not have thought of troubling you with such nonsense had not the King's name been mentioned in it, which renewed in me the horror of the late awful event arising from a person in a similar state of mind.' In fact, Pitt already knew about Withers because his brother had received a letter from her, but it was 'so sharply wrote he had flung it into the fire'. As the inquiry progressed, Sydney learned that a secretary at the Ordnance Office had also received letters from Withers but done nothing with them on account of her obvious insanity. Calling herself 'the Imperial Anne, surnamed Withers the First, Imperial of the Kingdom', Withers nursed political grievances about the loss of the American colonies and threatened to 'clear away' all 'rogues' from office.[54] Previously thought demented but harmless, Withers was suddenly reconstructed by ministers as a danger to the realm, but she could not be incarcerated because she could not be found.

The families or parish authorities responsible for lunatics in or from the provinces who threatened the King were expected to make every effort to keep them there. Wright, Nepean and Grenville were therefore concerned by the arrival in London of James Bull, 'a Madman' from Bedfordshire, in 1791. From his London lodgings, Bull advised his family that after April 23 he would 'not own King George to be my King'. In one letter, Bull threatened to 'kill or drive out of the Kingdom every man that honours King George the third ... I have no obgection to george more than Any Boody Else but it is the Powr that I do not like'. The Bedfordshire bench considered egalitarian language of this sort dangerous enough to charge him with treason. A county magistrate, who insisted Bull was 'more knave than fool', wrote to caution Grenville against indulging him as a poor madman and issued a warrant to have the man brought back to Bedford for a treason trial. But ministers had no intention of paying for one. Nepean ordered strict vigilance around the palaces but Wright's officers managed to capture Bull before he went anywhere near them. They immediately packed him off to his parish to be 'looked after', but indignant local magistrates still refused to accept Bull's insanity and committed him to the summer assize instead.[55]

The imputation of madness to anyone whose politics were 'wrong-headed' became increasingly common. Just as Lord George Gordon was derided as mad after the riots of 1780, so the pro-reform sympathies of one Major Billiere earned him in 1786 the epithet 'politic mad-man', and a man who caused a disturbance in Whitehall in 1801 was jocularly assumed by the anti-ministerial *Morning Chronicle* to be under 'some derangement of mind' because 'he said that Mr Pitt alone could save the country'. He was 'taken care of'.[56] The facility with which radical politics and madness were maliciously conflated by the loyalist media during the 1790s saw the concerns of the Bedfordshire bench over the confusion of punishment and sympathy amplified as the decade wore on. After stones were thrown at the King's coach in 1796, *The Times* reported:

> In times of tranquillity we should consider the outrage the deed of a madman, more deserving a place in BEDLAM than in NEWGATE, but in the present period, when an anti-royalist faction is indefatigable in propagating its regicide principles and putting them in practice, these repeated attempts to insult the monarch demand the most serious attention.[57]

It is not, perhaps, so surprising to find the discourses of madness and treason, of reform and iconoclasm (or innovation) and of iconoclasm and madness so intertwined in these years. Radicalism, insurrection and rebellion were, in the opinion of George Man Burrows, very bad for the brain. 'Insanity bears always a striking resemblance to public events', he explained in a treatise on mental illness in 1828 that drew exemplary lessons from the madness of France and America. Revolutions produce enthusiasm and, 'as all extremes in society are exciting causes, it will occur that in proportion as the feelings are acted upon, so will insanity be more or less frequent'.[58] So, not only did loyalists associate the apparent madness of Dennis Collins with the insanity of reform in 1832, or the assassination-mania of Edward Oxford with the lunacy of Chartism in 1840, but radicals inverted the argument and fought back. The *Northern Star* blamed ministers for undermining Victoria's popularity by consistently preventing her from hearing the petitions of the poor. 'The insane seem to resolve upon obtaining notoriety for their deeds and are content with nothing less than royal personages or royal things', it noted, trailing a list of failed regicides from Ravaillac to Oxford. 'What have we to add to these but the one crowning instance – viz., the numberless attacks made upon royalty by our insane rulers!' Victoria's Court of in-bred advisers were all smitten with idiocy, producing a polity of madness degenerating to royalty itself. 'Every physiologist is aware of this fact', the paper proclaimed. 'The royal blood of Europe, through the very means employed to keep it pure, is fast flowing to insanity.'[59] The known imbecility of George III gave this argument considerable strength. Similarly, the *Statesman* argued that it was not radicalism or revolution in themselves that produced popular madness and 'enthusiasm'; the fault lay in the social conditions that gave rise to discontent. The distresses of the poor at the time of Victoria's accession had themselves produced a 'period of mental excitement'.[60]

Disruptions to the more conventional lexicons of madness also brought about an occasional blurring of distinctions in cases of prosecution for seditious speech. Richard Smith, a labourer who believed the King owed him nine shillings, 'for boring of holes' on the royal estates, walked into a public house in 1794 and said: 'Damn the King. If anyone was to hire me to kill the King, damn my eyes but I would do it immediately.' Arrested for seditious speech, Smith first tried, unsuccessfully, to convince a magistrate he had been drunk when he spoke the words. He then claimed that he was insane, but the examining magistrate chose not to believe that either.[61] However, when John Taylor, well known to the Home Office as a 'very dangerous lunatic who has frequently followed and been troublesome to His Majesty', made some ill-advised threats against the King's life a few days after the attack on the royal coach in 1795, it was sufficient reason to have him removed to Bethlem.[62]

It is worth remembering that the Hadfield Act of 1800, which empowered the courts to confine defendants who might otherwise be acquitted after using an insanity defence, was devised partly to prevent both the mad and the not-so-mad from escaping retribution altogether. The Act enabled ministers and magistrates to continue treating troublesome subjects as lunatics without any likelihood of them walking free from court as a consequence. This was most convenient, for the only legal alternative open to the authorities was commitment to the expensive and unpredictable theatre of a full-blown trial for high treason. Few of the people who harassed the Royal Family at this time committed crimes sufficiently grave to warrant hanging, drawing and quartering, and a conviction for treason in such circumstances would have been unpopular with the public and difficult to get past a jury. The Hadfield provisions were also far more convenient than committals under the vagrancy laws because defendants became wards of the State, their detention controlled and paid for by Whitehall. This was of particular benefit at Windsor, where the parish authorities had previously been responsible for a disproportionate number of confinements. When a lunatic arrived in the parish in 1812, therefore, 'under the usual pretext of introducing himself to Her Majesty and the Princesses', the mayor simply had him locked up and asked the Home Secretary to make the 'regular communication' to the Treasury Solicitors for reimbursement. Similarly, in 1837, Charles Stuber, a writer of threatening letters to the Queen and Duchess of Kent was ordered by Bow Street into the custody of his parish authorities at Chelsea. This resulted in spells first in the workhouse, then at the private Hoxton asylum at parish expense, but, within six months, the Chelsea relieving officer was applying to have Stuber removed to the county asylum at Hanwell, the cost of which could be met centrally.[63]

In cases of 'mad politics', however, treason trials remained an occasional option when the 'humanity' of the Hadfield Act was felt inappropriate. The best evidence ever produced by Government for a radical conspiracy to assassinate George III was that collected for the treason trial of Colonel Despard in 1802. Unsurprisingly, the colonel's sanity was questioned. Building, perhaps, on the colloquial usage of Richard Ford, who, by September 1802, was convinced by his spies that some 'mad enterprise' was in the offing, retrospective suggestions that the failed 'leader' of the *putsch* was insane were levelled by diverse contemporaries, including Cobbett and the aristocratic Irish nationalist Lord Cloncurry (who had earlier been suspected of complicity).[64] Men such as these were perfectly prepared to accommodate Whitehall's marginalising of Despard, his treasonous schemes and his unrepresentative band of hopeless followers as a means of distancing themselves from his failure. Aware, no doubt, that the 'madness' of Despard's plot might be taken too literally by the trial jury, Lord Ellenborough pointedly steered them from the temptations of mercy. Despard's treason, he conceded, had been contained 'only in words', as defence counsel had argued, and 'if it consisted only in loose words, the ebullation of an irritated or crazy mind, it would not be treason'. But these had been words freely and consciously spoken in public meetings with the intention of inspiring action in others, and that was very different. Despard would not therefore be indulged as a lunatic in the eyes of the law, but that would not necessarily shield him in the eyes of society. In 1798, it was alleged he had tried to pass himself off to a Jewish sympathiser as the Messiah. He might be a 'man of education', but putting his faith in such a motley band of revolutionaries as he did 'surely argues something little short of madness'.[65] Cobbett thought the polarised discourses of madness and heroism equally unsuitable for Despard. 'Among the well-informed classes of society, detestation of the man is disarmed by assurances that he must have been insane when he talked of such wild designs', he objected. 'If you abhor treason, you are told Despard was a madman; if you are discontented with public affairs, you are told he was a hero.'[66]

Radicals were still being dismissed as lunatics at the end of the Napoleonic Wars. Seizing on Government's use of language in the composition of a national prayer of thanksgiving when the Regent evaded assassination in 1817, Thomas Wooler wrote in *Black Dwarf*: 'By petitioning you have been called *Madmen*, and a prayer has been composed by the bench of Bishops praying heaven to shield the Prince, your Royal Master, *from your Madness!*' In speaking of the 'madness of the people', thought Leigh Hunt, Government had insulted the whole nation. 'It is as gross at the very least, as if the people had put up prayers for themselves against the madness of the King and the Lords; – it is a phrase of treason against the popular part of the constitution.'[67]

Confusion of this kind was actually strengthened by the fact that mad people who troubled the King were rarely short of some constitutional justification for doing so. It was not difficult for political connections to be made between the madness of well-known 'regicides' like Nicholson and Frith and constitutional radicalism. Government dealt with many similar cases that were not so well publicised. John Duncan may have been 'mad' to urge the Regent to make him the next prime minister, pledged as he was to 'subdue all oppression' and combat the influence of Satan, but the theological grounds on which he made the request were not devoid of reason or constitutional logic. Duncan's argument went like this: the contractual duty of the Crown was to appoint ministers in accordance with the 'public mind'. The Earl of Chatham, he said, had always claimed he was called to office not because he was the King's favourite, but by 'the voice of the people ... which implies the legal power of the people in that appointment'. God had made it known to Duncan that it was the will of the people that he become prime minister. Moreover, the hand of God must lie behind every ministerial appointment because it was for God alone to 'secretly' communicate the public mind to the monarch. Because the power of the people was thus mediated by the agency of heaven, he assured the Prince, 'no invasion of prerogative' was implied.[68]

The idea that all regicide was, *ipso facto*, a form of madness continued to find expression at the outset of Victoria's reign when she was fired at three times in the course of two years. By confirming the 'otherliness' of the assailants, theories of regicidal insanity were one way of making sense of assaults on such a virtuous and defenceless young woman. Oxford's successful use of the insanity offence in 1840 drew approval from the liberal *Statesman*, because 'shooting at the Queen ... is the maddest of all acts' and 'it would be anything but satisfactory to quiet folks to hear of rational men firing pistols at the Queen'.[69] The *Court Journal* had no doubt that 'the assassins of sovereigns are, in most cases, mad; that with respect to the Queen, beloved as she is by every party in the State, however violent, they will always be mad nine hundred and ninety nine times out of a thousand'.[70] But, at the same time, middle-class public opinion was losing its patience with the idea of criminal non-culpability. Victorian regimes of corrective punishment were founded on the notion of personal responsibility, but these were difficult to reconcile with the endorsement by early psychiatry of such subdivisions of madness as 'moral insanity' and the 'uncontrollable impulse'. Something of a retreat from the Enlightenment-influenced eighteenth-century concept of criminal insanity began to influence public opinion in early Victorian Britain, and Peel's Royal Protection Act of 1842 provided an institutional framework for a regime of unforgiving physical punishment for individuals who fired off guns near the Queen. In 1850, the barrister William Townsend observed that Oxford's 'moral insanity' defence was 'fraught with danger to society'. Any criminal might claim to have committed a crime 'when preoccupied, deluded or impassioned, but it is the duty of a Christian and a rational being to keep down these unruly passions ... The law cannot tolerate the doctrine of making the crime itself proof of irresponsibility, without inflicting the greatest individual injustice, and undermining the safeguards of society.'[71]

Concern about the Oxford verdict was heightened by the successful insanity defence of Daniel McNaughten, who tried to assassinate Peel in 1843 but murdered his secretary by mistake. A series of eminent medical practitioners trooped through the witness box to lend scientific validity to the 'uncontrollable impulses' assumed to be behind McNaughten's involuntary crime. In response to escalating public fears that insanity was fast becoming the last refuge of every reprobate and murderer in the country, the Law Lords drew up a new set of guidelines, known as the McNaughten Rules. Defendants would now only be entitled to claim non-culpability if they could prove they had not known their crime was either morally wrong or illegal at the time they committed it. The intention was to make the 'irresistible impulse' defence morally inadmissible and to suggest that all such impulses, whether real or imaginary, were best deterred by the threat of capital conviction.[72]

Notes

1 *Morning Chronicle*, 7 August 1786; *The Times*, 8 August 1786.

2 N. Walker, *Crime and Insanity in England*, (Edinburgh, 1968), vol. 1: *The Historical Perspective*, pp. 185, 186.

3 A letter from 'The Ghost of Alfred', *True Briton*, 9 February 1796.

4 Useful discussions of the scope of the treason laws may be found in John Barrell, 'Imaginary treason, imaginary law: the State trials of 1794', in J. Barrell (ed.), *The Birth of Pandora and the Division of Knowledge* (Basingstoke, 1992); Barrell, 'Imagining the King's death'; A. Wharam, *The Treason Trials, 1794* (Leicester, 1992) and *Treason: Famous English Treason Trials* (Stroud, 1995). The remaining counts provided by the Act were: having sexual relations with the king's wife, his eldest daughter or the daughter of the heir apparent; levying civil war against the king (a charge that also covered serious rioting); assisting the king's enemies at home or abroad, counterfeiting coinage or fabricating the royal seal; and slaying the king's chancellor, treasurer or justices.

5 *Gentlemen's Magazine*, 26 (1756), 147.

6 Walker, *Crime and Insanity*, pp. 53–7; R. Porter, *Mind-Forg'd Manacles: A History of Madness in England from the Restoration to the Regency* (London, 1987), p. 117. For the debate over intention and culpability in these trials, see J. P. Eigen, 'Intentionality and insanity: what the eighteenth-century juror heard', in W. F. Bynum, R. Porter and M. Shepherd (eds), *The Anatomy of Madness: Essays*

in the History of Psychiatry, vol. II, *Institutions and Society* (London, 1985), pp. 34–49.

7 The definitive account is still Macalpine and Hunter, *Mad-Business*, but see also R. Porter, *A Social History of Madness: Stories of the Insane* (London, 1987), ch. 3: 'Madness and power'.

8 Quoted from the *Two Treatises of Government* in Condren, *Language of Politics*, pp. 128–9.

9 Sack, *Jacobite to Conservative*, pp. 135–6; N. Rogers, *Crowds, Culture and Politics in Georgian Britain* (Oxford, 1998), pp. 184–8.

10 Michel Foucault's well-known argument is set out in *Madness and Civilisation: A History of Insanity in the Age of Reason* (New York, 1965). For a critique questioning the usefulness of the model to English history, see Porter, *Mind-Forg'd Manacles*, pp. 5–9.

11 Cited in Lady Llanover (ed.), *Autobiography and Correspondence of Mary Granville, Mrs. Delany* (London, 1862), vol. 2, p. 377.

12 *Sketches in Bedlam, or Characteristic Traits of Insanity as Displayed in the Cases of 140 Patients of Both Sexes ... By a Constant Observer* (London, 1823), pp. 164–5.

13 PRO, HO 42/13, T. A. Smith Murray to Colonel Goldsworthy, 20 October 1788. Murray's claims caused the Home Office genuine anxiety for several years, during which he remained 'at different times very troublesome to the King'. He had allegedly entrusted into the care of the Treasury a number of letters from the late Prince to his mother, and these supposedly proved the Prince's paternity. On investigation, Nepean discovered that this story at least was true but that the Treasury had passed the letters on to the King, who had since 'lost' them. Murray was committed to keep him quiet; in HO 42/19: Notes in Nepean's hand, dated 14 June 1790.

14 *The Times* 31 August; 1, 3, 8 and 10 September; and 28 December 1787; Royal Bethlem Hospital Archive, Committee Book, October 1783–February 1791: entries dated 8 September 1787 and 27 September 1788; PRO, PRO, 30/8/64 pt. 1, Chatham Papers: Georgiana Townshend to Lady Chatham, 29 August 1787.

15 *The Times*, 3 June 1788 .

16 PRO, HO 42/18: Letter to the King signed Philip P__, 1 February 1791.

17 Fargé, *Subversive Words*, p. 134.

18 PRO, HO 44/3: Anon. to Sidmouth, 16 November 1820.

19 E. Sheppard, *Memorials of St. James's Palace* (London, 1894), vol. 1, pp. 321–2. For the contrasting experience of France, see Fargé, *Subversive Words*, pp. 134–42.

20 McCalman, *Radical Underworld*.

21 *The Trial of Josiah Phillips for a Libel on the Duke of Cumberland and the Proceedings Previous thereto ... to which is added in an Appendix 'A Minute Detail of the Attempt to Assassinate the Duke of Cumberland'* (London, 1833), pp. 109–11, 126, 129.

22 J. E. Kromm, 'The feminisation of madness in visual representation', *Feminist Studies*, 20:3 (1994), 507–35.

23 *The Times*, 4 May 1813.

24 W. Perfect, M.D., *Select Cases in the Different Species of Insanity, Lunacy or Madness, with the Modes of Practice as Adopted in the Treatment of Each* (Rochester, 1787), pp. 67–78.

25 Royal Bethlem Hospital Archive, Criminal Lunatics Case Book, 1816–50; entries dated 27 November 1837, 21 March 1843 and 15 September 1840.
26 London Metropolitan Archive Centre, H11/HLL/B4/1: Register of Male Admissions, 1839–50.
27 For example, S. H. Palmer, *Police and Protest in England and Ireland, 1780–1850* (Cambridge, 1988), pp. 83–92, 164–6; Emsley, *Crime and Society*, 216–25.
28 *The Times*, 21 September 1791.
29 PRO, HO 42/67: Earl of Euston to Lord Pelham, 29 April 1803; Lord Cathcart to Lord Pelham, with enclosures, 13 May 1803.
30 J. A. Hone, *For the Cause of Truth: Radicalism in London, 1796–1821* (Oxford, 1982), pp. 69–70.
31 *Report From the Committee on the State of the Police of the Metropolis* (London, 1816): evidence of John Townsend.
32 *Court Journal*, 4 August 1832.
33 PRO, HO 65/1: John King to Major General Manners, 15 July 1796. John Townsend was to become the best-known officer at Bow Street through his connections at Court. The services he consequently performed on behalf of some of the wealthiest victims of crime earned him an estate valued at £20,000 by the time of his death in 1832. He became a personal friend of George III and was frequently in his company at the theatre: J. J. Tobias, *Crime and Police in England, 1700–1900* (London, 1979), pp. 47–9; E. F. Clark, *Truncheons: Their Romance and Reality* (London, 1935), pp. 226–8; W. L. Melville Lee, *A History of Police in England* (New Jersey, 1971), p. 193; *Court Journal*, 28 July and 4 August 1832.
34 PRO, HO 42/13: 'Report of Patrick Macmanus, October 1788'; Sir Sampson Wright to Lord Grenville, 27 October 1788.
35 *The Times*, 17 February 1796; *Newcastle Chronicle*, 20 February 1796; Anon., *A True and Particular Account of the Behaviour of Charlotte Georgina Mary Ann Guelph* (London 1796).
36 Historic Manuscripts Commission, *Manuscripts of J. B. Fortescue esq., Preserved at Dropmore* (London, 1894): J. B. Burges to Lord Grenville, 13 October 1793 (vol. 2, p. 445); Francis Drake to Lord Grenville, 9 November 1793 (vol. 2, pp. 459–61); Marquis of Buckingham to Lord Grenville, 6, 10 and 22 August, 20 September 1794 (vol. 2, pp. 611–12, 614, 622–3, 634); PRO, HO 42/19: Henry Dundas to Lord Massereene, 2 August 1791; Hampshire County Record Office, William Wickham Papers, 38M49/6/4/16: George III to William Wickham, 18 March 1799.
37 Noted in *The Times*, 31 January 1817, after the very similar attack on the Regent's coach.
38 *St. James's Chronicle*, 31 October–3 November 1795. PRO, HO 65/1: Portland to Addington, 18 December 1795; J. King to Bow Street magistrates, 21 January and 17 February 1796.
39 PRO, HO 65/1, Police entry book, 1795–1811: various letters from John King and William Wickham to London magistrates, e.g. 5 October 1796, 17 December 1797 and 28 June 1798.
40 BL Additional MS 33122, Pelham Papers, fol. 79: 'Draft of the present state of the police of Middlesex, with observations', 22 January 1802.
41 PRO, HO 65/2, Police entry book, 1811–20: Orders from Henry Goulburn, 19 June 1811.
42 Palmer, *Police and Protest*, p. 171.

43 *Report from the Committee on the State of the Police of the Metropolis* (London, 1816): Evidence of John Townsend and John Sayer; J. Wade, *Treatise on the Police and Crimes of the Metropolis* (London, 1829) p. 58.
44 PRO, MEPO 2/30: Memoranda and correspondence for the funeral of William IV, July 1837.
45 Palmer, *Police and Protest*, p. 314. The Buckingham House station superseded the old Guard House, established after the Gordon Riots in 1780. For nightly military guard, see *The Times*, 13 June 1839. This was the origin of the present royal protection squad, SO14, which is responsible for security at all royal residences. In 1999 it was announced that the ever-expanding cost of royal protection, then estimated at £30 million a year, was to be dramatically slashed: 'Security for royals cut to save money', *Electronic Telegraph*, 19 July 1999.
46 *John Bull*, 7 December 1840.
47 *Court Journal*, 4 June and 9 July 1842; *Illustrated London News*, 1 July and 26 August 1843.
48 Porter, *Mind-Forg'd Manacles*, pp. 117–21.
49 H. Mayhew and J. Binny, *The Criminal Prisons of London and Scenes of Prison Life* (London, 1862), pp. 359–63. A. Babington, *The English Bastille: A History of Newgate Gaol and Prison Conditions in Britain, 1188–1902* (London, 1971), p. 107 (quoting Howard's *The State of the Prisons in England and Wales*, 1777).
50 L. D. Smith, 'Levelled to the same common standard? Social class in the lunatic asylum, 1780–1860', in O. Ashton, R. Fyson and S. Roberts (eds), *The Duty of Discontent: Essays for Dorothy Thompson* (London, 1995).
51 PRO, HO 49/1: Law officers' letter book, 1762–1795, E. Weston to the Attorney General, 3 May 1763; with John Painter to the King, 1 May 1763, enclosed; Attorney General to E. Weston, 4 May 1763; J. Gravenor to E. Weston, 13 June 1763; Attorney General to Lord Halifax, 16 June 1763.
52 PRO, HO 42/13: 'Report of Patrick Macmanus, October 1788'; Sir Sampson Wright to Lord Grenville, 27 October 1788.
53 *Bath Journal*, 7 August 1786; *Annual Register*, 1778.
54 PRO, HO 42/9: Sydney to Pitt(?), 19 August 1786, plus enclosures.
55 PRO, HO 42/18: William Lowndes to Lord Grenville, 22 and 26 April 1791; Reverend William Hooper to George Brookes, 24 April 1791; Lt Col. Manners to Evan Nepean, 26 April 1791; George Brookes to Evan Nepean, 14 June 1791.
56 *Morning Chronicle*, 25 January 1801.
57 *The Times*, 4 and 5 February 1796.
58 G. M. Burrows, *Commentaries on the Causes, Forms, Symptoms and Treatment, Moral and Medical, of Insanity* (London, 1828), quoted in H. Small, *Love's Madness: Medicine, the Novel and Female Insanity, 1800–1865* (Oxford, 1996), p. 105.
59 *Northern Star*, 25 January and 27 June 1840.
60 *Statesman*, 14 June 1840.
61 PRO, TS11/1119/5766: Case papers for King v. Richard Smith, Middlesex Sessions, 3 May 1794.
62 *Star*, 3 November 1795; Royal Bethlem Hospital Archive, Committee Book, February 1795–September 1800: entry dated 7 November 1795.
63 PRO, HO 42/123: John Secker to Colonel Taylor, 9 May 1812; C. Hayden to John Beckett, 12 May 1812; *The Times*, 5 June 1838.
64 Hone, *Cause of Truth*, p. 105.

65 *Morning Chronicle*, 11 and 14 February 1803.
66 *Cobbett's Political Register*, 26 February 1803.
67 *Black Dwarf*, 28 May 1817; *Examiner*, 16 February 1817.
68 PRO, HO 42/123: John Duncan to the Prince Regent, 31 May 1812.
69 *Statesman*, 19 July 1840.
70 *Court Journal*, 4 June 1842.
71 W. C. Townsend, *Modern State Trials*, vol. 1 (London, 1850), p. 108.
72 M. J. Wiener, *Reconstructing the Criminal: Culture, Law and Policy in England, 1830–1914* (Cambridge, 1990), pp. 83–4, 87–9

4

The madness of Margaret Nicholson

On 2 August 1786 George III survived what was to become the best-known attempt on the life of a British monarch. It was not a unique incident, for George had survived the attack of Rebecca O'Hara eight years earlier, but that case had aroused little public interest. What was it about the Margaret Nicholson affair that secured it such a prominent place in the nation's collective memory and in contemporary constitutional discourse?

Margaret Nicholson, a 36-year-old London needlewoman, was ushered to the front of a small crowd waiting by the garden entrance at St James's for the King's carriage to arrive. Seeing her standing there with a rolled petition in her hand, George III crossed the courtyard to accept it, but as he did so Nicholson produced a knife and stabbed at him with it. He was not hurt. As the King recoiled, she was prevented from making a second lunge by a yeoman and a footman who pulled her away to the guard house. Although at first refusing to answer any questions until she was taken before the 'proper persons', her examination over several days by the Privy Council allowed a story to be pieced together. Nicholson was the daughter of a barber from Stockton on Tees. Since coming to London she had secured several appointments in the service of respectable families, but had recently been forced to leave the service of Lord Sebright after a love affair with one of his footmen. In a state of distress over the loss of her livelihood and lover, Nicholson had petitioned the King more than twenty times for assistance and, on receiving no reply, she went to St James's to remonstrate with him physically. Construing both her actions and her language as signs of lunacy, the Privy Council ruled her unfit to stand trial for high treason and instead committed her to Bethlem 'for her natural life' under the 1744 Vagrancy Act.[1]

Treason negated: Nicholson and the familial nation

Following the public relations disasters of the previous two decades, the 1780s was the decade in which things finally started to go right for George III. In dismissing the Fox–North coalition in 1783, he was publicly congratulated for putting the nation back in order; a process mirrored in some respects by his efforts to promote economy in his own household. The deteriorating relationship between the King and the Prince of Wales over the latter's personal expenditure and accumulating debts came to a head during the summer of 1786 when the King refused to instruct his ministers to increase the Prince's income through the civil list. This decision undoubtedly had as much to do with placating public disapproval of the Prince's lifestyle as with the King's personal interest in good housekeeping, and the ministry was anxious to exploit both the King's economic sagacity in inflationary times and his fatherly firmness over a son who was becoming increasingly associated with the politics of opposition. In acknowledging the reciprocity of domestic and public retrenchment, commented the admiring *Bath Journal*, the King had reminded his son 'that he was the father of the People as well as of the Prince'.[2] The Prince was not the only one to have his memory jogged. Margaret Nicholson, one of the King's more frustrated 'children', may have taken the royal paternalism more literally than anyone had intended. Her real father was not a rich man and she had not seen him since she was 12. Tracked down in Yorkshire by inquisitive civil servants several days after the attack, Nicholson's father declared that he had recently received several letters from his daughter, most of which had convinced him she was unstable, but that, like George III, he had not replied. After discovering that their prisoner had sent more than twenty rambling petitions to the King, Privy Councillors asked Nicholson what she had wanted from him. 'That he would provide for me', she answered, 'as I want to marry and have children like other folks.'[3] The Nicholson affair was a perfect vehicle for the interlinking of healing processes within both the Royal Family and the nation. If the King had been killed, wrote an anonymous pamphleteer, the blow would have been fatal to the nation as well as to 'his most amiable family by whom he is perfectly adored; and never did a husband, a father or a master of a family deserve more truly their love, esteem, respect and admiration'.[4] Despite the efforts of opposition papers to paint the post-Nicholson reunion of King and Prince as a botched affair in which George III refused to see his son at all, leaving his 'filial duty' to the Queen, most papers celebrated the Prince's arrival from Brighton as the return of the prodigal son.[5]

The ongoing elevation of the King as a unifying factor in the national consciousness would play a crucial part in the Hanoverian State's self-portrayal as tempered, 'humane' and judicious in its handling of the Nicholson affair. The tone was set by the significance attached in the public sphere to the King's immediate reaction to the assault. Quickly recovering his dignity, he ordered the guards to treat Nicholson gently, for he was unharmed and she was insane. His magnanimity and composure were widely celebrated by the direct quotation of his words in the newspaper press. Accounts of the incident vary slightly in their reporting. The *Public Advertiser*, for instance, had him saying two slightly different things in two different accounts, both published on the day after the attack. On the one hand, the King is reported to have said: 'Secure the woman, I am not hurt', and then, 'Don't hurt the woman, she must be insane'. On the other, his reported words were: 'I am not hurt, take care of that woman.' On the following day, the paper further amended the statement to: 'Don't hurt the woman; she is mad; pray take care of her.'

How is the very imprecision of these accounts to be read?[6] Each of the *Advertisers'* four phrases transmits a slightly different signal. When taken in order of presentation, the King's attitude becomes steadily and subtly more progressive. Phrase one is matter-of-fact, the emphasis on his own escape from danger. In phrase two, he implies that only insanity *can* explain her behaviour and that therefore she should be treated gently. In the third phrase he judiciously and rather democratically balances his own survival with hers, and in the fourth his concern is entirely devoted to her, the *certainty* of her insanity and the necessity for her gentle treatment.

George's sympathy for his assailant was no less important than his nobility and bravery. The *Advertiser* explained the importance of the King's words in two subsequent editions; '"Spare the woman, she must be insane"', were the words which give the most lively idea of his Majesty's greatness of mind – of his command of temper – fine sensibility – humanity and everything laudable and amiable!' His 'generous emotions of compassion to the wretch' would surely leave all Europeans 'lost in wonder', and 'even Eastern despotism admire the virtue [of it]'.[7] Fanny Burney was convinced the King was 'the only calm and moderate person then present' and it was to 'the mob' that he shouted his instructions for Nicholson's protection.[8] Invariably, the King's dignified forbearance was tellingly contrasted with Nicholson's excitable enthusiasm, drawing further attention to her presumed derangement . The King, remarked one paper, was 'calm and composed' after the attack. 'It indicated that cool courage which ever attends a collected mind.'[9] The King's mind was more collected, indeed, than the group mind of his loyal subjects, who had been unable to prevent the outrage and whose immediate reaction was more instinctive. As a Home Office report put it: 'His escape was owing under providence to his own calmness and resolution, and his humane interposition to rescue this miserable wretch from the treatment she would have met with from the rage of those who surrounded her has naturally attracted the attention and admiration of everybody.'[10]

Reports like these were not uninfluential. After reading various newspaper accounts the Earl of Guildford, for example, confessed himself 'exceedingly shocked', and at the same time moved and uplifted for, 'I hear the King's behaviour was *great*, *composed* and *generous*'. The papers had also assured him of Nicholson's insanity; a point of further comfort to him, 'for tis shocking to conceive any person in their senses could be capable of such a crime'.[11]

The King's great sensibility and composure also found an outlet in an endearingly flawed concern for the nerves of his family. Burney and Delany were both impressed by the King's determination to prevent the Queen and the Princesses from hearing of the attack until he had shown himself to them unharmed. Unfortunately, they heard about it before he could reach them and were in fits of tears when he burst in 'with a countenance of striking vivacity and said: 'Here I am, safe and well, as you see. But I have very narrowly escaped being stabbed!' George's masculine and matter-of-fact British bluntness is here celebrated at the expense of his demonstrably non-British wife and delicate daughters who 'wept even with violence':

> His own conscious safety, and the pleasure he felt in thus personally showing it to the Queen, made him not aware of the effect of so abrupt a communication. The Queen was siezed with a consternation that at first almost stupefied her ... The King, with the greatest good humour, did his best to comfort them, and then gave a relation of the affair with a calmness and unconcern that, had anyone but himself been his hero, would have been regarded as totally unfeeling.[12]

The contrast between the King's cavalier cheerfulness in the face of death and the nervous agitation of the Queen and the Princesses became a theme often revisited in future representations of assaults and assassination attempts. In several respects, then, the Margaret Nicholson affair was to be a significant marker in the development of George III's fatherly style, an interesting conflation of sensibility and bullishness which did much to recommend British approaches to monarchy.

The King's sensibility also provided his ministers with an opportunity to distance the modern Hanoverian State from the circumstances leading to the trial and execution of the boy Shepherd for threatening the life of George I in 1718. A humanitarian approach to Nicholson's insanity negated her usefulness to the opposition as a symbol of discontent, and in avoiding the unpleasantness of a treason trial also denied the accused any kind of public platform. 'The consequences', considered *The Times*, 'will render the minister essential service by drawing off the attention of the people from other serious considerations and kindling their loyalty to that warmth and zeal which will raise them above all complaint and grievances'.[13] British jurisprudence was also loudly signalled. 'Nothing can demonstrate the justice and impartiality of our constitutional customs more than the manner in which the woman was dealt by. Imprisonment for some days, or confinement in a madhouse were rejected as being arbitrary modes of proceeding', explained the *Advertiser*.[14]

More direct references to the 'arbitrary' proceedings of non-constitutional and non-protestant nations soon followed:

> It must be a circumstance of pride to every Englishman to observe the very different manner in which those are dealt with in Great Britain, who, while under the influence of insanity, attempt the life of the sovereign of the country, compared with that in which criminals of a similar description have been treated in France – When Damiens, an absolute and acknowledged madman, assassinated the French King, he was subjected to every torture that savage ingenuity could suggest, and put to death by means the most horrid and shocking to humanity.[15]

Nicholson was also useful to Pitt as a symbol of the insane consequences of 'disloyal' opposition. Some Foxites believed themselves victims of a whispering campaign to associate them with both Nicholson and Gordon. Civil servants, it was alleged, had asked Nicholson's landlord Jonathan Fiske whether friends of the Prince of Wales, including Mrs Fitzherbert, or Gordon himself had ever called on the house. The language of madness was played upon and politically satirised by Pitt's opponents, the *Morning Herald* transcribing fictitious interviews between the Privy Council and Nicholson in which ministers themselves were presented as political lunatics. For example, 'Mr Dundas questioned her about the place of her nativity; she said it bordered upon Scotland, where rebellion was no crime, regicide a virtue, and treachery an hereditary principle of the people. Mr Dundas declared her quite mad.' These 'Proofs of Margaret Nicholson's Insanity' as the paper called them, all tended to imply that ministers were following their own ill-informed agenda in calling her mad.[16]

The Government's determination to avoid a treason trial was however, also pragmatic. Ministers were not confident that Nicholson's overt act was the expression of a clear intention to assassinate the King and did not relish the necessity of having to prove it. To begin with, there was the matter of the weapon. According to the Home Office report, Nicholson's first thrust with the knife 'did but just reach his waist coat which was not cut by it'. The knife itself was

> an old one and of the form used at breakfast or desserts; it was much worn but seemed to have been sharpened lately, it was round at the end. The weapon (though God forbid that it should have been put to the trial) was of a sort that was far from being proper for the intended wicked purpose as it would probably have been bent by a little resistance.[17]

Press reports took a similar view: 'a gentleman present at her first examination tried the point of it against his hand, when the knife bent almost double without piercing the skin'.[18] When the author of *Sketches in Bedlam* interviewed Nicholson in 1824, she told him 'she had not the remotest intention to injure His Majesty, on the contrary, that she had a great notion of him'. Her nervousness as she waited for him at St James's resulted in her producing the knife instead of her petition, but it had all been a mistake.[19] In his own critique of insanity and the State, the republican Richard Carlile repeated the evidence cited in the *Sketches* as proof of Nicholson's wrongful confinement. The obviously 'blunt' knife showed just what a 'trivial affair' the so-called assassination attempt had been.[20] If she was found insane, her inept thrusts with an inadequate knife could be interpreted as contextual evidence, but if not she might be acquitted and thus given the opportunity to re-offend. As the *Morning Chronicle* observed, many of the loyal addresses then flooding into the palace were composed in words which 'undoubtedly consider the attack to have been so feeble and so ill-conducted as to have threatened little danger.[21] Second, there was the unwelcome prospect of Nicholson using the platform given her by the trial to expose the lack of attention given to petitions submitted to the throne. The Pitt ministry's popularity was still reeling from wounds inflicted by the public outcry against the Shop Tax in 1785, a revolt that had been expressed not only in disorderly demonstrations but in a co-ordinated mass petitioning exercise.

Some contexts: Damiens, Byng, Tyrie and Gordon

Traditional Francophobic prejudices helped direct the British response to Nicholson's outrage. Overt attempts by aggrieved individuals on the lives of kings had previously been associated more easily with autocratic regimes than constitutional ones. Francois Damiens, who in 1757 assaulted Louis XV, was by no means the first Frenchman to assault a French king, and the Parisian police were well versed in the detection of plots and the incarceration of plotters. Although Nicholson's attack on George III was an altogether more surprising incident, comparisons between the two cases were nevertheless drawn by British commentators. Louis XV, like George III, was credited with composure and humanitarianism under attack. 'That man has given me a violent blow', he is supposed to have said, 'he must be either mad or drunk. I am wounded – seize that fellow but do not kill him.' Damiens, like Nicholson, was assumed to be insane rather than drunk. He had not wanted to kill the King, he told his interrogators, only to 'touch' him into 'restoring all things to order' and 'hearing the remonstrances of his parlement'.[22]

There was no similarity, however, between the reactions of the French Government to Damiens and the British Government to Nicholson. Nicholson's inquisitors in the Privy Council did not believe her to be the tool of a wider conspiracy; on the contrary, Pitt's ministry was determined to establish that she acted alone and in a state of mental distraction. Damiens, on the other hand, was assumed from the moment of his arrest to be an agent of either the Jesuits or the Jansenists and was subjected to the most gruesome tortures in pursuit of a confession. The savage theatricality of his eventual death was never in any doubt. Publicly flayed with red-hot pincers and with molten lead poured into his wounds, Damiens was pulled apart, fully conscious, by six wild horses and the executioner's knife. The English press had looked on with a mixture of fascination and horror at the awful consequences of divine-right Catholic justice on the one hand and Innocent III's famous approval of regicide in cases of heresy on the other. Walpole was shocked by such a 'lamentable spectacle', for, he reasoned, 'what punishments can prevent madness?' In 1786, reported the *Morning Chronicle*, the French argued over Nicholson's fate very 'inhumanely':

> A conviction for insanity, they say, should not save her from exemplary punishment; for who that attempts murder may not be proved insane? In reply to this it may be observed that if maniacks are to be punished for the crime of murder, it will not be means of preventing its commission, for what punishment, or what tortures can intimidate a maniack?[23]

In 1757, in fact, British criticism of the trial and execution of Damiens stood in stark contrast to the unforgiving popular and judicial condemnation of the unfortunate Admiral Byng. The trial and execution of Byng – for withdrawing an expeditionary force from Minorca instead of deploying it against a superior French army of occupation – were widely demanded by popular demonstrations and 'instructions' to Parliament. The public debate about Byng's fate took place at almost exactly the same time as judgements were being made about the trial of Damiens. As an example of abject treasonable cowardice, Byng's crime was considered unpardonable, particularly since he was believed to be perfectly rational and sane. The English were not, it seemed, willing to be seen as 'soft' on treason or on cowardly acts *per se*; on the contrary, the firm justice of Byng's execution was effectively amplified and delineated by the expression of disapproval over the treatment of Damiens.

The doomed efforts of some members of the court martial and a number of peers to save the disgraced admiral from execution were widely scorned and led to a deal of private lobbying of the King, 'lest', wrote Walpole, 'these aches of conscience should be contagious'. A number of MPs expressed concern that 'without doors the sentence was thought extremely cruel', and Pitt 'owned he thought more good would come from mercy than rigour'. In the debate that followed, questions were raised about the propriety of Parliament's presuming to advise the King on the exercise of his prerogative, and about the language in which the prerogative should be expressed. Members were clearly uncomfortable because, or so it was asserted by Fox, the warrant for Byng's death contained the innovative phrase 'His Majesty's pleasure' rather than the traditional and less emphatic 'His Majesty's consent'. George II, however, was unmoved, and in fact received a number of anonymous threats to help him make up his mind. If he expected his subjects to raise money for Hanover, he was reminded in one, he had better let Byng die. Another came in simple doggerel verse: 'Hang Byng, or take care of your King.'[24]

The disclosure that popular opinion 'without doors' was divided over the 'cruelty' of Byng's treatment may explain some of the caution with which the British authorities approached the possibility of a new trial for high treason in 1786. The humanitarian leniency extended towards Margaret Nicholson was in stark contrast not only to the moral line pursued in the case of Byng but to the bloody execution of David Tyrie in 1782. Tyrie, a naval clerk, was convicted for passing confidential information to the French and executed on Southsea Common. With no well-placed or influential friends to plead on his behalf for public or Royal sympathy, Tyrie was hanged, decapitated and quartered for his treason, as the law required. The execution, before a huge crowd, was extremely gory and provoked a distasteful and brutish public response, his dismembered body was fought over, and his limbs and fingers torn off for souvenirs. No-one emerged with much credit or decorum from the death of Tyrie; indeed the scenes beneath the scaffold reflected so poorly on the solemnity of the occasion that he became the last treason convict ever to be quartered.[25]

Finally, connections were made between Margaret Nicholson's case and the 'insanity' of Lord George Gordon. Although acquitted of high treason in 1781, Gordon remained a potent figure of opposition in London and a staunch critic of ministerial accommodation to international and domestic Catholicism. The Pitt regime was anxious to re-invent British protestantism as the domain of humane and tolerant values, not solely from a desire to silence residual public murmurs about Hanoverian imperiousness, but from the necessity of laying the over-enthusiastic protestantism of the Gordon Riots to rest. Gordon's continuing exertions were therefore less than helpful to Pitt, who considered having him apprehended and committed as a dangerous lunatic during 1785–86. Gordon and his crowd were steadily remodelled as harbingers of revolutionary and regicidal iconoclasm in much contemporary writing, particularly, as Iain McCalman has noted, in Edmund Burke's celebrated *Reflections on the Revolution in France* in 1791. Gordon's predictable championing of Margaret Nicholson, as a victim of Pittite tyranny who had been illegally confined without due process of law, was seized upon by the pro-Government press as further evidence of her lunacy. Gordon was reported to be interviewing Nicholson's friends and acquaintances with a view to establishing her sanity, but for sympathisers with the ministry the two were perfectly suited bed-fellows whose mutual derangement only confirmed the danger each posed. Some papers even suggested that the deluded couple planned to marry 'to preserve the current of their blood unadulterated'.[26]

Madness constructed

How was the madness of Margaret Nicholson read and determined? Despite the King's perceptive remarks on the spot, the first evidence heard by the Privy Council on the afternoon of 2 August was regarded as less conclusive. Jonathan Fiske, who had been Nicholson's landlord for the past three years, described her as 'industrious, sober and regular', and did not consider her insane. Recalled the following day, he admitted that he had 'often considered her behaviour extraordinary, but had never observed any marks of insanity in her conduct, except that she frequently moved her lips as if talking'. A number of other witnesses were equally uncertain about Nicholson's madness, but also found her habit of talking to herself a little odd. *The Times* helpfully sought the opinion of a 'medical correspondent', who confirmed that 'there cannot be a stronger symptom of madness or a heated imagination than talking to oneself', and then suggested that Nicholson's disappointed love life had caused the kind of distress that 'cannot but produce paroxysms of madness'. The notion that Nicholson was suffering from an Ophelia-like love-lorn melancholia captured the interest of several papers. Nicholson had 'abandoned herself to solitude', explained one provincial newsheet. 'Intense thought upon one subject debilitates the mind and, with a temper already prone to melancholy, an accumulation of thought and distress must increase intense thinking, which cannot but produce paroxysms of madness.'

The Times was afraid ministers had jumped the gun. 'They first announced her to be mad by the *London Gazette*', it noted, 'and then called a council and sent for a mad doctor to examine whether she was so or not.'[27] The mad doctor in question, Thomas Monro, could not be sure on a first examination, although Nicholson's behaviour under questioning became increasingly 'wild and incoherent', evincing 'strong marks of insanity', in the *Morning Chronicle*'s opinion.[28] Ministers knew they could temporarily confine Nicholson as a lunatic under the vagrancy laws, but they were looking for a permanent solution while being anxious not to be thought draconian at a time when the eyes of the nation were on them. Her present wildness and incoherence were probably enough to convince a jury that she was unfit to stand trial, but ministers did not want to give their political opponents the opportunity to suggest Nicholson had been feigning madness since her arrest. Privy Council investigations continued therefore in an effort to establish her insanity at the time she committed the offence, and preferably as a prior condition as well. Opposition papers like the *Chronicle* were already ridiculing the Government's position. Of course Nicholson was not mad, it snorted:

> Did she know that the King was the chief magistrate of the nation? Yes, for she applied to him for relief of grievances. Did she think that were he stabbed with a knife he would die a violent death? Yes, for she had threatened regicide. Did she know how to combine the perpetration of the horrid deed? Yes, for she took all the steps the wisest man could devise to approach the person of the Prince: she waited for him at the gate where His Majesty is used to alight; she imparted to some bystanders her intention of being ready at the coach door to present her pretended petition; always cool, collected, unmoveable in her design, guarding against betraying the least symptom of revenge. She plans, proceeds, executes with uninterrupted deliberation – and such a woman is pronounced insane![29]

The longer the uncertainty dragged on, the more nervous ministers became. The prisoner had to be confined somewhere while Monro examined her, but without contravening either *habeus corpus* or the rules of confinement for state prisoners. Technically, Nicholson was a treason suspect, and could not therefore be lodged with common prisoners in the bridewell. So Nicholson was privately boarded at the house of Cotes, a King's messenger. The arrangement had the additional advantage of a humane appearance.[30] Six days of observation had passed before the Monro brothers and a nurse were ready to go before the Privy Council and pronounce her madness authentic. The council decided then and there to send Nicholson to Bethlem for the rest of her life on the Monros' recommendation.[31]

The decision was not universally welcomed, however. Hard-line Conservatives like Pitt's Chancellor Edward Thurlow feared a backlash from a public thirsty for Nicholson's blood. 'Notwithstanding the marks of insanity in the woman, the subject is a very grave one', he told Sydney, 'and I think you should summon all the King's servants of the profession of the law to give better satisfaction to the public if she is not to be prosecuted.'[32] But Liberal opinion was also outraged. In the first place, many observers failed to understand a 'dangerous lunacy' that took so long to diagnose and which often seemed masked by composure and self-awareness. Nicholson was often 'volatile and cheerful', could talk 'very rationally' to her interrogators and 'appeared perfectly collected' en route to Bethlem.[33] But, in the second place, her removal for life bypassed due legal process and smacked of arbitrary rule. *The Times*, for example, did not question Monro's medical advice, but objected strongly that committal to Bethlem was the business of an impartial jury, not a panel of experts.

> Mad or not mad, Margaret Nicholson should be tried ... If she be insane, a jury will find her so and, after their verdict, let her be confined. If a jury should not find her insane but convict her, mercy still rests with the Crown and she may be pardoned conditionally. It is true, in her case, the overt act of treason is established and a jury could have no doubts upon the facts, but it would be a dangerous precedent to confine even her upon an *imputation* of madness.[34]

Ministers had also exceeded their authority in 'dooming' Nicholson to Bethlem for life. In denying Nicholson the right either to be released when cured or to even receive visitors without their approval, they were challenging the integrity of the asylum's governors and converting Bethlem into a 'government hospital for lunatics'. If that were allowed to happen, 'every man, however innocent, who may have incurred the jealousy of a minister may be dragged to a prison of the most horrid nature, under the pretence of insanity'.[35] It was 'little less than Star Chamber business', in the *Herald's* opinion.[36] In fact, the Privy Council knew it had no powers to confine Nicholson for life under the vagrancy laws, and knew too that Bethlem's governors reviewed the progress of every patient annually. But Government was determined to prevent her from ever regaining her liberty for, if she were freed and suffered a relapse, 'by what human precautions can she, in a country like England, be prevented in her next fit from repeating her atrocious offence?'[37] A parliamentary Bill conferring the required powers upon the Privy Council was therefore prepared for introduction in the autumn.

Nicholson and the public

The scale of public interest in Margaret Nicholson was extraordinary. In fact, it was sublime. 'The blow', according to one writer, was 'like the shock of electricity; it vibrated through the whole body, from the metropolis to the most distant and unimportant petty village in the extremities of the Kingdom: all felt, all trembled at the shock and recovered with a painfully pleasing sensation from its severity.'[38] It was not just the sensationalism of her assault on the King. George III's concern over her welfare tapped straight into a fashionable current of sensibility towards the melancholic afflictions of unrequited love. Nicholson's disappointment was inspired not only by her lost lover but by the inattentiveness of her spiritual father, the King. Melancholia, induced by the failings of civil servants to deliver Nicholson's earlier letters to the King, and the tragedy of a King made insensible to the suffering of a subject through the ineptitude of his own advisers, provoked in Nicholson an outpouring of what Helen Small has termed 'hyperbole'. This hyperbole was reflected not only in the deranged 'incoherence' of her answers to the Privy Council, but in the physicality of her final petition and remonstrance. The idea of the love-mad woman, turned by the 'desolation of betrayal', was an agreeable context for insanity and suitable to the more empathetic demands of the later eighteenth-century imagination.[39] Nicholson's case, it is fair to suggest, was not insignificant in the development of public sympathy for the mental distractedness of the King himself two years later. By signalling his own vulnerability both to physical attack and mental illness, George III became more loved as a man than feared as an omnipotent autocrat. John Barrell has argued that the language of sentiment evoked by the death of Louis XVI in 1793 played a significant role in creating public support for the vulnerable George, securing the constitutional Settlement and making it less likely he would be assassinated.[40]

There was also the matter of her gender. The idea that a woman could commit such a crime was both fascinating and horrifying to public opinion. As the anonymous author of the *Authentic Memoirs* saw it, Nicholson had 'renounced all the decent tenderness of her sex' by striking at the helpless monarch just as he was 'manifesting a wish to serve her'. And to the poet Jane Moore, the unnatural presumption of Nicholson's 'torrid zeal' had made her the 'scorn of thy sex!'[41] Within days of Nicholson's arrest, Jonathan Fiske was entertaining 'all ranks of curious people' who flocked to his house to ask questions about his celebrated lodger and look at an engraving of her. Two weeks later, he was the first to publish a cheap biography, *The Life and Transactions of Margaret Nicholson*.[42] The Home Secretary had to impound the key to her room to prevent visitors poring over her effects.[43] Others capitalised in more imaginative ways. The public, it was reported, would gladly part with a penny to see an 'identical' knife to Nicholson's, a fragment of the true knife at a public house in Devon, or even its accompanying fork, kept at an enterprising hostelry between Marlborough and Devizes. A woman exhibited by her husband as Margaret Nicholson's double was apprehended at Stirbeck by a party of constables who mistook her for the real regicide, on the run from Bethlem. This woman's forcible delivery to London was only prevented when a crowd of outraged onlookers rescued her from her captors because they thought Nicholson had been 'illegally confined long enough.'[44] In the more 'sophisticated' public sphere of the capital city, debating societies wrestled with the political issues behind the main event. The question 'Does the late frantic attempt at regicide furnish sufficient reason for the numerous addresses to the throne?' was considered at the Mitre, while in the Coachmaker's Hall there was little support for the proposition that an act should be passed for the perpetual confinement of every lunatic who tried to commit murder.[45]

Popular objections to Nicholson's arbitrary consignment to Bethlem were founded partly on a libertarian belief in right to trial by jury, but partly too on a suspicion that Government was covering up a sinister conspiracy for which Nicholson was merely a scapegoat. The very idea of conspiracy would not accommodate the Government's insistence that Nicholson was insane, moreover, because madness was not understood to be a shared or social experience. On the contrary, madness was a lonely and melancholic affliction. Ministers were very sensitive to allegations of this kind and, 'it was judged most advisable to discourage as much as possible every disposition to imagine plots and conspiracies, to which menkind are often inclined to give credit upon the slightest grounds'.

One Robert Mundy wrote to Pitt demanding to know why a 'conspiracy' he had reported earlier had not been followed up. A confederacy of twenty, including a royal equerry's servant, had been plotting the death of the King for some time, according to Mundy, and he was now convinced of Nicholson's complicity with them. A woman from Godalming, Surrey, thought the knife had been dipped in poison and that someone called 'Frances of Bristol' was implicated, and another informant accused a Shoreditch bookseller named James Herbert. Fiske, too, had a sinister story to tell. Nicholson had been seen in the company of a 'tall well-dressed woman', sharpening her knife in the park, and one of his other lodgers had been told some secrets by Nicholson 'that she will not repeate to me'. Finally, there were letters to the Home Office from Lord Deerhurst about the desirability of confining two people who were 'too dangerous for the present times, or for any time' – a 'Mrs Bellas, the footguard soldier's wife who is as mad as Margaret Nicholson' and Major La Billiere 'whose conversation savours too much of the politic mad-man, saying that the last parliament was a parliament of the Devil, and that a free-chosen parliament of the people should make a free choice'.[46]

The King himself had never been a greater celebrity. The terrace at Windsor was 'constantly full' because 'people have come from many, many places in England to see the King', the princess Elizabeth recorded.[47] Some people went to extraordinary lengths. William Harris, a poor brewer and gardener from Wiltshire, left home in the middle of August, determined to pass 'knowledge' to the King and to force secret information out of Nicholson, despite having no means by which to support himself on the journey. By the time he got to Windsor, he had been compelled to sell his horse and pawn his shoes for food and lodging. He saw the King's coach surrounded by guards and, recognising that he would never get near it on his own, continued to London where, along with two labourers he met on the way, he paid a visit to Nicholson's brother

George, who kept an inn on the Strand. After questioning him about his role in the affair, Harris went inside and wrote a letter to Margaret Nicholson: 'So I ham a messenger sent from my God from a Bouve and ief you do not Deth will be your posoune in this wourld and Damnaisoun the next From a persoun unnoun to you and your Temter the Divel.' Then he wrote one to the King: 'Ser may it ples your magisty I ham a man sent from God to fiend ought your privet Enimies if your magisty will gieve me a comisone to speck to the woman that atemted to teik your lief a way. From your afecttenet Souldear.'[48] Neither letter was delivered. George Nicholson had Harris taken up by two constables and he was marched off to tell his story to a magistrate, before being released with a caution.

Nicholson and petitioning

'Confiding in the loyalty of a generous and enlightened people', boasted the *Newcastle Chronicle* a few days after the attack on the King,

> the present Royal Family assume less state than any crowned heads in Europe and appear in public with all the ease and affability of private individuals. To prevent, however, the future attacks of *insanity, fanaticism* or *faction*, more precaution if not more parade, is necessary, as well for the security as the dignity of His Majesty's person.[49]

Precautions were indeed taken. First, there was an immediate tightening of security around the King as he got in and out of his coach at St James's. The customary two guards and two yeomen were augmented by seven grenadiers, and two extra yeomen with orders to closely escort the King in double file to and from the palace door. The first time this was done, a large crowd of well-wishers pressed close around his guard and so alarmed the King that he drew his own sword as a precaution.[50] Second, the custom and practice of presenting and acknowledging petitions to the throne was reviewed. It was understood in theory that the King personally passed every petition he accepted to one of the lords-in-waiting, who then prepared a short summary of its prayer and communicated it to him. The King would then direct an answer. But Nicholson's experience showed that this process was not working. The *Advertiser* would find no fault with the King, believing that most petitions never reached his ear because they were entrusted to 'some inferior attendant who seldom or never takes the trouble of reading them'. *The Times* agreed and thought the Nicholson outrage would almost certainly 'be the means of putting an end to the practice' of personal petitioning altogether. 'It would be a privilege highly beneficial to the public if the petitions were afterwards noticed, but they are ... committed to a chest destined for their reception, from which they never stir, till at a stated time the rubbish is cleared away and burnt to make room for more.' The failure to read petitions was certainly a scandalous affront to contractualism, but as a number of loyal addressers pointed out, it had also proved to be extremely hazardous to the King. 'Had the least attention been shown to Margaret Nicholson's first petition', observed the *Herald*, 'such evident marks of absurdity or insanity would have appeared, as must have prevented the lamentable effects which the citizens so lamentably deplore.' Other papers thought it ridiculous that the King should waste his time responding to petitions that were 'such stuff and nonsense'. In the end it was not thought politic to prevent the King's subjects from petitioning him in person just when his paternal domesticity was doing so much for his public image, but the practice was nevertheless discouraged and petitioners were expressly forbidden any more to 'stand before the guards' in the courtyard of St James's Palace.[51]

For most contemporaries, the purpose and meaning of Nicholson's behaviour was somewhat overshadowed by the elevation of the King's sensibility and the disagreement over the arbitrary incarceration of unproven 'lunatics'. These issues are not unimportant, but to fully understand the Nicholson case, we need to direct our attention to her grievance and behaviour.

Whether insane or not, Margaret Nicholson's answers to the Privy Council's initial questions were coherent and rational. She gave her personal circumstances and employment history succinctly and clearly, and explained that, since April, she had 'petitioned His Majesty twenty different times upon a Property due to her from the Crown of England; that she wrote her petitions herself and delivered them herself'. The most recent, containing a request that her case be heard before a judge, she had placed in the King's own hand seven days prior to this interrogation. When asked to restate her grievance for the benefit of the Council, she called it a 'mystery which she did not know how to relate', but she offered to write it down for them. What followed was a word-perfect replication of that final petition, including:

> I mean by this earnestly to request your Majesty will assist me now in preventing Regicide if possible which, on my side of the question I am inevitably obligated to commit unless your Majesty's accommodating circumstances enable me to withstand it – my cause is concerning the right in blood and understanding for the Crown of England by which I am sensible of securing the right Kingly marriage, in case I could obtain a Property answerable to bring him up upon, and unless I do this, I am sensible of the most fatalist catastrophe for some thousand years that ever was imagined in the mind of Man, owing to a foreign marriage, that in length of time causes a confusion of tongues.

There are two possible meanings. Either Nicholson, disappointed in love, out of regular employment and far from her own father, was requesting property and the King's hand in marriage to rescue him from an ill-advised match with his own foreign wife; or else a property dowry to help her marry somebody equally 'Kingly', like the Prince of Wales whose own secret marriage to Mrs Fitzherbert in 1785 was rendered 'foreign' by her Catholicism. Nicholson had been in 'very poor circumstances owing to the neglect shown to her Petitions', and if she received no reply now she would be 'obligated' to the physical resistance of regicide, although it is still not clear that she meant any bodily harm to the King. In an earlier petition, Nicholson had repeated her request that a judge be found to hear her case, 'or I am obliged to assault St. James's with vulgar insults till I am taken into custody'. Physical remonstration was, for Nicholson, the means to an end: a fair hearing. The knife with which she poked at the King was an intentionally poor weapon, her action no more than a pretext for arrest. Her first remarks under questioning, it will be remembered, were a refusal to answer anybody but a judge.[52]

Corroboration for part of Nicholson's story came from a publican at Twickenham who had met and spoken with her on 25 July. Nicholson had just spent two fruitless days at Windsor trying to present one of her petitions to the King, 'and ... she was determined to see him within a fortnight to give it him, having already delivered several without any notice being taken of them'. She knew the King would think her mad, she said, but he would be 'mistaken'.[53] All of her former landlords and employers had been asked to present petitions to the King on her behalf, it was said, and she was sure he 'would provide for her.'[54] While staying at her brother George's house, Nicholson had written a number of petitions, not only to the King but to the Duchess of Northumberland. She had been telling George about her entitlement to 'a considerable property' for about six years, 'that she wished to have a property and hoped she should have it', and she wrote to the King about it because he was 'the best King, that he was a good father and things to that purpose.'[55] The idea, therefore, that she had ever wanted to kill the King was, as she said herself in a letter to her father from Bethlem, 'the most mistaken idea that can be represented to the mind of man', for she wanted only to make him attend to her petitions. Nevertheless, she had been 'stigmatised' for it and was desperate to regain her liberty from a 'bondage worse than death'.[56] The most pressing questions posed by the Nicholson case were therefore not really about the security of the monarch or the insanity of the petitioner, but concerned the impracticalities of contractual theory when put to the test through the associational theatre of petitioning.

Nicholson was never to secure her release. At the end of her first year of captivity, the Home Office Under Secretary Evan Nepean instructed Bethlem's

Figure 1 Troublesome subject confronts contractual monarch. Margaret Nicholson, with a petition in one hand and a dagger in the other, advances on an open and vulnerable George III in Robert Smirke's contrived academic treatment of the celebrated assault outside St James's Palace in 1786.

governors to hold her for life and Thomas Monro duly pronounced her 'incurably insane'. Despite the King's plea for her humane treatment, she was kept in chains in her room until 1791.[57] Neither did the King's apotheosis secure him from discontent. He was hissed and groaned at when he went to open Parliament in January, and in a separate incident a man was taken up for shouting insults at his coach as it passed through the park.[58] Nicholson's crime was not, however, quickly forgotten. The Royal Academician Robert Smirke immortalised in oils the King's providential escape, less from a desire to create an enduring history painting, it seems, than to exploit the growing market for cheap engravings. The painting was sold to Robert Pollard, who reproduced it as a popular print. In 1790, divine intervention received its due reward when a bas-relief of the attack was carved on a pew in St George's Chapel in Windsor Castle. By this time, indeed, the King's recovery from his first bout of porphyria had made his earlier rational and measured triumph over the madness of Margaret Nicholson nothing less than portentous. Nicholson was also celebrated in poetry. The best-known example, Shelley's

Posthumous Fragments of Margaret Nicholson in which 'Kings cannot hear/ For passion's voice has dulled their listless ear', appeared anonymously in 1810.[59] Like a harbinger of the *fin de siècle*, Nicholson's name would continue to evoke the apparent madness of modern life throughout the 1790s. Walpole thought she had made her appearance a decade too early, 'or she might have been entitled to the honours of sepulture with Mirabeau, Marat and other felons of this consecrating age'.[60] In 1795, *The Times* concocted a phoney and sympathetic correspondence between Nicholson and the millenarian–democratic prophet Richard Brothers, who had himself been recently consigned to an asylum on a charge of high treason. Nicholson was still writing letters to secure her freedom in 1822, but she died in Bethlem in 1828 having outlived her King by eight years. On the day of his funeral she had worn a black riband.[61]

Notes

1 *High Treason Committed by Margaret Nicholson* (London, 1786); *Authentic Memoirs of the Life of Margaret Nicholson who Attempted to Stab His Most Gracious Majesty with a Knife as he was Alighting from his Carriage* (London, 1786); Jesse, *George III*, vol. 2, pp. 532–7; *Annual Register*, 1786, pp. 233–4; *The Times*, 3 August 1786; *Morning Chronicle*, 10 August 1786; *Newcastle Chronicle*, 12 August 1786.
2 *Bath Journal*, 31 July 1786.
3 *Gloucester Journal*, 7 August 1786.
4 *High Treason Committed by Margaret Nicholson.*
5 *Morning Herald*, 9 August 1786.
6 *Public Advertiser*, 3 and 4 August 1786.
7 *Public Advertiser*, 4 and 5 August 1786.
8 Cited in Sheppard, *Memorials* (London, 1894), vol. 1, pp. 328–9.
9 *Newcastle Chronicle*, 12 August 1786.
10 PRO, HO 42/9: 'Account of Margaret Nicholson's attack upon the King', 2 August 1786.
11 Cited in Llanover, *Mrs. Delany*, vol. 3 (London, 1862), pp. 376–7, 378–9.
12 Burney's account is cited in Sheppard, *Memorials*, vol. 1, p. 327–8. Mary Delany described the 'animated manner' of the King's arrival in front of his womenfolk, which left the Queen 'stood struck and motionless for some time' (Llanover, *Mrs. Delany*, vol. 3, p. 392).
13 *The Times*, 5 August 1786.
14 *Public Advertiser*, 5 August 1786.
15 *Morning Chronicle*, 10 August 1786.
16 *Morning Herald*, 9 August 1786; *Public Advertiser*, 8 August 1786.
17 PRO, HO 42/9: 'Account of Margaret Nicholson's attack'.
18 *The Times*, 7 August 1786.
19 *Sketches in Bedlam*, pp. 253–8.
20 R. Carlile, *A New View of Insanity* (London, 1831), pp. 28–9.

21 *Morning Chronicle*, 25 August 1786.
22 D. K. Van Kley, *The Damiens' Affair and the Unravelling of the Ancien Régime, 1750–1770* (Princeton, NJ, 1984), pp. 33, 36, 39, 43, 246; The king's words have been taken from *Felix Farley's Bristol Journal*, 22 January 1757.
23 *Felix Farley's Bristol Journal*, 22 January; 2 and 9 April 1757; for a number of contemporary French descriptions of the punishment, see Foucault, *Discipline and Punish*, pp. 3–6. Innocent's injunction was made at the Council of Lateran; Horace Walpole, *Memoirs of King George II*, vol. 2: *March 1754–1757* (1985 edition, ed. John Brooke, Yale), p. 198; *Morning Chronicle*, 26 August 1786.
24 Walpole, *George II*, vol. 2, pp. 216–21. See also Wilson, *Sense of the People*, pp. 178–85 for the popular provincial reaction to Byng's 'treachery'. Nicholas Rogers' *Crowds, Culture and Politics*, pp. 58–64 has recently put the case into broader political and economic context, but his interest is in the popular condemnation of Byng and not in public sympathy for his treatment by the Admiralty.
25 For Tyrie's case, see the long series of letters in PRO, HO 42/1: Robert Serle to Thomas Townshend, 19 August 1782 and *passim; and The Trial of David Tyrie for High Treason at the Assize at Winchester, August 10 1782* (London, 1782). In 1781, the French spy La Motte had been the last to be disembowelled, although even he was allowed to die by hanging before his heart was cut out. See Gatrell, *Hanging Tree*, p. 317.
26 McCalman, 'Mad Lord George' pp. 359, 361; Douglas Hay, 'The laws of God and the laws of man: Lord George Gordon and the death penalty', in J. Rule and R. Malcolmson (eds), *Protest and Survival: The Historical Experience. Essays for E. P. Thompson* (London, 1993), pp. 66–70. In 1786, Gordon attacked Pitt for refusing to aid the Anglican community in Canada and Quebec against Catholic expansionism: *Public Advertiser*, 8 August 1786. He was also an important magnet for popular opposition to Pitt's notorious Shop Tax in 1785. Gordon's approach to Nicholson's landlord Jonathan Fiske is alleged in HO 42/9: Jonathan Fiske to Lord Sydney, 6 August 1786. See also, *The Times*, 12 August 1786 and 3 June 1787.
27 *The Times*, 3, 4, 5, 11 and 24 August 1786; *Morning Chronicle*, 10 August 1786; *Morning Herald*, 10 August 1786; *Bath Journal*, 14 August 1786. Others who doubted her madness were a neighbour, Ann Southey, and a former employer, Watson.
28 *Morning Chronicle*, 4 and 5 August 1786.
29 *Morning Chronicle*, 25 August 1786.
30 *The Times*, 4 August 1786; *Morning Chronicle*, 4 August 1786.
31 *Morning Chronicle*, 10 August 1786; *Morning Herald*, 10 August 1786.
32 PRO, HO 42/9: Edward Thurlow to Sydney, n.d. (August 1786).
33 *Morning Herald*, 10 August 1786; *The Times*, 11 August 1786; and *High Treason Committed by Margaret Nicholson* (London, 1786).
34 *The Times*, 8 August 1786.
35 *The Times*, 10 and 12 August 1786, and 12 October 1786.
36 *Morning Herald*, 9 August 1786.
37 *Public Advertiser*, 8 August 1786; *Morning Chronicle*, 9 August 1786.
38 *Authentic Memoirs*.
39 Small, *Love's Madness*, pp. 72–9. See also her following comments on the meaning and gendering of hyperbole in Regency literature.

40 J. Barrell, 'Sad stories: Louis XVI, George III, and the language of sentiment', in K. Sharpe and S. N. Zwicker (eds), *Refiguring Revolutions: Aesthetics and Politics from the English Revolution to the Romantic Revolution* (Berkeley, CA, 1998), p. 93. See also E. Schor, *Bearing the Dead: The British Culture of Mourning from the Enlightenment to Victoria* (Princeton, NJ, 1994), ch. 3, 'Burke, Paine, Wordsworth and the politics of sympathy'. Barrell's argument rather overlooks the possibility of George's representation as a 'man' making him *less* popular. As Bolingbroke had warned during the previous reign, 'a king who lives out of the sight of his subjects, or is never seen by them except on his throne, can scarce be despised as a man, though he may be hated as a king. But the king who lives more in their sight and more under their observation, may be despised before he is hated, and even without being hated' (quoted in Jephson, *The Platform*, vol. 1, see pp. 25–41).

41 *Authentic Memoirs*; J. E. Moore, 'On Margaret Nicholson', in *Miscellaneous Poems on Various Subjects* (Dublin, 1796).

42 In September there were at least three cheap biographies of Nicholson in circulation, and, by the end of the year, a growing number of published sermons. See notices in the *Monthly Review*: September 1786 (p. 235), and December 1786 (p. 454).

43 *Public Advertiser*, 8 August 1786.

44 *The Times*, 15 and 17 August; 2, 6 and 10 October 1786.

45 D. T. Andrew (ed.), *London Debating Societies, 1776–1799* (London, 1994): entries dated 28 September and 31 August 1786.

46 PRO, HO 42/9: 'Account of Margaret Nicholson's attack'; Alison Robinson to the King, 7 August 1786; A loyal subject of the King to Lord Sydney, 16 August 86; Examination of James Herbert, 21 August 1786; Petition of Robert Mundy, n.d. (1786); J. Fiske to Sydney, 6 August 1786. The excitement in and around Fiske's house appears to have all been too much for Fiske's pregnant wife, who became so 'alarmed' that Fiske was obliged to employ doctors and a nanny. He later tried to forward the bill to Sydney, 'as those troubles and expenses are caused by the proceedings of government': J. Fiske to Sydney, 21 August 86; M. Barthelemon to Sydney, n.d. (August 1786).

47 R A GEO/Additional MS 9/12: Princess Elizabeth to Prince Augustus, 5 August 1786.

48 PRO, HO 42/9: Examination of William Harris, 21 August 1786, with enclosures.

49 *Newcastle Chronicle*, 12 August 1786.

50 *Gloucester Journal*, 7 August 1786.

51 *Morning Herald*, 14 August 1786; *Morning Chronicle*, 4 August 1786; *The Times*, 5 and 7 August 1786; *Public Advertiser*, 5 August 1786.

52 PRO, PC 2/131/366–70: Examination of Margaret Nicholson, 2 August 1786; various letters and petitions from Margaret Nicholson to the King, the first dated 26 July 1786, the rest undated.

53 PRO, HO 42/9: Samuel Goodwin to Pitt, 5 August 1786; Statement of Samuel Goodwin, n.d. (August 1786).

54 *Authentic Memoirs*.

55 PRO, HO 42/9: Examinations of George and Jane Nicholson, 3 and 4 August 1786. Other references to Nicholson's belief in her 'property' entitlement may be found in the testimony of the hatter, Watson, and in remarks she made to the

magistrate William Addington: *Morning Chronicle*, 4, 5 and 10 August 1786, *Morning Herald*, 10 August 1786.

56 PRO, HO 42/9: M. Nicholson to her parents, 28 August 1786, and to Sydney, 31 August 1786.

57 Royal Bethlem Hospital Archive, Committee Book: entries dated 11 August 1787 and 12 March 1791.

58 *The Times*, 20 and 23 January 1787.

59 N. Rogers (ed.), *Complete Poetical Works of Percy Bysshe Shelley*, vol. 1: *1802–13* (Oxford, 1972), pp. 67–78.

60 W. S. Lewis and A. D. Wallace (eds), *Horace Walpole's Correspondence with Mary and Agnes Berry* (London, 1994), p. 117: letter to Mary Berry, 29 September 1794.

61 *The Times*, 3 and 24 April 1795, 2 January 1822 and 15 May 1828.

5

Treason compassed: popular mobilisation and physicality in the 1790s

Madness, law and the levelling stone of John Frith, 1790

In contrast to the years following the foundation of the French republic in 1792, the first three years of the Revolution were not a great cause of alarm or controversy in England. Until the execution of Louis XVI, few profound changes were expected in the French State beyond the establishment of constitutional monarchy, land reform, equitable taxation and religious tolerance. Between 1786 and 1792, the British Government remained alert to the possibility of regicidal assaults against George III and did its best to apprehend the writers of threatening letters, but it was scarcely concerned about republican plots. The case of John Frith in 1790 was taken extremely seriously, however, partly because his was the first physical assault on the King since Nicholson's, but partly also because, despite his apparent insanity, there were political elements at play.

Frith believed he had been unjustly retired from a promising military career in Jamaica in 1787 after the Governor, Jeffery Amhurst, fabricated evidence of insanity against him. The half pay he received in consolation was insufficient for the support of his dependent family and he was additionally haunted by Amherst's 'supernatural agents' who tormented him by whispering in his ear. But, believing himself under the protection of Christ and St Paul, Frith began a long crusade for reinstatement and recompense.[1] He first complained to his old regimental commanders 'that the King had put him on half pay without his consent which he said demanded the interference of the Lords and the Commons', then sent a memorial to the King and waited fruitlessly outside the palace for a reply. Frith's grievance was therefore a double one: that as Commander in Chief of the armed forces George III was responsible for the 'illegal warrant' depriving him of his commission; and that as a constitutional monarch he had ignored previous appeals for redress.[2]

In December 1787, Frith 'constitutionally addressed' the House of Commons 'to desire His Majesty to enforce his executive power of martial prerogative' and order the army to pay him his money. 'Until His Majesty is better advised and gives a Martial Redress', he later told the Bow Street magistrate Sampson Wright, 'the Liberty of the British Soldier and Subject are Infringed by Despotism which may end in Anarchy and Confusion'. If the King did not act, he would effectively 'Depose himself, and our chartered rights in the Tower will Supply the Deficiency to Carry on the Law of the Land. Now the Compact is Disolved as in the case of James II, June 1688.'[3] And, a year later, in a manuscript entitled 'Manifesto and Declaration', Frith offered further evidence of his constitutional ideas:

> The King's Majesty levies war with his military servant and subject by Tyranny in not redressing grievances – The subject has a similar power of retaliation and may besiege the King's throne with a bold complaint for Justice and what, in a simple case, would be High Treason, in this Crisis is a lawful constitutional resistance ... [I] have constitutionally addressed the King through the Three Estates by a memorial petition to the Honourable House of Commons that they will be pleased to address His Majesty ... After waiting upwards of four months and no attention paid, I don't hesitate to pronounce our Ancient Constitution has given a mortal blow to her libertys and we have only the outward form of government.[4]

In January 1790, Frith went to St James's Palace and posted up a signed and hand-written notice headed 'A Protest against the Democracy of the People in the Kingdom of Great Britain'. This somewhat incoherent and rambling address asserted that 'the people' had 'overturned the Body Politic and established their Natural Rights by which a Revolution, as in Sweden in 1772, is established without a struggle', but that, 'His Majesty having broke his coronation oath by not rendering me martial justice ... I openly declare my disapprobation of this late revolution and view this protest as a necessary act to guard the majestic prerogative of the subject'.[5] Frith tried to persuade the Treasury Solicitors' Office to take up his case on 21 January, the day of the State Opening of Parliament, but then walked to St James's Park to join the crowds waiting for the King. As the coach rounded the corner by Carlton House, he fell in beside it and produced a rolled petition. But instead of trying to present it at the window, he shouted, 'You tyrant! You villain! You are going to be hanged like a rogue, as you are guarded by a parcel of rogues of constables!', and threw a stone at the carriage. A constable grabbed Frith, who told him:

> There he goes, a Rebel. He is going like a common felon to be executed, escorted by a parcel of constables. He ought to be broke as he has broke

> me. I think no civil power has a right to lay hold of anybody in the Park, particularly an officer like me, the Park being private property, I think it is, under the government of the military.[6]

Before the Privy Council, Frith denied any intention of harming the King and said he had only been trying to draw attention to his case. But during four hours of questioning and depositions by witnesses, his eccentricity became abundantly clear. Since he had come under the influence of St Paul and Christ, he said, people had perceived him as 'a most extraordinary kind of man' and hailed him as a messiah. But, 'all I do is make myself memorandums daily to prove myself in my senses'. In Hampstead churchyard he had erected 'an extraordinary kind of monument with strange emblematical figures', sufficient in itself to convince the poor curate that he was deranged. However, a man who had heard Frith stamping on the floor of his room, pounding the walls and singing psalms, merely assumed him to be a Methodist.[7] That he had been under a mental affliction for some considerable time, the Council had little doubt. Whenever the moon was in the south, he told them, 'it attracted great quantities of water and produced such effects that he could not sleep near heavy buildings and was obliged to sleep out of town'.[8] But the Council remained uncertain about what to do. Even if Frith was mad *now*, they could not be sure he had been insane at the time of the offence, so they committed him for high treason and washed their hands of his fate. *The Times* considered it a shrewd move, for ministers had 'effectively silenced the clamour raised on Margaret Nicholson's business', and there was every possibility that the prisoner was fabricating his insanity to avoid punishment.[9]

Given the circumstances, and the relatively trivial nature of the 'overt act', there was never any question of Frith's being executed for treason, especially after the painstaking way in which ministers had used Nicholson's insanity to illustrate the nation's humanitarian legal code just four years earlier. Neither the Government nor the newspaper press seemed interested in the political nuances of his behaviour or his manuscript manifestos, despite the ambiguous language of 'revolution' contained in the 'Protest'. If Frith had posted his panegyric, shouted his insults and thrown his stone in an identical manner *after* the royal proclamations against sedition in 1792, it might have been different, but for now ministers were content to confirm a marginalising mental distractedness that rendered his politics and motivation irrelevant. Frith would therefore stand trial at the Old Bailey, publicly display his insanity to the satisfaction of a jury, and *then* be taken to Bedlam. The Privy Council was careful to make no public pronouncement of Frith's insanity before the trial, despite having him examined by Monro and a number of other physicians.

In April, Frith took his place at the bar.[10] Contrary to the wishes of the prisoner himself, defence counsel began with a request for postponement so that irrefutable evidence of madness could be produced. The motion was accepted by both the bench and the prosecution, but strongly challenged by Frith who demanded immediate judgement. His health, he said, had already suffered enough from confinement at Newgate, 'the King has broken the mutual obligation between him and the subject, and the assault is of such a simple kind of manner ... that I desire to speak by way of extenuation and to plead guilty or not guilty to the facts'. He reminded the court of his legal right to plead to the indictment, since both the Privy Council and the mad-doctors had found him 'in perfect health, fit to meet my trial'. But Lord Justice Heath ruled that the court was obliged to consider the defendant's state of mind, not only when the act was committed but when he rose to make his defence. If a doubt arose about the latter, an inquiry would have to be made and an adjournment was unavoidable. 'I know it is untrodden ground', explained one of the justices, 'though it *is* constitutional'.

Inviting the jury to assess the results, Heath now directed Frith to prove himself sane. He tried to do so in three pieces of testimony: the Monro brothers had failed to find him mad before the trial, his family's lawyers would confirm his sanity; and the evidence on which he had been retired from the army was maliciously fabricated. But as soon as his counsel prompted him on the subject of his millenarianism, Frith began to talk strangely again of the 'Christ-like powers' by which he had overcome the voices whispering in his ear. After a number of witnesses confirmed that they had heard him talk this way before, the inquiry was stopped and the jury ordered to reflect on Frith's mental ability to stand trial. They did not need to concern themselves with his state of mind when he committed the crime, ruled Heath, nor when he was examined, unless they first established his fitness to face trial. Frith protested that he had not been permitted to call any witnesses of his own and insisted once again that he was both sane and fit; but the jury was certain he was 'quite insane'. Heath stopped the trial, and Frith was returned to his cell in Newgate where he remained for the next eighteen months while ministers made up their minds what to do with him. The prison doctor twice advised the Privy Council that Frith was unmanageable in prison, subject to extreme fits of rage, and in need of proper care in an asylum. But it was not until December 1791 that Dundas ordered his removal to Bethlem.[11]

By the time the trial was over, *The Times* had abandoned its scepticism. Both the nature of his crime and his religious enthusiasm made his madness unquestionable:

> The very deed for which Frith was brought to trial is the strongest proof of his insanity. It is not probable that a man in his senses would be guilty

> of such an act of High Treason as throwing a stone at the Sovereign, attended by his guards in the open face of day – Methodism has made more maniacs than Frith – and Frith was one of the closest followers of that sect.[12]

Frith's insanity and enthusiasm made him an easy tool for ministerial propaganda. Cruickshank engraved him as Burke, conspiring with Sheridan and Fox to undermine the King's ministry while the satirical *World* linked him with radical, French and opposition causes. All radicals are maniacs, asserted the paper, and Frith was 'no more a maniac than any distempered wretch who makes treasonable speeches for hours together'.[13] With language of this kind, the politics of the Foxite opposition, together with its nascent Jacobin progeny, were cynically constructed as the politics of madness and enthusiasm, an argument made more persuasive by the death of the unfortunate James Sutherland in 1791.

Frith was the first ex-military man to achieve a high public profile as a frustrated petitioner to the throne, but he was certainly not the last. The eighteenth century had no word for 'shell-shock', but this was also an age in which unhelmeted soldiers were susceptible to mental damage from head wounds received in close range combat. Battle-related madness was a common cause of enforced retirement on half pay, and a source of understandable resentment among those who believed themselves sane enough to serve. As titular head of the armed forces, the monarch was often held ultimately responsible for the welfare of his soldiers, and the frequency with which they appealed to him for help should not surprise us. Insane discharged soldiers with a grievance were, therefore, of course, potentially dangerous to the king. Six months after the trial of Frith, Captain William Carlyon marched into the vestry of St Martin in the Fields and asked the curate to let him present his case during Divine Service and for a full report to be sent to the King. When he was refused, Carlyon fell on his knees and swore loyalty on the bible, then hurriedly left. Afraid he might be making for the palace, the curate alerted Bow Street but he could not be found.[14]

The Romantic tragedy of Sutherland's suicide made him an appealing symbol of constitutional frustration in the public press. In stark contrast to its instinctive diagnosis of Frith's insanity, *The Times* rejected the coroner's verdict on Sutherland's mental condition. A man who so calmly and rationally took his own life in the name of justice could not be mad, it reasoned, and although both Frith and Nicholson had both, in their own way, inspired fashionable feelings of sensibility, Sutherland's elevation was the more assured. 'He who condemns thee is a BRUTE', proclaimed *The Times*, 'he who pities thee a MAN. That your conduct was upright, the laws of your country have declared – that you were ill-treated – cruelly – very cruelly used, everybody believes.'[15] The full impact of the Sutherland case in the public sphere is hard to guage, but the insistence of *The Times* that his cause and method were legal may not have been uninfluential. A few days after Sutherland's death, William Wetton, a poor 46-year-old ex-soldier and shoemaker from Staffordshire, 'insisted in a boisterous manner' on an interview with the Queen at Buckingham House. Macmanus secured him for the night, then took him before Justice Addington at Bow Street who, after 'a very short examination', called him a lunatic and sent him back to his parish.[16]

Political plots and constructive treason: the LCS, petitioning and resistance

> Is there an impenetrable barrier between the oppressed and the magistrate? ... Think of the abyss between supplication and despair! [17]

Between 1794 and 1795 Pitt's ministry made three noteworthy attempts to destabilise the London Corresponding Society by associating its members with wishing the death of the King. The most important was the decision to prosecute the secretary, Thomas Hardy, and several other prominent members including John Thelwall, Thomas Holcroft and Horne Tooke for constructive treason; in other words, for being members of a body whose aims and objectives posed a potential hazard to the King's safety. The second centred on allegations of an actual conspiracy by LCS members to murder George III with a poisoned dart: the so-called 'Pop Gun Plot'; The third involved a merchant who was not even a member of the LCS, William Stone. Stone's case we need notice only in passing. Charged with aiding and abetting the enemy after co-operating with French inquiries about the likely reception in England of an invasion attempt, Stone spent several months in prison awaiting trial, but was acquitted of treason in January 1796.[18] The failure of all three legal initiatives only underlines the difficulties the Government faced in making any practical use of the treason laws, unless an undeniable overt act could be established.

Mass petitioning and address signing were absolutely central to the political debates between reforming radicalism and conservative loyalism during the 1790s. The force and passion of this dialectic, no less than the ease with which it involved and energised every section of British society, are perhaps the strongest indications we have of the extent of the late eighteenth-century public sphere. 'The open air is become the order of the day', announced John Gale Jones in the autumn of 1795.

> Dukes, lords and members of the House of Commons no longer think it a disgrace to harangue the people in the open air. Forty thousand men

> associated together will not very easily be separated. Men who have been delegates and sub-delegates, who have been used to the discussion of political subjects, to attend committees and to transact their official business, will not very easily return to insignificance.[19]

The London Corresponding Society, an organisation whose very existence was rooted in the inclusive rhetoric of 'members unlimited', found itself irresistibly drawn into the numbers game. While their first universal suffrage petition to Parliament attracted 2,000 names, John Reeves's loyalist association movement countered with a call for mass signatures to broadly conceived patriotic declarations of support for the status quo. Reformers felt compromised and 'dare not sign on both sides of the question'.[20] Beyond turning out to watch Tom Paine's effigy burnt on bonfires stoked with sequestered copies of *Rights of Man* over the winter of 1792–93, 'membership' of the loyal associations was undemanding. Patrician unease about 'the consequence of making every man a politician and drawing the attention of the lower ranks from labour to thinking',[21] ensured the virtual death of the movement within six months.

Through the medium of the loyal associations, however, reform was wilfully construed as republicanism. Royal proclamations against sedition in May and November 1792 encouraged the 'loyal' to detect and report anyone whose written or spoken language was defamatory to the King or his ministers. The prosecution and extra-legal intimidation of known and suspected radicals followed on a vast scale. In a well-known essay Clive Emsley has estimated a total of 200 prosecutions under the sedition laws in England during the 1790s, but questioned the consequent radical appellation of a 'Reign of Terror' against progressive opinion. As I have argued elsewhere, Emsley's figure, unhelpfully based upon prosecutions rather than custodial arrests, is almost certainly a considerable underestimation of the true total,[22] but whatever language we may care to use, one thing is clear. People were frequently inclined to insult the Royal Family in these years, and did so openly, sometimes violently, and often without fear of the consequences. Anonymous letters to Government threatening all manner of retribution against the King if he did not stop the war with France were commonplace by 1795, as were enthusiastic declarations by frustrated individuals. 'Let us all join and rebel', crowed a pamphleteer from Norwich. 'Down with the present government! Off with King George's head! and a REPUBLIC in Great Britain! Huzzah!' Other outbursts were more emblematic. A Liverpudlian gaoled for wishing the King's death in 1794 produced a pack of playing cards and impressed his friends by taking out all the Kings and cutting their heads off.[23]

Radical language was robust, irreverent and difficult to silence. Even jailed seditionists seemed sustained by gallows' humour. After three years in Cold

Bath Fields' bridewell, the Spithead mutineer Joseph Hudson remained a 'very quarrelsome man' much given to 'damning and blasting the King and [royal] family and the country', and two LCS prisoners, Joseph Burke and John Smith, had to be banned from the prison chapel for 'laughing and nodding at particular parts of the service' or proclaiming their atheism to the chaplain. Their 'posture was at times irreverent and unbecoming', and they made a display of 'smiling, winking and nodding their heads', laughing or making 'a nod or a shrug' during all prayers in which sedition, Parliament, the magistrates or the King and Royal Family were mentioned.[24] This was a culture in which the presumptions of majesty were simply regarded as funny. Laughter stripped the King of all mystery and magic. In 1795, this is why John Thelwall was rewarded with a 'loud laugh in the room' when he alluded to the 'Glorious reign of George III, whom God long preserve', and why John Gale Jones was so delighted to find the walls of a public house in Chatham so 'well stored with political caricatures', including one celebrating the 'Royal Assault' a few months afterwards. For Jones, humorous comment on regicide was a sign of conviviality.[25]

The logical outcome of the legal offensive against radicalism was the arrest and trial of Hardy, Thelwall, Horne Tooke and other leading figures in the LCS for the capital crime of high treason in 1794. By building a case around the *potential* insurrectionary outcome of LCS plans to call a Convention, the Crown did not have to prove any overt act of treason beyond the realm of the imagination. Circumstantial evidence was nevertheless produced to situate the defendants within a regicidal matrix. The spy Edward Gosling, for example, claimed that an army officer had suggested they should 'blow up the Family altogether', and that another soldier had promised armed support 'if the Society once showed themselves in force'. The LCS were said to be preparing an address to the army, and the committed revolutionist John Baxter was procuring 'thousands' of pikes, ostensibly for the defence of the proposed convention. 'Is there one man in the Society who believes a parliamentary reform is all we want? No, not one', Baxter is supposed to have said. Nevertheless, according to Gosling, Baxter 'did not wish the King or his family to lose their lives – he thought they might let him go to Hanover and take his family with him'.[26]

Gosling's allegations were used at Hardy's trial to suggest that since Baxter and Hardy were both prominent members of the LCS, they were complicit in one another's thinking. It did not matter that Baxter hoped to save the King's life; for, on the one hand, deposing him was treason enough; and, on the other, the King could not be seized or even physically opposed without endangering his life. Gosling was certainly the source of much of the prosecution's more salacious evidence about plans for armed insurrection.

John Hillier, an LCS member arrested but, like Baxter, not charged, is supposed to have told Gosling 'that the principal dependence of the Society was in securing the Royal Family and both Houses of Parliament', because the army would not oppose them if they had no 'Head to look up to'.[27] Thelwall, who wanted it known that he had always opposed 'the ridiculous project of procuring arms and exchanging [the pen] ... for pikes and guns', blamed spies like Gosling for maliciously spreading ideas like these within the LCS. Of course, regicide was a 'monstrous act', and the 'fences of the law' around the King must be 'thick and strong'; nevertheless constructive treason remained an 'absurd and inexplicable doctrine' unknown to English law.[28] But, Gosling's allegations aside, in the prosecution's case political agitation became itself an overt act of treason because the popular sovereignty invoked by a convention was simply antithetical to the existing sovereignty of George III. The Attorney General spelt it out: 'A representation of the people founded upon the principle of equal active citizenship of all men, must form a parliament into which no King, nor Lords, could enter.' The King, bound by his coronation oath to prevent such a calamity, might place his own life in danger as a consequence.[29] Thelwall thought it dangerous nonsense, for

> if it be true that to seek to alter or ameliorate the laws and constitution of your country is high treason, because the people may *possibly* become unreasonable in their demands, and the government may *possibly* oppose their wishes, and a contest may *possibly* ensue, in which the king may *possibly* be deposed or slain, then farewell at once to every boasted exercise of reason! – farewell to political improvement![30]

The jury shared Thelwall's view and voted for acquittal. In playing too many semantic games with the language of 'imagination', in seeking to equate imagination with intention and in trying, in Barrell's phrase, 'to expel all discourses from the court other than its own',[31] the prosecution had made a dreadful mess of its own case. The Government's case, argued Daniel Isaac Eaton, had undermined the Bill of Rights by calling every attempt to defend its provisions an act of treason:

> [To] form associations for the purpose of framing petitions, or of taking the sense of the people on the means to be used when petitions are found to be ineffectual for obtaining that and whatever else the Bill of Rights so solemnly insisted upon as the condition on which the throne was to be held by the family of our present gracious sovereign.[32]

Genuine treason, thought Jones, lay not here but in the neglect of popular petitions by any 'man who shall dare to oppose the will of the people, I care not whether he be a King or a minister'.[33]

In September 1794, three young LCS artisan apprentices were taken up on fresh evidence for plotting to kill the King with a poisoned dart. George Higgins, Paul Thomas Lemaitre and John Smith were joined in prison by a fourth suspect, Dr Thomas Crossfield, in February 1795. These conspirators, it was alleged, had intended to shoot the King through a brass tube either at Windsor or at one of the west end theatres. All denied the charges; but, however absurd the plot sounded, polite society expressed its outrage. 'You see', commented Horace Walpole, 'murder is not dead with Robespierre.' The plot was 'universally believed' in aristocratic circles, he said, and was proof of the regicidal intentions of 'our Jacobin clubs ... working underground'. Mary Berry told him the defendants were almost certainly 'mad'.[34]

The best evidence the Crown could muster centred on testimony that Crossfield had openly boasted about an air-gun he had invented and which he had already aimed at the King in both St James's Park and at Covent Garden. He was therefore prosecuted first. But it was unnecessary for the prosecution to prove that any attack had actually taken place: the overt act of 'compassing and imagining' the King's death was constituted in the manufacture of the weapon. Unfortunately, the State's key witness Thomas Upton was discredited because he had a personal grudge against the defendants, who had been trying to have him ejected from the LCS for fraud. Crossfield accused him of ordering the brass tube himself, and of acting as an *agent provocateur*; and, worse still, when the trial opened Upton could not even be found to give evidence. Since the evidence of two reliable witnesses was required to prosecute a charge of treason, the case collapsed and the four defendants walked free.[35]

No sensible motive was ever adduced for the conspiracy. Thelwall considered it 'infamous and ridiculous ... wickedly fabricated', and yet 'so politically believed by a certain circle, notwithstanding its monstrous absurdity and impracticability'.[36] Lemaitre believed Upton's tale had been seized on by Pitt against his better judgement because Hardy's prosecution was then in progress, and, 'as the bills of indictment were about to be presented to the Grand Jury, it was thought by the arch-traitor [that] a pretty little plot against the King's life would prove a powerful adjunct in the grand desideratum of alarm, and the Pop Gun Plot became instantly a ministerial measure'. It was, he maintained, a sure sign of the ministry's own corrupt condition and irrefutable evidence of the need for reform. Reformers had nothing to gain from assassinating the King, he maintained, for 'George IV would have succeeded George III'.[37] Smith pointed out that even a well-aimed dart would be more likely to wound than kill its intended victim: 'If instant death had not followed the unerring dart of wonder-working poison, of what advantage to any conspirators could have been the illness of a king? Has he not been for several months unable to hold the reins of government, yet the realm was not, in consequence of his madness, in a state of anarchy and confusion?'[38] The recently liberated Thomas Holcroft agreed:

> I met no man who was so void of understanding as to suppose that this was the true means of promoting reform. They all knew that if the monarch were to die, he had an heir to succeed; and it was not the change of the King but the change of the House of Commons, that, so far as I was acquainted with their designs, had been their general object.[39]

Lemaitre, Smith and Holcroft's remarks on the futility of king-killing are only in part disingenuous. The king's institutional body could not be destroyed simply by the murder of his person (although both the English and French republics had been prefaced by regicide). But resistance to individual monarchs who broke their contract might well result in a king's death, and few radicals rejected this possibility, at least in theory. In practice, as we will see, even those radicals who, like Despard, were willing to pursue resistance to the point of capturing and restraining the king cannot be shown to have intended his death. In this respect then, radical collective resistance to tyrannical monarchs differed little from the tactics pursued by individual 'non-political' but equally constitution-conscious remonstrators like Nicholson and Frith.

The first response of the LCS to the arrest of its leaders in May 1794 was to call for a 'spirited remonstrance' to be drawn up, but few members would contemplate sending it to Parliament. Citing the Wilkesite remonstrances of 1768–69 as precedents, John Gale Jones thought it should be sent to the King. He did not expect George III to help them because he was ruled by a *junto* of ministers,

> But if we remonstrate to the King, it will have this effect: It will convince the country that we have done everything in our power to do, and that if we resort to other measures, we do it as our last, our only resource. Let us, he then said, present a spirited remonstrance to the King alone. It will show our contempt for the two inferior branches of the legislature and, should he disdain to receive it, let us show him that we can also treat him with contempt and appeal to the Majesty of the People.

When some members expressed fears about language that could be interpreted as threatening to the King, Jones replied that, in that case, they should go straight to the people and forget about the King. A debate ensued about the propriety of issuing a remonstrance to the people rather than to Parliament or the throne, but no such document was drawn up.[40]

Daniel Isaac Eaton's *Politics for the People* meanwhile drew up its own 'Remonstrance of the Swinish Multitude to the Chief and Deputy Swineherds of Europe'. This document castigated all kings who ignored popular petitions and reminded them that the prerogative was conferred by the people only 'for their own good'. If the prerogative was used in any other way, added 'a Freeholder',

> [the people] have a right to resume it into their own hands ... [and] unreasonable opposition to their just demands has often been attended with such consequences ... In my domestic economy, I am authorised, both by natural and positive law, to discharge an unworthy servant: who will have the effrontery to assert that the nation is not entitled to a like right? It has, I own, been little exercised ... but as no custom, no prescription, can justify illegal acts, so no disuse can anul the natural charter, the birthright of a nation ... Since the people have adopted the mode of petitioning, they will wait and see what redress it will procure them. Should they be disappointed, they should strike into this path which I have pointed out.[41]

In a considered statement of qualification, the writer then explained that it was ministers he would have forcibly removed, not the king. If parliaments were chosen by universal suffrage, the king would necessarily be surrounded by ministers who would advise him to heed the prayers of his subjects. As usual, radicals were willing to ascribe the king's negligence to bad counsel because that offered them a constitutionally legitimate organisational lifeline. Other writers were less equivocal. If petitions and remonstrances were repeatedly overlooked, 'the conclusion is that the People must remedy their own grievances. To effect this they must unite and throw off at once their inactivity and their allegiance and then ... insurrection becomes a sacred and a solemn duty'.[42]

In 1795, an address to the King was mooted once again, although members were sceptical that their efforts would ever reach him. Few such addresses, they feared, ever progressed much further than the Privy Council's arbitrary screening system. Nevertheless, an address to the King was drawn up and sent, and disregarded in June. A remonstrance, directly evoking the Whig 'martyrs' Hampden and Sydney followed in the autumn. In spirited language, the LCS reminded the King of the fate of the Stuarts for opposing the 'public will' in 1641. An 'Address to the Nation' was drawn up at the same time, and both documents adopted at a large open-air public meeting on Copenhagen Fields on 26 October, three days before George was attacked in his carriage as he went to open Parliament. The Address to the Nation expressed the Society's dismay at the King's disregard for their last approach to the throne:

> His Majesty should consider the sacred obligations he is bound to fulfil and the duties he ought to discharge; he should recollect that when he ceases to consult the interests and happiness of the People, he will cease to be

> respected; and that justice is a debt which the Nation hath a right to demand from the Throne! ... Our address was not attended to by your majesty's servants as it should have been. Are we to suffer and not complain? ... Is there an impenetrable barrier between the oppressed and the magistrate? ... Think of the abyss between supplication and despair! It is our right to advise as well as supplicate.[43]

A disinclination to petition Parliament was by now widespread amongst reformers. In Norfolk, local leaders urged radicals to look to themselves rather than to Parliament,[44] and at the Westminster Forum a day after the Copenhagen Fields' meeting Jones confirmed that the 'LCS disdains to petition any more to the present House of Commons'. There was concern from the floor that the remonstrance to the King was not worth sending either if they had to trust Pitt to deliver it. One man had the answer. 'The LCS ought to present the remonstrance to the King in a body, and not through the medium of a paltry secretary of state. He thought the voice of the people was the voice of God and that if the King did not attend to the voice of the people, God would speak to him in thunder.' But the chairman 'thought his Majesty was very wisely screened from receiving a remonstrance in that way, which would carry with it an appearance of force'.[45]

The problem of kings breaking their contract was widely debated in the radical clubs and presses in the autumn of 1795. The bookseller and pamphleteer Richard Lee produced a series of instructive polemics on the subject, and so earned himself a prosecution for seditious libel. Some, like the *Happy Reign of George the Last*, were little more than crude republican doggerel:

> Are we born for them alone?
> If by right divine they rule,
> Yonder *idiot* on a throne
> Reigns by right divine a *Fool*!

Others were more considered. The pamphlet causing the greatest affront to the Crown's law officers was called simply *King Killing*. Here Lee set out a robust defence not only of collective resistance to tyranny but of lone assassins like Margaret Nicholson:

> The infliction of terrible justice by the people when the people have it in their power is alone capable of checking the cancer of Tyranny. If an individual believes that an act of seasonable violence on his part will operate as a salutary example to his countrymen and awaken them to the Energy and dignity of their characters by breaking the wand whose magic power lulled them into sloth and inaction, does he not, in committing that Act of Violence, perform his duty as a member of the Community whose interests

> are closely connected with his own? ... Let us destroy this huge Colossus under which the tall aspiring head of liberty cannot pass.[46]

The awful consequences of these sentiments became apparent in an incident that, in many ways, represented the culmination of radical rhetoric throughout the autumn of 1795. On 29 October, George III was attacked in his state coach as he made his way through London to open the new session of Parliament.

'My lord, I have been shot at!' The St James's Park riot, 1795

In the Museum of London there is a small piece of worn and much-fingered eighteenth-century glass. It has an accession number, 31.117, and a provenance dating back to 1931 but no further. Picked up off the ground in St James's Park in 1795 by a Mr Gray, it once formed part of a window in George III's coach and it has survived the centuries, passed from unknown hand to unknown hand, like a piece of holy reliquary. Fragments of glass like this one were once 'sacreligiously' offered for sale on the streets of London for anything up to a shilling apiece, 'depending on the size', while thicker and larger shards from the back window could fetch half-a-crown.[47] The mobbing and near-destruction of the King's elegant coach as it trundled through Whitehall and St James's Park that autumn were unprecedented: an extraordinary cultural and constitutional event. Yet it has rarely received from historians the attention it deserves, despite being 'one of the most famous incidents of the decade'.[48] More often than not, the affair is reduced to a functional footnote in which it is assumed to have been an unfortunate incident of relatively minor importance, over-amplified by Pitt as justification for his repressive measures against the radical clubs; or else it is treated as an uncontrolled expression of popular frustration over the economic privations of war and famine. Few historians have taken seriously contemporary claims that the King was shot at, and most recently the incident has simply become lost in the headlong rush to endorse George III's 'apotheosis'.

The crowd that gathered on 29 October to witness the royal progress to Parliament was considered by one newspaper the 'greatest concourse of people ever remembered on a similar occasion'. The whole park and the Mall, from the stable yard to the Horse Guards and the length of Parliament Street, were 'completely choked up with spectators'. The *Morning Chronicle* estimated 200,000 people there. Many waited quietly enough but this was not interpreted as a good sign given that the pageantry of the State Opening was intended as an opportunity for boisterous and patriotic cheering. As one observer, 'struck by the profound silence of the people', had noted when the King last opened Parliament in January, '*Le silence du peuple est la lecon des Rois*'. There were certainly some friendly faces, however. It was alleged in the opposition press that every civil servant in Whitehall had been ordered to 'attend in the Park and huzza'; that Lord Walsingham expressly ordered all the clerks in the Post Office to do so; and that a 'number of labourers were planted in the garden behind St James' Palace' who ran along the top of the wall, waving their hats and cheering.[49] Whether these stories are true or not, the scale of the problem had clearly not taken the authorities entirely by surprise. Not only had the platform meetings of the LCS over the previous few days concentrated public debate on the duties and responsibilities of the monarchy, but there had also been much speculation in the press about the contents of the King's speech on the subject of the war, in particular that it would 'tend to a safe and honourable peace'. That it would *not* was well known by the morning of the 29 October because all the papers carried intelligence of its main points. The day was also marked by an additional rise in bread prices which had 'alarmed' the Royal Family; a quartern loaf on a pole and covered in black crepe was paraded by the crowd in Parliament Street.[50]

In Whitehall, John King had spent three days assembling a sizeable force of soldiers, including fencibles, volunteers, two regiments of Dragoons and an artillery company. Magistrates at Worship Street were told to be in attendance all day, and extra constables were drafted from their regular patch in Holborn. In the morning, the King was escorted by 500 Dragoons all the way from Windsor to St James's, the largest military escort the King had ever had, thought Henry Hunt. Eyewitnesses saw the King's coach surrounded by two protective rings as it pulled away from Buckingham House at 2.20 p.m., one of constables (who were 'not to leave the procession as on former occasions at the Horse Guards, but to attend it to the Palace') and the other of soldiers – an unusual precaution.[51]

Most contemporary accounts confirm that although few people in the crowd appeared friendly, only 'a few hundred' were actively hissing and booing at the outset, and of these only a 'handful' got near enough to the coach to offer personal insults. 'Peace!', 'Bread!' and 'No War!' were the gist of the cries, and there were even shouts of 'No King!' One account insisted that the worst offenders were the group of about forty men who ran beside the King's coach all the way to Parliament, seeming to 'act in perfect concert and on a settled plan'. Two part-time constables, John Walford and John Stockdale, and Lord Onslow, who had every opportunity to observe the crowd from his place in the carriage, offered confirming testimony. The troublesome 'party' were all of the 'worst and lowest sort' and they 'kept by the side of the carriage ... the whole of the way'. The pressure of the crowd created two serious incidents while the King was still in the park. Lieutenant Fleming, an off-duty soldier, was knocked to the ground by 'several ruffians' in the crush around the coach, trampled on and relieved of his sword, but he escaped with a broken rib. Then, between St James's Palace and Carlton House, there was a sudden panic when the press of bodies temporarily separated the coach from its guards. The constables tried to secure the park gates at the Horse Guards as soon as the King had passed through them, to contain the crowd following, but people 'flew to the different avenues' and over-ran them. There was no serious violence offered until the King drew level with the Ordnance Office, however.[52]

It was here, at the end of Great George Street, that the thick glass of the coach window was suddenly punctured by a – still unidentified – projectile, creating a smooth round hole the circumference of a finger. Most witnesses thought it was either a marble or a bullet, and that it came from an upstairs bow-window of a house in Margaret Street with 'great velocity'. 'Good God!' exclaimed Walford, 'the glass is broke; that must surely be a ball.' He was certain the object had been fired, for 'nothing could throw it with that velocity except an instrument'. James Parker, one of the King's footmen, felt the missile as it 'whisked' past his face and was sure it had come from an air-gun of some kind, 'for he heard no report'.[53] There were few doubts among the occupants of the coach itself. The King immediately leaned forward to trace the outline of the hole with his finger, and said to Westmoreland, 'That's a shot!!'. According to Jesse's rather imaginative account, he rebuked one of his companions for looking afraid, and Onslow believed the King must be 'insensible' to fear. George further distinguished himself by shouting a 'humane' instruction to restrain one of the Life Guards who was trying to 'cut down' an innocent man. The coach finally gained the safety of the entrance to the Lords, and as the King climbed out he was met by an anxious looking Lord Chancellor. 'My lord', he informed him, 'I have been shot at!'[54]

Although the majority of radical and opposition commentators, including the influential Francis Place, refuted the bullet theory as yet another ministerial plot to discredit the reform movement and deflect criticism of the war,[55] most ministerial papers followed the administration's insistence that an attempt had been made to assassinate the King with a live round from some kind of gun. This had become 'generally believed', according to the *St. James's Chronicle* a week later, although the fact remained that no one had heard a shot fired. A reporter for the *Oracle* had studied some of the glass fragments, 'and the amazing thickness, half an inch, convinces us that no force that was not communicated by an engine could have driven a bullet and perforated the glass in such a circular figure'.[56] The pamphleteer John Gifford had also inspected the glass. He thought it 'pretty evident' that only a bullet could have caused 'such a perfect hole'. The perforated pane was carefully removed from the coach door when the King arrived at the Lords and taken away to the

Home Office for examination. A secret committee of peers was immediately convened to investigate the evidence.[57]

The house in Margaret Street, together with several of the adjoining properties, was thoroughly searched. The fact that its window had been left open while the house was apparently empty and untenanted was thought extremely suspicious, but nothing incriminating was found there. Some thought the shot had come from a group of 'ill-looking fellows; apparently intent on mischief', who had drawn up a dray to stand on immediately beneath the open window, but none of them could be identified and no arrests were made.[58] The police and the guards were clearly more concerned with the safe delivery of their royal charge than with making arrests. Even after the King had gone into the building, and although they were able to identify several people in the crowd who had run beside the coach the whole way, constables 'on consideration, declined' to take any prisoners.[59] It might have been a dangerous enterprise, given the imbalance of numbers.

If the King's outward journey to meet his parliament had been troublesome enough, the return journey was very much worse. George dutoriously ignored Onslow's advice to travel home in a different coach and said he had every faith in God's protection. In truth, he said, he was 'more chagrined at the silent indifference manifested by the general mass of the people than at the hooting and attacks of the desperate ruffians'.[60] To the firing of signal guns, the damaged coach swung away from the Lords at 3.00 p.m., followed by the hooting crowd. A house in Parliament Street from which a handkerchief of royalist white was seen waving was spontaneously pelted with mud.[61] As the coach turned towards the park at the Horse Guards, an attempt was made to reach it by a group of about thirty men. They were 'grinning at the King, groaning and calling out', and the Life Guards and constables had to struggle to keep them back.[62]

Then, as the coach drew level with Spring Gardens Terrace, a stone splintered the woodwork of the window frame. Another six or seven stones followed before the procession could clear Carlton House, then a great barrage of them. Suddenly, missiles were 'repeatedly flying from the mob'. Some hit the constables and yeomen; others found their target and another sideglass was shattered.[63] As the crowd 'pressed closely around the coach', the King, who was now 'in considerable agitation', began waving his hands at the Life Guards to keep the people back. At a snail's pace the battered coach at last reached the gateway to St James's Palace. Accounts differ as to the temper of the King at this point. The author of *Truth and Treason* found him 'sitting backwards in his carriage, pale and aghast, his countenance betraying all the symptoms of horror and dismay'. But Onslow, sitting opposite the monarch, could remember only the King's habitual calmness. 'The King took one of the stones out of the cuff of his coat, where it had lodged' he recalled, 'and gave it to me, saying – "I make you a present of this, as a mark of the civilities we have met with on our journey today".'[64]

As the coach turned into the gate, a large rock smashed against the remaining door window, showering the King's face with splinters of glass. Now that the disturbance had become so serious, some of the constables tried to seize ringleaders. Strenuous efforts were made to find the man who had thrown the last stone. George Gregory and Edward Collins were both arrested in this connection, but two witnesses went to Bow Street on 4 November and told magistrates they had seen the real culprit walk away unmolested. He had allegedly been with several others who shouted 'prepare!' as the King drew closer. 'Damme, but you shivered it!' commented a coachman admiringly as the stone-thrower hurried off. John Walford, with help of a Horse Guard, grabbed Kidd Wake by Carlton Gardens and pulled him through the cordon, marching him along between the guards and the coach to prevent any attempt at rescue. 'He kept repeating the whole way, he thought there could be no harm in acquainting his majesty with their grievances', said Walford.[65] There was also a casualty on the authorities' side. As the coach came to a halt beside the stable yard's gate and the King prepared to get out, the crowd pressed around it on all sides, causing a horse to rear and knock over an elderly groom named Dorrington, who fell under the wheels and broke his thighs.[66] No violence was offered to the King when he left the coach, and he walked with as much dignity as he could muster to the palace door. But the crowd had not yet finished with his splendid coach and it suffered 'great injury' as the footmen turned it round and drove it along Pall Mall to the Mews. With the King now gone from the coach, the crowd lost all sense of restraint. Outside the Mews gate, the coach, coachman and horses were liberally pelted with mud, stones and oyster shells until 'scarcely a piece of glass about it remained unbroken'. If a party of guards had not come racing up to clear the way, the vehicle would almost certainly have been demolished. John Dinham, seen pocketing pieces of broken glass, was followed away from the scene by constable Christopher Jones and arrested when he began proudly showing them to passers-by and telling them 'I did for it'. Robert Bryant was also followed and arrested at *The Rose* inn.[67]

Stopping only to 'change his wig' at the palace, and anxious to rejoin his family in Buckingham House, the King left again by the back stairs, at 4.00 p.m., with two footmen in a more anonymous coach. It was not anonymous enough, however, because as soon as he set off he was once again surrounded by a 'groaning' crowd and showered with stones, one narrowly missing his head. Under the assumption, perhaps, that the King was going to stay at St James's, the Life Guards had been dismissed and were now making their way in the opposite direction down the Mall to Whitehall. There was therefore no one to prevent a small group of about sixteen men from getting close enough to the carriage to pull at the wheels and hold it still. As the cries of 'Bread, bread! Peace, peace!' grew louder, George III could only look on helplessly as one man got his fingers on the door handle. This was probably the LCS member, John Ridley. The King was rescued this time by a civil servant named Bedingfield who pushed his way to the front and waved his pistol about to keep people back while someone else ran to fetch the guards.[68] Only when he had been inside Buckingham House for half-an-hour did the crowds outside begin to disperse.

Aftermath

> 'Only one stone was thrown at the King, but the Minister has thrown two stones at the People'.[69] John Gale Jones, 17 November 1795

There was further unrest on the evening of 30 October when the Royal Family went to Covent Garden to see *The Rivals*. Jumpy ministers did their best to fill every seat in the theatre with civil servants and police officers, but the streets outside were densely packed. A force of 200 Cavalry, 100 Foot Guards and 500 constables was deployed to accompany the procession and seal off the route so that nobody could come 'within a street's length of the coach'. Unusual routes were taken on both the outward and homeward journeys to confuse demonstrators, but even these precautions were not enough to prevent a stone finding its mark on the return trip. Several people were trampled and cut as the cavalry worked the crowd, estimated at 10,000 strong in the streets around the theatre, 'sparing neither age nor sex'. Several people were taken up for hissing the King. Covent Garden, complained an opposition paper, 'exhibited the appearance of a camp rather than a public space for the amusement of a free people'. There were signs of distinct unease among the soldiery. Outside the theatre, a cavalryman fired his gun by accident and felled his comrade's horse; and inside a fight broke out between two captains when one accused the other of disloyalty. There were certainly some disloyal people in the audience, because a near-riot ensued when the actor playing Captain Absolute obsequiously insisted on repeating the line 'You know, sir, I serve His Majesty', instead of the once demanded by the script. When catcalls were heard from the gallery, Patrick Macmanus suddenly appeared on stage and stood under the King's box as if guarding it. The hostile uproar this created did not cease until he left again.[70]

A number of people were arrested over the next few days for using 'treasonable' expressions. William Addington sent a man to Tothill Fields for wishing the King's death, and Portland received information about a hairdresser who wanted to kill the King and all of his family with a sword, then wash his hands in the blood of the judges.[71] George Elliot, a Birmingham master builder, was prosecuted for wishing the crowd had 'knocked his damned head off, and Pitt's too ... I wish I had been present at the time. I would have done everything in my power to have assisted. I hope in a little time I shall have it in my power to carry a musket myself ...' When a woman objected to his remarks, Elliot countered: 'Do you imagine that we receive any benefit from having a King, or that it would make any difference if he was dead?' In Newark, as Harriot Moss was reading about the riot in a newspaper and 'expressing her sorrow', William Unwin's comment was: 'It's to be hoped they'll take care of him soon, damn him. I should like to undo the button and let the chopper down to take the King's head off, damn him.'[72]

The prisoners taken on 29 October were examined over the next two days at Bow Street by magistrates whose line of questioning seemed designed to establish a case of high treason. Kidd Wake, a printer, continued to insist that he had been hissing and groaning at the King only to signify his 'dissatisfaction with the war' and seemed incredulous at his arrest. Treason would be difficult to prove, however, because no one could identify him as a stone-thrower or as a man who had shouted 'Down with George'. Dinham, a baker, and the shoemaker Bryant were charged with making a riot and throwing missiles at the empty coach. All were refused bail. Gregory, a young jeweller with impeccable personal references from his employer, denied everything and was later discharged.[73] By the end of the week, the ministry was ready to abandon its quest for a treason trial based on the premiss that George had been shot at. No new suspects had been arrested despite the offer of a £1,000 reward. Helpfully, then, on 3 November, six unidentified 'respectable housekeepers' trooped into Portland's office to swear that it had been a stone, not a bullet, that broke the King's window. They saw the man who threw it, described him and confirmed that he was not in custody. Their testimony was widely circulated to the press and the *Oracle* asserted that it was 'now ascertained beyond question' that the King had not been shot at after all.[74]

All hope of securing a conviction for treason now depended on the identification of Wake, Dinham, Bryant or Collins for throwing stones at the King.[75] The most promising suspect was Collins. When the prisoner was re-examined on 13 November, the arresting officer was prepared to swear on oath that Collins was the man who threw the final large stone at the King as the coach turned into the stable yard. The magistrate accordingly committed Collins for high treason and a December trial date at the Old Bailey was fixed. But the Crown traversed and finally abandoned the case on counsel's advice some time in the New Year.[76] Kidd Wake's trial before Lord Kenyon in the Court of Kings Bench in February 1796 for the high misdemeanour of riot, tumult and sedition was more successful. Erskine took the defence, but offered very little. His request to call some character witnesses in mitigation was turned down by Kenyon, who told him there was no defence to be had for such a heinous crime and directed the jury to convict. Wake received a gruelling five years' hard labour in a penitentiary cell at Gloucester Gaol and a spell in the pillory.[77]

There seems no very good reason for us to discount the possibility that George III was shot at on 29 October. From the perfectly formed round hole created in his coach window, it seems reasonable to conclude that he was either shot at with an air-gun or attacked with a slingshot. Either could have killed him. However flawed the Government's prosecution of the so-called Pop Gun Plot in 1794, the publicity given to the alleged conspiracy may at least have had the effect of giving someone the *idea* of shooting the King with a wind-gun in 1795. Burke believed that this is what happened,[78] and weapons of the sort were not unknown. A Fleet Street gunsmith who gave evidence at the Pop Gun Plot trial had explained, 'If it is discharged where the air passes briskly by, you cannot hear it yourself; but if it is in a confined room, where the external air does not pass freely, it makes a noise like that (clapping his hands).' The greater the space, the lesser the sound. Such a gun would be particularly accurate and easy to aim, even at a moving target, he said, because there would be no recoil. Chief Justice Eyre had interrupted him before he went into any further detail for fear, he said, of broadcasting dangerous information to the disaffected.[79] The 29 October incident was not the first time a window of the royal coach had been broken. On his last journey to open Parliament, on 21 January, a side-glass was mysteriously shattered. 'The circumstance gave rise to a report of some madman having thrown a stone at the window', reported the *Times* two days later, but the palace moved quickly to deny any such malicious motive. According to the official explanation, the glass was broken by accident when one of the yeomen guarding the procession lost control of his halberd and banged it against the coach.[80]

Despite having to make his way through a disaffected crowd 'of the very lowest sort' when he reprised his journey to Parliament on 12 December to give his assent to the Gagging Bills, most of their 'hissing and halooing' was expended upon Pitt and Addington.[81] George's apotheosis was not yet reflected in the behaviour of all Londoners, however. On 1 February, the Royal Family made its first theatre excursion of the new season, and although members received an encouragingly loyal reception from the Drury Lane audience the coach was twice attacked on the journey home. First, a footman riding on the back of the coach was struck by a brick thrown from a small crowd at the end of Southampton Street. Then, in Pall Mall, a large stone shattered the side window, hitting Queen Charlotte in the face and landing in the lap of the lady-in-waiting, Lady Harrington. The stone, which appeared to have been sharpened to cause injury, was examined by the Privy Council the following morning, and a reward of £1,000 offered for information about the culprits. It was not claimed, and no one was apprehended.[82]

Government's response to the October outrage was swift and punitive. A direct challenge was issued to the LCS's next outdoor meeting by royal proclamation on 4 November, drawing direct associations between previous meetings and the attack on the King and instructing magistrates to prevent any recurrence. On 6 November, the first Gagging Bill was introduced to the Lords. The Bill For the Safety and Protection of His Majesty's Person made it treason to 'intend any bodily harm tending to the death, wounding, imprisonment or restraint' of the King or his heirs, or to 'deprive or depose him of the style, honour or kingly name of the crown', either by direct action or, crucially, in words. Many offences previously only actionable as seditious speech or libel were therefore now technically punishable by death as high treason. The Seditious Meetings' Bill followed – a more explicit interference with the radical platform, restricting the numbers at public reform meetings to forty-nine without proper sanction.

In line with the Government's determination to use the St James's Park riot as justification for repression, ministerial papers laid the blame also on the platform rhetoric of the LCS and the liberality of local officials for accommodating them. It was all very well for Thelwall to claim he had urged the crowd to peaceful conduct on 26 October, it was noted, but what were the public to make of Jones's hope that the next time he saw so many people assembled it would be to 'witness the punishment of a guilty minister'? The *True Briton* looked forward to the installation of a new lord mayor on 9 November and trusted he would take a harder line in discouraging radical handbills and meetings. Fearing further disorder at the mayoral procession, John King enrolled extra constables to police it and ordered a close monitoring of the LCS's forthcoming outdoor meeting on 12 November.[83] Burke lamented the encouragement that had been given to the LCS by the failure of the 1794 treason trials: in suggesting to extremists that the courts would not punish treason, the acquittals were directly responsible for the attack on the King. By the time of the second attack in 1796 public attitudes to 'daily attempts on the sacred person' had so hardened that

> if ever God for our punishment should suffer some of them to take effect, it would pass for an event as much in the ordinary course of things as if he were carried off by a fever or a palsy. Already they begin to make less and less impression on the public mind. If these things are so in the time

> of our present Sovereign, let me assure you that in the time of his successor ... all this gathering of Evil will burst out into a distemper, which no human art will be of force to prevent being mortal.[84]

The *St. James's Chronicle* agreed with Burke. The LCS was 'a mischievous club where treason is hatched and thoughts of royal massacre rendered familiar'. Perhaps it was time to combat the 'savage licentiousness of an UNFEELING MOB' with 'the noble and generous exertions of AN ARMY; whose first duty it is to obey'.[85] Some private individuals offered the Government similar advice. Richard Chapman wrote to Pitt urging the complete reorganisation of the civil power to protect the monarch. The demise of royalty in France had begun with the surrender of the streets to the mob, the consequent reluctance of Louis XVI to pass through the streets of Paris and his fatal withdrawal to Versailles. On future royal outings in London, then,

> The streets must be so completely lined as to suffer his Majesty to go from the Palace to the theatre or the Senate at a rate that will gratify the curiosity of those subjects who always see him with pleasure, instead of that disgraceful speed which, though now prudent and necessary, impressed the mind with the idea of an army flying before a victorious enemy.

Nobody should be permitted to follow the coach; and any hissing and groaning should be met with immediate arrest.[86]

Such draconianism was not seriously considered; indeed ministers began a searching national inquiry into the extent of the distress caused by harvest failure[87] at the same time as they drafted the two Gagging Bills to silence the radical platform. Government also used the assault on the King to distract attention from Foxite criticisms of the war effort. This was no time, it was argued, to relax hostilities with a regicide republic. French agents were even suspected of being behind the London outrage; the Lords demanding to know whether any French accents had been overheard in the crowd. Concern for the safety of the King was an issue which, it was predicted, would reunite a politically divided nation, exemplified by loyal addresses from the provinces which would 'make manifest, however opinions may differ respecting the policy of continuing the war, that there is but one sentiment of love and affection for his Majesty among the great mass of the people'.[88]

Radical responses to accusations of complicity in the outrage against the King were measured. Notwithstanding attachments to resistance theories, few serious reformers were prepared to publicly countenance the mobbing of the monarch, and most were well aware that it would be used by Pitt as a pretext for their repression. Predictably, Thelwall denied any connection between his own oratory or the principles of the LCS and the attack on the King, and insisted that none of those arrested were members of the society. Responsibility for the outrage lay squarely with those 'oppressors who wish to destroy all knowledge but their own' and whose measures had provoked an underclass who, 'though they can feel the oppression, can neither write not read – poor, harassed and degraded beings who have neither opportunities nor inclination for inquiry ... The tumult arose, not in consequence of reason or enquiry, but from the misery in which the people are plunged.' The LCS believed assaults and assassinations were counter-productive, he said, being more likely to prevent reform than promote it.[89] An estimated 100,000 people attended the LCS outdoor meeting on 12 November to oppose the Two Bills. An address to the King, lamenting his inattention to their previous communications, but putting the blame on ministers, urged him to reject the Bills 'to prevent the possibility of intestine commotion'. A petition to the Commons ended by reminding MPs that the LCS knew how to 'cherish and to practice' the right of resistance as a 'last extremity'.[90]

But there was a distinct air of unease at the Wych Street debating club on 16 November, when members met to discuss the question 'Can the late outrage on His Majesty be a pretext for the introduction of a Convention Bill?' For thirty minutes, nobody would speak at all. Then Jones arrived to dispel the gloom. He wished no harm to the King, he assured them, indeed he would rather 'receive the stone on his own breast' than see him harmed by it. But the punishment of those responsible for throwing stones at the King was provided for by existing legislation, he said. And it was not as though there was anything novel about his being shouted at en route to Parliament. His subjects had been pleading for bread and an end to the war for two years. 'Is it to be wondered at that after intolerable burthens have been heaped upon the people, a few irritated and perhaps starving individuals should, in a much stronger manner, express their detestation of those measures which have occasioned their distress?' Furthermore, repressive laws would be more likely to destroy the monarchy than preserve it, 'for if we look to those countries where the people are denied the liberty of expressing their resentment with their tongues, we shall find that they resort to the practice of assassination.' The new Treason Bill was to be enacted for the lifetime of George III. 'May not this circumstance make an English Brutus consider the life of the monarch as a bar to the happiness of the people, may it not make him think it his duty to sacrifice the individual to restore the liberties of the nation?' If the King refused to give the Bill his assent, the people would forgive him all of his past errors; but if he allowed it to become law, then he, Jones, would take up physical force, for this was legislation that unequivocally justified resistance. 'At present', he advised, 'I have neither musket, sword or pistol, but should the Convention Bill pass into a law, I declare I will immediately procure arms ... And the moment the tongue shall be compelled to be silent, I hope the arm will be in action.'[91]

At Panton Street, one young debater announced that if the King gave his assent to the Bills, he would be breaking his coronation oath, in which case 'he would no longer be a King, but he would be a traitor to his country and if he shall dare attempt to trample upon the liberties of the people, I hope they will trample upon his head'. This was all perfectly constitutional, he added. Another contributor denied they had any right to resist the King through violence, but confirmed their right through Magna Carta to resist him by 'distraining his revenues'. Jones disagreed. 'There were cases in which the King's person was not inviolable', he assured them, and if the King signed the Bills, he might as well 'sign his own death warrant'. At a final platform meeting of the LCS on 7 December, it was announced that 15,000 people had signed a petition to the King, begging him to refuse his assent. Eleven days later, he gave it and the Acts became law. Looking back in old age on these months of crisis, John Binns believed the Government's tyranny had turned many LCS members in favour of the 'overthrow of the monarchy and the establishment of a republic'. Yet the 'general revolution' he had sensed was not forthcoming.[92]

Notes

1 PRO, TS 11/1026: Papers for the prosecution of John Frith, J. Amherst to Sir George Younge, 2 July 1786.

2 PRO, HO 42/16: Lt Col. Lindsay to Lord Dover, 22 January 1790; Memorial of John Frith to the King, 11 March 1790; John Frith to Evan Nepean, 29 June 1790.

3 PRO, HO 42/13: 'A general statement of accounts of defraud and robbery by his majesty's officers ... by John Frith', 25 March 1788.

4 PRO, TS 11/1026: Papers for the prosecution of John Frith; 'Manifesto and declaration to the people of Great Britain and the world at large', April 1788. The Treasury Solicitor's papers include a large number of densely packed folio sheets similar to this one, and all in Frith's hand. He wrote prolifically about his case.

5 PRO, PC 1/18/A21, Examination of John Frith before the Privy Council, 22 January 1790. A fuller account of Frith's examination may be found in the Council's Minute book, PC 2/134.

6 PRO, PC1/18/A21: Examination of John Frith.

7 T. B. and T. J. Howell, *A Complete Collection of State Trials*, vol. 22 (London, 1817), cols 312–13; PRO, HO 42/16: Rev. Humphreys to Sir Sampson Wright, 25 January 1790; TS 11/1026: J. Foley to the Secretary of State, 5 February 1790.

8 PRO, PC 1/18/A21: Examination of John Frith.

9 *The Times*, 26 and 28 January 1790.

10 For the trial, see Howell, *State Trials*, cols 307–18.

11 PRO, PC 1/18/A21: Dr Francis Milman to Mr Fawkener, 19 June 1790 and 5 November 1790. A copy of this order survives in James Hadfield's case papers (TS 11/223: Henry Dundas to the Attorney General, 5 December 1791).

12 *The Times*, 21 April 1790.
13 *World*, 28 and 30 January, 1790.
14 PRO, HO 42/18: Sir Sampson Wright to Evan Nepean, 14 January 1791.
15 *The Times*, 19 and 20 August 1791.
16 *The Times*, 19 August 1791.
17 From the London Corresponding Society's 'Remonstrance to the King', October 26 1795, quoted in M. Thale (ed.), *Selections from the Papers of the London Corresponding Society, 1792–1799* (Cambridge, 1983), p. 316.
18 *The Times*, 1 February 1796; Wharam, *Treason Trials*, pp. 85–7 and 234-6.
19 PRO, HO 42/37: Spy's report of a radical debate at Wych Street, London, 16 November 1795.
20 Thale *Selections*, pp. 53, 61, 63.
21 An unidentified loyalist quoted in N. U. Murray, 'The influence of the French Revolution on the Church of England and its rivals', D. Phil. thesis, Oxford, 1975, p. 227. At time of writing, publication of Nick Rogers's detailed study of Paine burnings is imminent: N. Rogers, 'Burning Tom Paine: loyalism and counter-revolution in Britain, 1792–3', unpublished conference paper delievered to the Pacific Coast Conference on British Studies, University of California, Santa Cruz, 27 March 1999.
22 C. Emsley, 'An aspect of Pitt's terror: prosecutions for sedition during the 1790s', *Social History*, 6:2 (1981), 173–4; 'Repression, terror and the rule of law during the decade of the French Revolution', *English Historical Review*, 100 (1985), 801–25. Professor Emsley has recently revised his view in *Crime and Society* (p. 50 n). See also S. Poole, 'Pitt's terror reconsidered: Jacobinism and the law in two south-western counties, 1791–1803', *Southern History*, 17 (1995), 65–88.
23 Quoted in M. Morris, 'The monarchy as an issue in English political argument during the French revolutionary era', unpublished Ph.D. thesis, University of London, 1988, pp. 116–17, 134.
24 London Metropolitan Archive, MA/G/GEN 348: Minutes of Cold Bath Fields Prison Committee, Middlesex, 9 February 1799.
25 PRO, HO 42/37: Report of a lecture by John Thelwall, 25 October 1795; John Gale Jones, *Sketch of a Political Tour Through Rochester, Chatham, Maidstone, Gravesend etc. ...*, ed. Bruce Aubry, ([1796] Rochester, 1997), p. 8.
26 Thale, *Selections*, pp. 156–7.
27 *Ibid.*, p. 146.
28 Claeys, *Thelwall*, pp. 9, 62.
29 Thale, *Selections*, p. 232;. Barrell, 'Imaginary treason', p. 126.
30 Claeys, *Thelwall*, p. 11.
31 Barrell, 'Imaginary Treason', p. 143.
32 *Politics for the People*, vol. 2, (1794): Letter from 'Forewarned, Forearmed', p. 18.
33 PRO, HO 42/37: Spy's report of Westminster Forum debate, 27 October 1795.
34 Lewis and Wallace, *Walpole's Correspondence with Mary and Agnes Berry*, pp. 115, 119, 121, 123: letters to Mary Berry, 29 September and 1 October 1794: letter from Mary Berry, 1 October 1794.
35 *London Chronicle*, 27–30 October 1794; Wharam, *Treason*, pp. 100–14; Thale, *Selections*, pp. 220–2.
36 John Thelwall, 'The natural and constitutional right of Britons to annual parlia-

ments, universal suffrage, and the freedom of popular association' (1795), in Claeys, *Thelwall*, p. 8.

37 P. T. Lemaitre, *High Treason!! Narrative of the Arrest, Examination before the Privy Council, and Imprisonment of Paul Thomas Lemaitre* (London, 1795), pp. 57–8; and his 'Account of the origins and progress of the Pop Gun Plot', 1833, in Place's narrative history of the LCS: BL Add. MS 27808.

38 John Smith, *Assassination of the King! The Conspirators Exposed or, an Account of the Apprehension, Treatment in Prison and Repeated Examination before the Privy Council of John Smith and George Higgins on a Charge of High Treason* (London, 1795).

39 Quoted by Morris, 'The monarchy as an issue', p. 138.

40 Thale, *Selections*, pp. 165-7.

41 *Politics for the People*, vol. 2, pp. 5 and 9 (1794).

42 *Politics for the People*, vol. 2, p. 26 (1795).

43 (R. Lee) *Account of the Proceedings of a Meeting of the London Corresponding Society, held in a Field near Copenhagen House, Monday October 26, 1795* (London, 1795).

44 PRO, HO 42/37: Robert Fellowes to Duke of Portland, 19 October 1795.

45 PRO, HO 42/37: Spy's report of Westminster Forum debate, 27 October 1795.

46 R. Lee, *King Killing* (London, 1795) and *The Happy Reign of George the Last: An Address to the Little Tradesmen and the Labouring Poor of England* (London, 1795). See also Lee's *A Summary of the Duties of Citizenship; Written Expressly for the Members of the London Corresponding Society; Including Observations on the Contemptuous Neglect of the Secretary of State with regard to their Late Address to the King!* (London, 1795); and *The Rights of Kings* (London, 1795). Copies are to be found among the indictment papers in PRO, TS 11/837/2832, Case against Richard Lee for seditious libel, October 1795.

47 *Morning Chronicle*, 30 October 1795; *Truth & Treason! or A Narrative of the Royal Procession to the House of Peers, October 29th, 1795. To which is Added, an Account of the Martial Procession to Covent Garden Theatre, on the Evening of the 30th* (London, 1795), p. 5. I am grateful to Edwina Ehrman at the Museum of London for information about the provenance of the shard.

48 J. Stevenson, *Popular Disturbances in England, 1700–1870* (London, 1979), p. 173. See also E. P. Thompson, *Making of the English Working Class*, pp. 158–9 and p. 192 in which the trial of Kidd Wake as a ringleader is somewhat disingenuously presented as evidence of the harsh sentencing of defendants for mere seditious words; Morris, *British Monarchy*, pp. 127–9; J. Ehrman, *The Younger Pitt*, vol. 2: *The Reluctant Transition* (London, 1983), p. 455; R. Wells, *Wretched Faces: Famine in Wartime England, 1793–1801* (Gloucester, 1988), pp. 140–1. Wells is curiously uninterested in the incident in his earlier study *Insurrection;* and Hone barely gives it a mention (see *Cause of Truth*, p. 18).

49 *Oracle*, 30 October 1795; *Morning Chronicle*, 30 October 1795; *Morning Post*, 2 November 1795.

50 *St. James's Chronicle*, 24–7 October 1795; *Oracle*, 29 October 1795; Royal Archive, Windsor Castle, RA Add. MS 15/8168: Princess Elizabeth to Lady Charlotte, 6 November 1795; *Morning Post*, 2 November 1795; *Morning Chronicle*, 3 January 1795.

51 PRO, HO 65/1: J. King to Lord Onslow 26 October 1795; J. King to Lord Leslie,

Col. Brownrigg and Lt Col. Herries, 27 October 1795; J. King to Hatton Garden magistrates, 28 October 1795; Hunt, *Memoirs*, vol. 1, p. 234; *Morning Chronicle*, 30, 31 October 1795.

52 *True Briton*, 4 November 1795, *St. James's Chronicle*, 31 October–3 November, 3–5 November 1795, *Minutes of the Evidence of Witnesses examined by the House of Lords* (London, 1795): evidence of John Walford and John Stockdale; Jesse, *George III*, vol. 3, pp. 214–15; *Morning Post*, 30 October 1795; M. Thale (ed.), *The Autobiography of Francis Place* (Cambridge, 1972), p. 146; John Gifford, *An Account of the Attack Made Upon the King* (London, 1809); *Truth and Treason*, p. 2.

53 *Oracle*, 30 October 1795; *Morning Post*, 30 October 1795; *St. James's Chronicle*, 29–31 October 1795; *Minutes of the Evidence*: evidence of Walford, Parker and Sayer.

54 *Morning Post*, 30 October 1795; *Morning Chronicle*, 2 November 1795; *St. James's Chronicle*, 31 October–3 November 1795; Jesse, *George III*, vol. 3, p. 214.

55 See for example, Thale, *Francis Place*, p. 146; and *Morning Chronicle*, 30 October 1795, in which the missile is pointedly referred to as a 'pebble'. A gun could not have been fired without someone hearing the shot, it was argued.

56 *St. James's Chronicle*, 3–5 November 1795; *Oracle*, 2 November 1795.

57 Gifford, *Account of the Attack; St. James's Chronicle*, 31 October–3 November 1795.

58 *St. James's Chronicle*, 31 Oct–3 Nov 1795; *Oracle*, 4 November 1795.

59 *Morning Chronicle*, 31 October 1795.

60 *St. James's Chronicle*, 3–5 November 1795.

61 *Morning Chronicle*, 30 October 1795.

62 *Ibid.*, 31 October 1795.

63 *Morning Post*, 30 October 1795; *Morning Chronicle*, 31 October 1795; *Oracle*, 30 October 1795.

64 *Truth and Treason*, p. 4; Jesse, *George III*, vol. 3, p. 215.

65 *Oracle*, 30 October, 5 November 1795; *Morning Chronicle*, 31 October 1795; *Minutes of the Evidence*: evidence of Walford.

66 *Morning Post*, 30 October 1795; *Oracle*, 30 October 1795.

67 *Morning Post*, 30 October 1795; *Oracle*, 30 October 1795; *Morning Chronicle*, 31 October 1795; *Truth and Treason*, p. 5.

68 *Oracle*, 30 October 1795; *Morning Chronicle*, 30 October 1795, Gifford, *Account of the Attack*; *Morning Post*, 30 October 1795; *Truth and Treason*, p. 5; *St. James's Chronicle*, 29–31 October and 31 October–November 5 1795. Francis Place accepts that the man who tried to open the carriage door was Ridley, but is characteristically adamant that he meant no harm. According to Place, his 'foot slipped, he was thrown towards the carriage and was in great danger of falling under the hind wheel; to save himself he thrust his hand against the coach door' (Thale, *Francis Place*, p. 147). Binns, on the other hand, was at a meeting that evening where a man publicly boasted that he had been prevented from pulling the King from his carriage only by the arrival of the guards (*Recollections of the Life of John Binns, Twenty-nine years in Europe and Fifty-three in the United States* (Philadelphia, 1854), pp. 55–6).

69 PRO, HO 42/37: Anonymous report of Panton Street debating club meeting, 17 November 1795.

70 *Morning Chronicle*, 31 October 1795; *Morning Post*, 2 November 1795; *Truth and Treason*, pp. 6–8; *Star*, 31 October 1795; *St. James's Chronicle*, 31 October–3 November 1795; *Oracle*, 31 October and 3 November 1795. All those arrested for hissing the King were released as drunk. The author of the play, Sheridan, was of course also a leading Foxite MP, and he appears in caricature as one of the King's assailants in Gillray's cartoon of the St James's park riot *The Republican Attack* (BMC 8681). The play the King did *not* see that evening was Otway's *Venice Preserved* at Sheridan's own Drury Lane Theatre; a production contemporaries identified with opposition. For an illuminating discussion, see G. Russell, 'Burke's Dagger: theatricality, politics and print culture in the 1790s', *British Journal for Eighteenth-Century Studies*, 20 (1997), 14–15. In fact, the King *could* not have seen it, even if he had wanted to, because Sheridan prudently closed his theatre for the evening! Sheridan's next production was Thomas Holcroft's *Man of Ten Thousand*, a play considered deeply seditious by the loyalist press, 'libelling the army and holding up the highest orders of society as objects of disgust' (*True Briton*, 3 February 1796).

71 *Morning Chronicle*, 4 November 1795.

72 PRO, TS 11/1045/4504: Case against George Elliot, information of J. Davis and J. Waldron, 4 November 1795; and Case against William Unwin, information of Harriot Moss, 10 December 1795.

73 *Morning Chronicle*, 31 October and 4 November 1795; *Oracle*, 4 November 1795.

74 *Oracle* 4 November 1795. See also identical stories on the same date in *Morning Post, The Times, Morning Chronicle* and *St. James's Chronicle*.

75 Sporadic arrests of suspected stone-throwers continued throughout the winter. Thomas Macmillan was briefly gaoled at Oswestry when someone thought he answered the description of the wanted man. Unfortunately, he had never been to London in his life, so he was released on John King's orders (PRO, HO 65/1: J. King to Rev. J. R. Lloyd, 12 December 1795; HO 42/37: F. Fitzwilliam to Duke of Portland, 17 December 1795).

76 *Morning Chronicle*, 16 November 1795; *Star*, 7 December 1795.

77 *Oracle*, 22 February 1796; PRO, TS 11/927/3272: Crown brief for the prosecution of Kidd Wake, 20 February, 1796; *Gloucester Journal*, 23 May 1796.

78 R. B. McDowell (ed.), *Correspondence of Edmund Burke*, vol. 7 (Cambridge, 1969), p. 338, letter to William Windham, 8 November 1795.

79 Quoted in Wharam, *Treason*, p. 108.

80 *The Times*, 23 January 1794.

81 PRO, PRO 30/8/112, Chatham Papers: V. Stuckey to Countess of Chatham, n.d. (December 1795).

82 *The Times*, 2, 3 and 5 February 1796, Duke of Portland to the King, 5 February 1796, in A. Aspinall (ed.), *The Later Correspondence of George III* (Cambridge, 1962–70), vol. 2, p. 457.

83 PRO, HO 65/1: John King to London magistrates, 2 November 1795; and to Lt Col. Herries, Col. Le Mesurier and Lt Col. Brownrigg, 2 November 1795; with similar letters dated 6 and 13 November 1795; *True Briton*, 4 November 1795; *Gloucester Journal*, 2 November 1795.

84 McDowell, *Burke*, vol. 8, p. 432: letter to Lord Loughborough, c. 17 March 1796.

85 *St. James's Chronicle*, 29–31 October 1795.

86 PRO, PRO 30/8/122/1, Chatham Papers: R. Chapman to Pitt, 31 October 1795.

87 See the huge quantity of letters received by the Home Office in response to the Duke of Portland's circular to the deputy-lieutenants of every county; for example PRO, HO 42/36: Reply of Walter Laurie of Kirkcudbright, 14 November 1795.
88 *Felix Farley's Bristol Journal*, 7 November 1795.
89 J. Thelwall, 'Warning voice'; Claeys, *Thelwall*, pp. 314–27.
90 Thale, *Selections*, pp. 322–4.
91 PRO, HO 42/37: Informer's report of a debate at the Temple of Reason and Humanity, Wych Street, 16 November 1795.
92 PRO, HO 42/37: Spy's report of Panton Street debates, 15 and 25 December, 1795; Thale, *Selections*, p. 330; Binns, *Recollections*, pp. 45–6.

6

Lunacy and politics at fin de siècle, *1800–3*

The extraordinary flurry of physical interference with the King during the months between the assassination attempts of James Hadfield and Urban Metcalf in 1800–1, and the consequent 'Despard conspiracy' of 1801–2, may perhaps be seen as the *fin de siècle* climax of popular–royal physicality. It is not, however, simply a question of evaluating the extent to which the language of resistance in post-1794 radicalism may be considered contextual. If one of the consequences of the Two Acts was the forcing of radicalism underground into a world of clandestine association and uncertain policy, Government too quickly adopted a form of conspiratorial logic in which traitorous subversion was assumed to lie behind every covert circumstance. Mass arrests of United movement activists in 1797–98 failed to uncover a single clear plan of insurrectionary intent. Coming as it did at a time of growing confluence between militant radicalism and popular discontent over food scarcity in which anti-monarchical and quasi-republican panegyrics were commonplace, James Hadfield's sudden and unexpected attempt on the life of the King in 1800 was a gift for ministers still on the look-out for republican conspiracies. These expectations coloured Hadfield's reception in the public sphere.

Cheating death twice, 15 May 1800

On the morning of 15 May 1800, George III went to Hyde Park to watch a field exercise of the Grenadier Guards. In the middle of a display, in which blank cartridges were to be fired, a live round went off 'by accident', missing the King by twenty feet. William Ongley, a clerk in the navy pay office, was not so lucky. The ball hit him in the thigh.[1] Later that evening, James Hadfield, an ex-soldier, fired a pistol at the King as he arrived for a performance of *She Would and She Would Not* at Drury Lane. Once again, the bullet missed him, instead chipping a plaster pillar near the roof of the royal box.

The Hyde Park incident has never been adequately explained. The soldier who fired the shot was not identified, despite an immediate inspection of every man's cartouche box. The belief that it was an accident is rooted in the regiment's wishes that it should be seen as one and in the acquiescence of the loyalist press. After an inspection less than a week later, however, eight further illicit live cartridges were found in the guards' possession. 'It seems', observed the *Morning Chronicle*, 'that some of the ball cartridges had been made up in the same coloured paper as the blank ones. Such mistakes are very scandalous'.[2] Was it a mistake? The press had picked up on rumours of disaffection amongst the guards over the recent withdrawal of their beer allowance. That this measure had caused discontent was true enough; beer was understood by the men to be a rightful part of their daily rations. The decision of the War Office to withdraw it had been taken in the name of retrenchment and in response to spiralling grain prices but, as the *Morning Chronicle* put it, 'there is no misrepresentation so artful as that which has some truth for its basis'.[3] Discontent over beer allowances is hardly proof of a rank and file conspiracy to assassinate the King, however, and Ongley's distance from the King inspires little faith in the 'assassin's' marksmanship. Nevertheless, the presence of at least a handful of guards in the Despard affair two years later leaves some room for speculation.

Suspicions about a conspiracy behind the Hyde Park incident may be a consequence largely of what happened at the theatre later that evening. The 29-year-old Hadfield, sitting close to the front of the pit and two rows back from the orchestra, had been watching the royal box and waiting for the King's party to arrive. As George moved towards his seat, Hadfield climbed onto his own chair, levelled a pistol and fired twice. The first ball hit the top of the Princesses' box before falling into the orchestra; the other lodged in the top of Lady Milner's box immediately below the Princesses' seats. The King remained standing as the rest of his family filed through the door to take their seats while, below them, Hadfield was pulled to the ground by members of the audience.

Having assured the frightened Queen that it was nothing but a firework, the King characteristically insisted on behaving as though nothing had happened. He stayed to watch the play and then went home. The audience cheered him continuously and were greatly impressed by his coolness. His assailant, meanwhile, was bundled into a room behind the stage and questioned by Sheridan, the Bow Street magistrate William Addington, the Prince of Wales and the Duke of York. Hadfield gave his name, a brief patriotic résumé of his military career, and warned that 'it was not over yet – there was a great deal more and worse to be done'. He was visibly battle-scarred. Four years earlier, Hadfield had been invalided out of the Fifteenth Light Dragoons after suffering such terrible head and body injuries at Lincelles that he had become insensible to the pain. He became convinced that 'his Maker … felt it for

Figure 2 James Hadfield fires his pistol at George III as he enters the royal box at Drury Lane Theatre in May 1800.

him'. Back in London he found work as a spoonmaker to support his family, but felt depressed and 'weary of life' now that his military career had been terminated. God had told him that when he died the world would die too. So in May 1800 he bought a brace of pistols and some powder, cast himself two lead slugs, and paced the streets for some hours with 'a deal in his mind, whether he should make away with himself or do what he did do. He knew his time was pretty near come, and he wished for it'.

He denied trying to kill the King. He was 'as good a shot as any in England', but he had deliberately fired high over his head, he said, not to harm him or anyone in the audience, but to 'raise an alarm' and perhaps cause his own death as a consequence. He was afraid that if he had simply committed suicide, he would have 'gone to the Devil'. Addington was dissatisfied with this explanation. For a case of treason to be brought against Hadfield it was necessary to establish him either as the agent of an as yet undetected conspiracy, or as a lone assassin. If it was to be the latter, then it was important to prove a treasonable *intention* behind the overt act of shooting, but Hadfield had just denied having one. Addington's first concern was to find witnesses who would tell him 'whether the pistol was levelled at the sacred person of His Majesty or fired at random, as the one case would be High Treason, the other not'. His second was to see whether Hadfield could be connected with Jacobinism, for if there was a wider political conspiracy to prosecute, his wide aim would be less material. But Hadfield denied that too.

A Privy Council was hurriedly convened and witnesses who knew the prisoner were fruitlessly examined about his political connections. Most considered his character good until he took alcohol; but then his head wounds would cause him to lose all self-control and fly into a rage. Since Hadfield had seemed calm, collected and not at all drunk at the time of the shooting, ministers were more reluctant than ever to suggest that he was simply insane. It was true that the messianic language in which he answered their questions was suggestive of some form of 'mental derangement' but, as *The Times* pointed out, it was quite 'possible for ... madness to be counterfeited'. At any rate, Pitt emphatically instructed his subordinates to treat the matter as a consciously political act of treason in any public statements before the House the following morning. Since 'the evidence of firing at the King's person will turn out quite direct', Pitt confidently told Grenville, 'I therefore conclude you will not describe the act in your address as anything short of a horrid and treasonable attempt against his Majesty's sacred person. The description will not be the less true, even if the plea of insanity should (as it probably will) be hereafter established; and therefore all reference to that point seems as well avoided'. It was decided before the end of the evening therefore, that Hadfield would stand trial for high treason – and by special commission, to avoid unnecessary delay – despite the likelihood of mental illness. Portland believed there was 'not a doubt in the mind of any person present at the examination of the man's mind being deranged', nor that there was any real political conspiracy behind the attack, but ministers were clearly hoping to keep alive the possibility of premeditated treason long enough for some associative guilt to rub off on their political opponents, and were still hopeful of unearthing a Jacobin plot. Moreover, if Hadfield, who was not obviously insane at the time of committing his crime, were to evade a death sentence on grounds of insanity, difficult questions might be raised about the execution in 1760 of Earl Ferrers, whose defence plea had been similar. In Buckingham's view they would effectively be making a choice between convicting a poor ex-soldier for treason or declaring that 'Lord Ferrers was foully murdered by the judgement of his peers'; the former unfortunate, but the latter unthinkable. Extending mercy to Hadfield when his insanity was so much in doubt would, in any case, only 'encourage Jacobinical treason' amongst any malcontents who thought they could get away with it.[4]

For four full days, therefore, the examinations and inquiries continued; Richard Ford now heading a team whose members made it 'their most anxious interest to discover whether the outrage was the result of a treasonable design, or a wanton act of barbarous insanity'. Further blows were dealt to the plot thesis, however, by witnesses' testimony to Hadfield's exemplary war record, and to his lonely melancholic preoccupation since receiving his wounds. But evidence also began to emerge of a possible accomplice in the shoemaker Bannister Truelock, 'who either is, or effects to be, touched with a religious frenzy'. Hadfield's wife said her husband believed Truelock was on a 'divine commission' to 'purify the Earth', that he thought 'great changes will soon be brought about' and that 'there was a great work to be done' to make a 'strange alteration in the country'. Truelock's landlady considered him 'a seditious bad character', always complaining about the high price of provisions and blaming the King and Pitt. 'In the month of April, May or June', Truelock had once told her, 'the King would be assassinated and we should have no more Kings to reign at all'. Evidence of Truelock's involvement potentially strengthened Ford's hand in the search for premeditation and conspiracy; but the shoemaker's millenarianism did little to recommend him as a rational figure, and there was nothing to link him with radical organisations. Ford interviewed Truelock, who answered him in apocalyptic language; but the magistrate was undecided about his insanity. He and Hadfield had 'had some discourse about religion', he confirmed, 'that Gog and Magog were about to appear very soon, that all Kings are then to be put down and their power taken away'.[5]

Truelock's influence upon Hadfield was thought to be worth exploiting, for it was suggestive of both rational thought and a predetermined motive. Hadfield was tried for High Treason before Lord Chief Justice Kenyon on 26 June. The prosecution was led by the Attorney General John Mitford, and Erskine took the defence. Mitford opened by arguing that Hadfield was in full possession of his faculties when he fired the gun, and that he aimed it at the body of the King. He was therefore as fully responsible for his actions as Arnold had been in 1723, or Ferrers in 1760. A defence of insanity would simply not do.[6] But Erskine challenged Mitford's interpretation of the law regarding insanity and responsibility. In practice, he said, it served no useful purpose to define insanity as tightly as it had been applied in the Arnold case, for they would be very hard put to find any individual idiotic enough to fit the description. He demonstrated the seriousness of Hadfield's wounds and the likely effect they would have had on his behaviour. A doctor confirmed that two or three of his head wounds were sufficiently deep to have entered and damaged the brain. It was quite possible, he argued, for a mentally disturbed man to have long periods of lucidity and apparent self-composure. His apparently rational actions could still be influenced by his latent insanity. Hadfield's workmates and family all testified to the prisoner's *general* insanity, and blamed Truelock for making it worse. Hadfield's gloomy depression had even led him to try to kill his own child a few days before he shot at the

King. His madness was characterised not by a raving frenzy, explained Erskine, but by 'delusions'.

Kenyon interrupted him to observe that unless Mitford could produce witnesses to contradict the defence evidence, Hadfield must indeed be regarded as deranged at the time of the shooting. Mitford gave way, and Kenyon summed up. 'The prisoner, for his own sake and for the sake of society at large, must not be discharged', he ruled, for he was a potential danger to everyone, 'from the King upon the throne to the beggar at the gate'. Hadfield would have to be 'properly disposed of, all mercy and humanity being shown to this most unfortunate creature'. Kenyon's problem however, was that the court was not empowered to commit him to a madhouse at public expense. He could only deliver Hadfield back into the 'safe custody' of prison, and that would be inappropriate. The jury was then directed to acquit the prisoner of the charge because he was 'under the influence of insanity at the time the act was committed', and Hadfield was delivered temporarily back into penal custody. 'Means will be used to confine him otherwise', Kenyon assured the court, 'in a manner much better adapted to his situation'.[7]

The Hadfield Act

Four days later, Mitford introduced a Bill to the Commons to give these measures legal sanction. Poor lunatics like Hadfield should not be convicted of treason for attacks on the monarch, he argued, but it could not be in the public interest to acquit them. It was no good relying on defendants' friends and relatives to keep them secure for they tended to be 'of low habits and connections and seldom have any friends to take care of them'. Frith was exceptional; the law could not *instruct* relatives and friends to commit an offender to an asylum. Theoretically, magistrates in the offender's parish could be persuaded by the court to confine the defendant under the 1744 Vagrancy Act as soon as he left the court, but detention could not be guaranteed indefinitely and, once again, the court had no power to direct. The Safe Custody of Insane Persons Charged with Offences Bill therefore proposed empowering the court to confine insane defendants at the king's pleasure and at government's expense, provided the jury made it clear that this was the only reason for acquittal. The provisions applied equally to defendants adjudged insane at the time of committing their offences, insane at the time of their trial, or who might otherwise be acquitted and freed for want of prosecution. Pitt wanted to extend the Bill to prevent treason defendants enjoying any more privileges than those accused of civil murder and Windham was unhappy about the prospect of permitting lunatics who endangered the king to evade punishment. Madmen were not only as susceptible to deterrence as the sane, 'but he conceived that they were influenced by the fear of punishment more than by any other consideration, and to a degree much beyond the impression it made on other men'. He did not press his case, however, and the Bill became law on July 28.[8]

One further clause must be noted. The Act specifically provided the same terms of confinement for lunatics who attempted to gain access to any of the royal palaces. This was crucial, for it did not require proof of an overt act other than the desire to enter. Any determined individual demanding the right to see the king for any reason could be committed to an asylum for an indefinite period without trial and on the direct orders of the Privy Council or the Secretary of State, provided a court pronounced them insane. The Vagrancy Act was also amended to allow magistrates to order the confinement of lunatic vagrants beyond the period in which they appeared 'dangerous to be abroad'. Suspected lunatics could now be detained for far longer without trial provided two justices found 'a purpose of committing an indictable offence' and, if the offence involved the security of the royal family, central government money could be applied to meet the cost.[9]

The 'Hadfield Act' is usually subjected to a Whiggish interpretation,[10] that in its genuine intention to prevent the harsh treatment of the afflicted it was both enlightened and modern. Contemporary reception was similarly triumphalist. In language recalling press attitudes to the treatment of Margaret Nicholson, *The Times* was pleased that 'the French journals ... praise the discrimination, integrity and impartiality which mark the proceedings of an English court of justice'. The 'dispassionate' investigation and trial 'ought to serve as a model to the Tribunals of every civilized nation'.[11] Such interpretations, however, invariably overlook the contextual circumstances of Hadfield's crime: the security of the monarch at a time of domestic unrest, impending famine and fear of invasion. In these conditions, the choice between mounting a political trial for high treason, confirming disaffection on a grand scale, or risking the acquittal of any 'insane' regicides who might appear in Hadfield's wake was an unenviable one.

There was not only the unfortunate 'accident' in Hyde Park to consider. On 13 May, two days before either incident, an anonymous letter addressed to the Prince of Wales and alleging that a 'diabolical conspiracy' against the King 'involving more than one person' was imminent was forwarded to Portland by the Countess of Albemarle. The minister at first treated the letter as a hoax, but the two incidents of 15 May persuaded him to instruct Richard Ford to investigate. 'Great fears' were reportedly entertained 'by government of risings in the metropolis – of fires etc., and all the military were under arms' throughout the night of 15 May. Some reports certainly suggest hostility to the King among sections of the crowd outside the theatre immediately following Hadfield's arrest. Soldiers were ordered to seal the doors to prevent any accomplices either leaving or entering, and there was 'something like tumult' when horse guards tried to disperse the crowd before the King came out at the end of the performance. These clashes were fierce enough for one soldier to be carried off with a broken thigh, despite press insistence that people in the 'excessively crowded' streets had 'displayed great loyalty'; their tumultuous noise and 'shouts of joy' an expression only of profound relief.

In fact, at least two men were arrested that night as soldiers struggled to prevent the crowd from attacking the King's coach. John Dutton was one of about twenty people who had waited for the King at the corner of Southampton Street and the Strand, and then ran alongside the coach, keeping up a barrage of hisses and hoos. Dutton was arrested by a Bow Street officer, examined by Portland and later convicted for seditious speech. Robert Chapman was arrested in a crowd at Westminster for shouting 'I wish I had a pistol. I would shoot the King and it will not be long before I do it!' Further attempts on the King's life were feared. 'The public ear is daily and hourly assailed by fresh rumours', commented the *Morning Chronicle* as false reports began to circulate of a follow-up attempt at Windsor on 18 May. There were signs of disloyalty in the provinces, too. Although tactfully overlooked by the town's own papers, the *True Briton* reported a serious riot at Nottingham Theatre, two days after the close of Hadfield's trial, when a section of the audience tried to prevent the orchestra from playing *God Save the King* and wounded three constables with flying stones.[12]

Ford discovered a London whitesmith named James Martin who had issued threats against the Royal Family and had been in contact with guardsmen at Holborn 'who were in the same way of thinking and who had told him they only waited for an opportunity to kill the King'. He was sorry Hadfield had failed and went to a review to kill the King himself a few days later, but 'it was owing to the wet day that His Majesty did not lose his life as there was not a crowd of people sufficient for a person to act without being noticed'. In November, three more men were arrested for 'hissing and hooting' the King as he returned from opening Parliament in an atmosphere of intensifying discontent and popular politicisation over the response of the State to the subsistence crisis. Even in the famously loyal Borough of Windsor, an anonymous note was delivered to the mayor calling for a lowering of prices in the market and demanding action from the town's most eminent resident. The Corporation was unusually alarmed, 'particularly as the last mentioned paper more directly points at the person of His Majesty'.[13] In such a turbulent atmosphere, then, what we must recognise above all else in the passing of the Hadfield Act are its political and pragmatic dimensions in the continuing war against attacks on the Royal Family at the end of the 1790s. The genius of the Act lay in the sleight of hand by which it represented deterrence or arbitrary confinement as humanitarianism. Far from rescuing the apparently insane from the punishment of confinement, the Act made it far more likely that they would lose their liberty; it may, indeed, have deterred some prisoners from entering a defence of insanity in the first place.

Hadfield spent several months as a prisoner in Newgate before being moved to Bethlem in October.[14] He spent the rest of his days at the asylum but never came to terms with his confinement. In July 1802 he and another troublesome millenarian, John Dunlop, briefly escaped but were recaptured, and in September he was temporarily readmitted to Newgate as a consequence. Ironically, Mitford's Act for the Safe Custody of Lunatics was also the means by which the executive, or indeed the king, became legally entitled to move insane prisoners *into* jail as easily as moving them *out*, for as Treasury Solicitor, Joseph White reminded John King as soon as the Act was passed, Hadfield could be removed to Bethlem because 'His Majesty may order Hadfield to be kept in such manner as to His Majesty shall seem fit'.[15] According to the MP, E. J. Littlejohn, who visited him at Bedlam in 1818, Hadfield 'much wished he had suffered at the time. The loss of liberty, he said, was worse than death. But he appeared clearly mad'. This was not the opinion of the anonymous author of *Sketches in Bedlam* in 1824, who found Hadfield apparently sane and protesting his incarceration. He applied several times for release. In 1838, he petitioned Queen Victoria to let him become a Chelsea Pensioner, claiming he was now sane and deserving of a review. Victoria, who was not even born at the time of the crime, was unmoved and Hadfield 'gave up all hope' in 1840. He died in Bethlem in January 1841.[16]

Bannister Truelock was removed to Bethlem without trial on the instruction of the Duke of Portland, for aiding and abetting Hadfield. For a quarter of a century at least, he was kept in solitary confinement, to prevent him proselytising his dangerous religious ideas among fellow inmates and because, 'being a discontented and uneasy subject, he might soon excite commotions and disaffection amongst all the patients'. Having escaped, once, in a bid to persuade William Hone to publish his 'seventy eight signs' of the approaching millennium, he died in the asylum in November 1830. Despite his obvious 'enthusiasm', no proof was ever offered that he was insane; indeed, 'in his ordinary conversations of life, he betrays not the smallest symptoms of a disordered intellect'.[17]

An epidemic of lunatics: troublesome subjects after Hadfield, 1800–2

In the months following Hadfield's attack on the King, the Royal Family was assailed by an unusually large number of unwelcome visitors, petitioners and attention-seekers. While it is quite possible that public interest in Hadfield's case provoked at least some of them, it may also be that the case and the Act conferred unaccustomed visibility upon a common phenomenon. Whichever it was, Richard Ford, newly appointed to the post of Chief Magistrate at Bow Street, certainly began interning troublesome subjects at an unprecedented rate. As we have seen, the Hadfield Act specifically encouraged justices to arrest and confine individuals whose behaviour suggested they were contemplating an offence in the vicinity of the King or the palaces. Ford did his best to follow the spirit of the Act by consigning suspects to the Westminster bridewell. He could hold them there pending Whitehall's approval for a trial if a sufficiently grievous offence had been committed, or under the extended terms of the Vagrancy Act if it had not. He was reticent, however, about confining suspects to prison for lengthy periods without charge.

The first man brought to Ford's attention after 15 May was Joseph Purslove, who was neither committed nor examined. Immediately after news of the Hadfield outrage reached him, Purslove travelled 160 miles to St James's to tell the King of 'a great secret' and warn him that the nation's laws and religion could be 'overturned to ruin'. Assuming insanity, the palace guards sent him away.[18] 'Another madman', posing an unspecified 'danger', was apprehended at Windsor Castle on 9 June but released after questioning. This may have been Joseph North who had been 'extremely troublesome' about his chancery suit at St James's and at Windsor for several months by the time of his eventual incarceration in July. He may have been only 'pretending to be a lunatic', but Ford had him locked up in the bridewell.[19]

The scale of the problem undeniably took the London press by surprise. By the time John England – the fourth 'lunatic or person pretending to be a lunatic' to seek access to the King since Hadfield's arrest – was taken into custody, intruders were turning up at the royal palaces week by week. England, a drawing master, 'supposed to be a maniac' but recently released from hospital, was spotted striding through the Presence Chamber at St James's. He was evicted by guards after trying to get into the locked Levee Room. Minutes later he was back at the gate with a knife. The weapon was taken from him and under questioning he claimed to have been 'induced by the public' to give a message to the King. In September, Ford committed North for riotous conduct before he was removed to Bethlem under the Hadfield Act. He died there.[20]

Two more would-be intruders were apprehended in November. Richard Neale, a journeyman chair painter from Birmingham, went to Buckingham House and asked to see the King. Christ had revealed to him that George III was his father, he told Ford, who sent him to the bridewell. John Stickes was arrested in St James's Park a few days later, a 'harmless' lunatic, in Ford's opinion, and an old offender. On several occasions since 1798, Stickes had been apprehended at one or other of the palaces, questioned and released, but only now was he 'taken proper care of' in the bridewell, on Ford's instructions. In practice, offenders like Neale and Stickes who posed no obvious physical threat were more likely to be released than committed for trial and removed to Bethlem. In 1800, Whitehall remained wary of sanctioning committals to an asylum unless an indictable offence or intention could be established. However, Ford was perfectly aware that removals were rarely ordered publicly and before a jury as specified in the Act, because removal orders were usually prepared by him and authorised by Under Secretary John King. Such ambiguities of policy sometimes puzzled Ford. In January 1801, for example, he was unsure what to do with Palmer Hurst, despite clear evidence of threatening behaviour. Hurst, a frequent uninvited visitor of the palaces, had damned the Queen and struggled with constable Sayers outside Buckingham House after demanding entry, apparently to take the Princesses to the theatre and to counsel the King about the ministry. In his pocket were a number of manuscript panegyrics about the Government's subversion of the Constitution. Ford sent Hurst to Tothill Fields, but did not think he could be charged under the Act, nor sent back to his Oxfordshire parish for fear local officers 'will perhaps be glad if he should escape from them and by that means rid them of the burthen and expense of his maintenance'. Given that Whitehall had just reconvened the Committee of Secrecy to assess the strength of forces 'hostile to the existence of the present monarchy', Portland could not understand Ford's cautious stance and ordered Hurst's permanent removal to Bethlem, a resting-place from which he did not emerge.[21]

Similarly, Ford committed to the bridewell John Dunlop, a millenarian 'lunatic' with a 'deep and fixed enmity against the King'. Dunlop promised his gaolers: 'You know not what an enemy you have in custody both to your King, your Laws and Religion, all of which I will strive to overturn.' Ford gently prodded the new Addington administration, suggesting ministers might like to continue the *ad hoc* practices of the Pitt regime and quietly sanction Dunlop's committal to Bethlem, for 'unless some steps are taken, he will be discharged in a few days'. Dunlop was accordingly despatched by Home Secretary Thomas Pelham.[22] The new administration was less inclined to interpret its powers under the Act as broadly as Pitt's had done, however. When Catherine Kirby was arrested in June 1801 for the unequivocally overt act of throwing stones at the King, her transferral to Bethlem should have been a formality once the Home Office convinced itself of her lunacy. After recording law officers' advice to use the Hadfield Act, however, nobody seemed confident enough to make the first move, and Kirby remained in the bridewell for the next two-and-a-half years while ministers and civil servants discussed the correct procedure for obtaining a Commission of Lunacy. After a close reading of the Act, Pelham believed that he was not empowered to sign Kirby's removal order on the King's behalf, and that to do so would not anyway be legal unless she was first judged insane in an open court of law. A commission of lunacy would then be required to ratify the decision. Kirby was finally transferred to Bethlem without trial in October 1803.[23]

The tightening of royal security in the months after Hadfield's arrest rendered the King all but inaccessible to his subjects in London. Ministers were apprehensive about the removal of the court to Weymouth in July 1801, however, and so Ford was sent, together with a small posse of Bow Street officers, to take charge of security. This was zealously attended to – from the prevention of voyeurism while the Princesses took the waters, to the prevention of petitioning. Indeed, Ford's draconian response to the attempts of 68 year old Neil Maclean to hand a petition to the King on the sea front are indicative of Government's alarm at this time. Maclean had been trying without success to present a personal petition to the King since the summer of 1799. He was a veteran of the American war who had fallen into 'poverty and distress and, for an unjust debt', forced to serve thirteen months in a debtors' gaol. He wanted an 'adequate allowance' from the State in recognition of his past services. In May 1801, he had twice tried to gain admittance to the palace at Kew, and on being turned away by Macmanus 'became very violent and swore that he would speak to the King and that nobody whatever should prevent him'. He followed the King to Weymouth but was recognised by Macmanus, who saw him waiting for the royal yacht one morning. As the King approached, Maclean reached inside his jacket to retrieve a petition, but was pinioned by several officers and hauled before Ford. Having read through Maclean's forthright – if rambling – petition, Ford decided that the old man was dangerous. The high price of bread, a direct consequence of the economic policies pursued by 'wretched' ministers, had so deepened the distress of the poor that there was now both 'the most dangerous disaffection to government throughout the whole United Kingdom' and a widespread sympathy for the French. Only the dismissal of the ministry and a massive redistribution of wealth through a punitive land tax would restore public patriotism, Maclean advised the King. At Ford's behest, a local magistrate committed the petitioner to the Dorset assize for 'outrageous behaviour in front of the King'. No prosecution was offered as there had been no offence, but Maclean was nevertheless detained in Dorchester prison and his case traversed. Ford thought it likely that Maclean 'would have been still continued from assize to assize, in custody' at Dorchester had he not been summoned to London for questioning some eight months later.

In August 1802 Maclean was transferred to Tothill Fields under the Vagrancy

Act as a prisoner who 'appears to be insane'. But Ford wanted the Hadfield Act invoked so that Maclean's permanent removal to an asylum could be accomplished. In his view, Maclean should have stayed at Dorchester and been prosecuted for a breach of the peace, then committed to Bethlem. With the assistance of a prison visitor who thought Maclean's 'principles and understanding sound', the luckless petitioner argued for release in an open letter to the King published in the *Morning Chronicle*. For the offence of 'greeting to present a most just and dutiful and necessary memorial and petition to his sovereign', he wrote, he had been seized and confined 'in this bridewell, yet no crime of any kind! No breach of any law hitherto charged or alleged against him!' It was not until October 1805 that a report on Maclean's likely insanity was procured from Dr Monro, and a Commission of Lunacy was ordered by John King in 1806. He had by then been in the bridewell for five years without trial, and it is quite possible that he died there.[24]

Maclean was not the only man for whom the wheels of 'humanitarian' justice under the Hadfield Act moved decidedly slowly. In 1806, John Zorn was acquitted of using seditious words against the King at a quarter session in Devon, but was nevertheless pronounced insane under the Act and ordered into the county gaol 'until His Majesty's pleasure be known'. This took nine years, during which time Zorn, with a severe wound in his leg and clearly in a state of extreme distress, remained in his cell and appealed in vain for release. In December 1816, he was admitted to Bedlam on the order of the Secretary of State for 'threatening the life of His Majesty'. This was something of an exaggeration. The 'threats' for which he had been acquitted in 1806 had been merely remarks inspired by his belief that as a distant relation of George III 'he was entitled to the Crown and that Bonaparte was ordained to uncover it for him'. Despite being 'perfectly orderly, honest and inoffensive', in the opinion of his keepers, Zorn stayed there until he died, aged 63, in 1825.[25]

Ford did not treat every case brought to his notice at Weymouth with such indifference. His principal concern with the avoidance of what he called 'public *éclat*' persuaded him that the 'harmless' Sir Francis Gordon, for instance, a man infatuated with one of the Princesses, ought only to be watched, 'hoping that he would leave the place'. It was only when he persisted in following the Royal Family that Ford had Gordon 'quietly apprehended' and confined to his room. He then pressed Gordon's doctor 'to send proper reasons to remove him to London'. Ford had no wish to send Gordon to join Maclean in Dorchester prison because 'this is not a case to be made the subject of confinement in prison'.[26]

Ford's determination to avoid 'public *éclat*' was, however, also the cause of what amounted to a news blackout on another serious attempt on the King's life. On the evening of 31 August George III was attacked in the

Weymouth theatre. Ford and his constables had already identified one 'drunken fellow who seemed likely to be troublesome', but the trouble ultimately came from someone else. As the performance ended, a man suddenly leapt onto the bench on which he had been sitting, ran along it towards the royal box and attempted to pull himself inside. The Bow Street man pulled him down and took him into custody, but not before the Queen and the Princesses had been 'greatly frightened'.

The culprit was Urban Metcalf, a 25-year-old lace and garter hawker from London who eight years previously had been a short-stay patient at Hoxton and Plaistow asylums. Ford's initial reaction was to treat Metcalf as though still insane, however, and he wrote to Pelham soliciting his approval for the man's subsequent admission to Bethlem under the Hadfield Act. He reminded the Secretary of State of the 'inconvenience' they had experienced over Whitehall's recent reinterpretation of the Act's powers to detain Kirby and Maclean, and said he would 'strongly recommend sending the man at once to Bedlam, as we have repeatedly done during the last twelve months'. But a day later it was discovered that Metcalf had not only caused a disturbance in front of the Royal Family but had thrown a penknife. It was found embedded in the stage door beside the box. 'There is no doubt he meant to have killed the King ... Perhaps he had better not now be treated as a lunatic but under suspicion of High Treason', mused Ford. Committing Metcalf to Bethlem under the Hadfield Act was in any case going to be difficult, for Ford was a long way from his own jurisdiction 'and the magistrates here would never take such a step'. But a trial for high treason would depend on evidence that Metcalf threw the knife, an overt act he had not admitted and to which Ford could find no witnesses. At this stage, neither the Royal Family nor the general public knew anything about the knife, and since he had no wish to publicise the matter he was forced to make inquiries 'as quietly as I can'. Consequently, no evidence was uncovered. 'If no legal trial is to take place, I had better let the matter quite drop', he conceded. But when Metcalf escaped from his Weymouth lock-up one night and caused a second disturbance outside the King's Lodge, Ford had no choice but to send him to London for further questioning. Although Metcalf's family came forward at this point to confirm the prisoner's insanity, Ford by then had information from an 'entirely dependable' source that the prisoner was a former member of the LCS and believed Metcalf deserved to stand trial for treason. 'I shall always think he had his senses when he threw the knife', he told John King, 'and that he enjoyed a lucid interval sufficiently to know well the criminal nature of what he was attempting'.[27]

There would be no trial. Urban Metcalf remained in the bridewell while the Government's law officers and Home Secretary Pelham collected evidence of his derangement. This was established to their satisfaction by mid September, first on grounds of previous illness and, second, because his assassination attempt was deemed irrational. 'The idea of attempting to take away the life of any man by flinging a knife at him in a playhouse from a considerable distance, considering the great improbability of its succeeding and the almost certainty of its being observed and discovered, of itself marks an extravagance bordering on madness.' Government remained determined to keep the matter from both the King and the public however, making an open trial to test Metcalf's insanity before a jury out of the question. As Pelham and his advisers understood the law, this meant they could not use the Hadfield Act for Metcalf's removal and to have done so would, in any case, only have resulted in 'publicity and delay'. The law officers therefore desired Ford to make use of the crucial secondary clauses amending the Vagrancy Act and to commit Metcalf to Bethlem under them 'to save the necessity of further publicity'.[28] Thomas Pelham was still not convinced of the legality of the measure and both Metcalf and another offender, Patrick Rooney Nugent, who had tried to get into Buckingham House in January 1802, were left in the bridewell until Lord Hawkesbury took office in 1804. Hawkesbury sent both men to Bethlem without further delay, but Metcalf's 'madness' did not greatly impress his doctors and they recommended release a year later as he had been 'free from any symptoms of derangement whilst in the hospital'. Hawkesbury prevaricated for a month before agreeing to set Metcalf free, but sent him back to Bethlem two weeks later, the patient 'having relapsed since his discharge'.[29]

Pelham's reluctance to use the Hadfield Act to commit lunatics to Bethlem was not a consistent policy. The 'recovered' Richard Neale was sent to the bridewell when he reappeared at Buckingham House demanding in November 1802 to be made Lord Mayor of London, and the same treatment was meted out to Robert Ingram when he declared himself the Messiah in 1803. Yet, at the same time, William Wake was delivered to Bethlem on Pelham's instructions for an offence very similar to Neale's; and he was followed by John Oldfield and John Whitehouse who tried to gain admittance to Buckingham House in 1803.[30]

The guards' plot of 1802: Despard and king killing

Addington's recalling of the parliamentary committee of secrecy in 1801 culminated in the arrest, trial and execution of the small group of English and Irish radicals associated with Colonel Edward Marcus Despard over the winter of 1802–3. The 'Despard conspiracy', as it became known, has been comprehensively reassessed in recent years by historians of popular politics,[31] but their scholarship has been chiefly concerned with the political strength and depth of the alleged plot rather than the fine detail of Despard's planning. However, an important component of the prosecution's case was the group's intention to assassinate George III as he went to open Parliament in the autumn of 1802. The intricacies of the intended rising were never fully revealed either at the trial or since, so the evidence for Despard's regicidal intentions remains thin and circumstantial. There is little reason, however, to suppose that either the murder of the King or the overthrow of the monarchy was an explicit intention.

In the light of the Government's failure to prove constructive treason against the LCS in 1794, the prosecution case at Despard's trial made as much capital as it could from the alleged assassination plot.[32] In the course of some opening remarks to the jury, Crown counsel conceded that the bulk of the evidence concerned an alleged plan to attack the Tower, but nevertheless 'the principal thing which will require your consideration is the plan of intercepting the King'. By the fifth count, the conspirators were accused of an intention to 'lay in wait, attack and murder' the King, and by the eighth, specifically to shoot him on his way to Parliament. Yet the evidence for these intentions is not conclusive. There was certainly *talk* of attacking the King as he went to open the New Session on 16 November, but little indication that it was being seriously considered by the circle's leaders. This is not to deny the existence of an armed conspiracy to force a reform on Parliament, and since the King was inextricably linked to his Parliament by the Constitution the seizure of Parliament could not be realistically contemplated without an attempt to incapacitate the King. The State Opening offered a clear opportunity to achieve both aims, with the securing of the King as a *consequence* of the prime objective – constitutional reform.

In law, and especially since the passage of the 1796 Treason Act, any distinction between killing, seizing or deposing the monarch is largely academic. The Act had bought any intention to impede or restrain the King more clearly within the meaning of an 'overt act', and the court did its utmost to clarify this for the jury. It did not matter, explained Lord Ellenborough, that no actual attempt had been made to kill, depose or restrain the King. Any 'consultation, agreement or resolution ... compassing the imprisonment of the King' would be as substantive an act of treason as assassination itself. However, as a factor in constitutional rather than republican discourse – and as a factor in Despard's own politics – the distinction is important. Despard may have had little to say during his interrogation and trial, but he did deny any intention to take the King's life in a petition for clemency composed as he awaited execution.[33] The jury, perhaps impressed by Despard's character referees – Evan Nepean and Horatio Nelson – perhaps suspicious about the role played in the affair by spies and *agent provocateurs*, and perhaps unsettled by the absence of solid evidence for the conspiracy, found the accused guilty but recommended them to mercy. Such liberality puzzled Ellenborough. Despard's referees may have 'rendered the guilt of the party more doubtful – but when the guilt was once fully ascertained it seemed to me, considering the nature and quality of the crime, *which was intended assassination of his Majesty*, to operate very materially in aggravation of it' (my italics).[34]

The most useful *tangible* evidence found on the prisoners and produced at the trial were printed copies of the United Englishmen's constitution pledging 'independence' for Britain and Ireland, equal rights, 'a liberal reward for distinguished merit' and 'ample provision for the families of the heroes who shall fall in the contest'. Only the last of these clauses was openly suggestive of rebellion, but it still did not amount to republicanism, much less regicide. In adopting the language of impending martyrdom rather than aggression, the phrase suggests a violent response from the State, but does not identify the 'contest' as either physical or legitimate. The ambiguity was probably deliberate.[35] The importance of these documents lay less in their language than in their function however, for they were designed for use during oath-taking in direct contravention of the 1797 Act against Administering Unlawful Oaths. The case for conspiracy was thus considerably strengthened, although its precise nature remained in doubt.

The best evidence for an intended attack on the King came from the repeated examination of the guardsman Thomas Windsor, who turned King's evidence. The Crown did its best to confer credit on his testimony, but Henry Hunt would later claim that Windsor 'confessed upon his death bed that he had been bribed to swear against the Colonel, that what he had sworn was false, and that he had been instructed what to say, and he did so, for doing which he received a considerable sum'. There may be no truth in Hunt's allegation, but the evidence of informers must certainly be treated with caution.[36] Windsor's first examination on the evening of his arrest confirmed the State Opening as a signal to attack the Tower, but lacked detail on the assassination of the King. Despard had apparently told him that 'His Majesty must be put to death', but the words were spoken in private so that nobody else heard. The destruction of the Royal Family was simply part of the conspiracy's 'general purpose'. At his second examination, Windsor was more helpful. He remembered hearing Despard make an identical remark to another soldier, Thomas Winterbottom. But his reliability as a witness was not helped by Winterbottom's disclosure that Windsor himself had suggested sending for every revolutionary 'within a twenty mile radius of Chatham' to come and help seize the King.[37]

Government put some energy into discovering the means by which the King was to be killed. According to two informers, the defendant John Wood, another soldier, offered either to 'post himself sentry over the Great Gun in the Park and load it and fire it at His Majesty's carriage as it passed in going to the House', or to fire it as the King rode back to Buckingham House from the levee, 'because there would be no Horse Guards there'. Alternatively, he could seize the King here with a force of just thirty or forty people, he thought.[38] Thomas Broughton too wanted to fire the Great Gun at the King's coach. The informer Emblin claimed that he remonstrated with Broughton about the number of innocent people who would be killed in the crowded park. Broughton was unconcerned. If the ball missed the King, 'then, damn him, we must manhandle him', he said.[39] On other occasions, however, Emblin, Broughton, Arthur Graham and Despard had confined themselves to the problem of capturing the King. Broughton thought it best to 'take and shoot two of the horses and then the carriage must stop ... then seize him directly', but Emblin objected. The Life Guards would be 'riding close by the carriage with their horses' heads almost in the window and any person attempting such a thing would be cut to pieces'. Despard said he was prepared to do it nevertheless.[40]

Despard was aware that some of the soldiers he had enticed into the conspiracy were impatient to 'begin and kill the Tyrants', but he appears to have wanted men like Broughton to lead the rebel guards against the King's soldiers rather than kill the King. There would be plenty of soldiers protecting the coach, he told John Connell, but the guards would 'do the business and they would take the King as he came out into Parliament Street and secure him until all the rest of the business was done ... When the guards had secured the King and taken the Parliament House, the members [the United Englishmen] were to take possession of them while the soldiers took possession of the Tower.'[41] Broughton's preference for attacking the King's coach from a distance with cannon was a reckless one, and perhaps unlikely to have been favoured by Despard, who still nursed faint hopes of support from 'great men' like Burdett for a non-regicidal *putsch* against the Government.[42]

Yet there remains some evidence that Despard, at least, had been considering regicide the previous February. A heavily indebted baronet, Sir Edward O'Brien Pryce, approached magistrates on the day of the conspirators' arrest and volunteered information about his own connection with Despard. Producing promissory notes from several unnamed English and French gentlemen, Despard had offered him unlimited sums of money in exchange for some expert advice about making underground bombs. Pryce said he was shown a diagram of a 'machine' to blow up the King. Three powder barrels surrounded by ball and metal spikes for bringing down horses were to be placed in boxes and fitted with spring locks. These would be buried under the road and detonated by means of a connecting wire from a safe place. Despard hoped the resulting explosion would 'blow the road up for a considerable distance and the balls placed in the machine would destroy any person whom they might strike'. After studying the diagram, Pryce told him it would certainly work, and Despard said he intended to plant three such devices in London: the first on the road to Windsor, the second between Buckingham House and Hyde Park Gate and the third close to Buckingham House, opposite the gate into the lower part of Green Park. This was Despard's favoured option. The wire could be stretched under the garden wall to a place from which the assassin 'could not miss, the wall would be his guide; if he did there would be no doubt His Majesty would be killed as the horses might, through the report, take the carriage among the trees, and then the Prince of Wales would be King'.[43]

Pryce wrote all this information down and sent it to Pelham together with a diagram. His evidence stands alone, unsupported by any of the testimony offered by known conspirators turning King's evidence, and it was not used during the trial. There is no indication that Pelham took it seriously, and he may indeed have wondered why Pryce had not volunteered the information in February when Despard had approached him. If the story is true, Pryce had every reason to suppose Despard would name him under interrogation and so may have come forward to disclaim his own complicity as soon as he heard of the latter's arrest. The alleged date of February 1802 does coincide with Despard's reappearance in London's radical circles after a quiet sojourn in Ireland. As Marianne Elliott has shown, this was the point at which Despard was persuaded by the United Irishmen to come out of political retirement and exploit the public sympathy he had attracted as a State prisoner. In February, therefore, Despard was 'back in England attempting to attract a better class of leader into the English movement'.[44] This alone would give a pretext for an approach to Pryce.

That Despard and his colleagues at least intended to attack the King's procession and take him prisoner is no more implausible than the notion of achieving reform through an insurrectionary strike. Over-awing Parliament and the King may be read as a physical remonstrance for a wider suffrage; there is certainly no good reason to read it as part of an attempt to overthrow the constitution and establish a republic. The British experience of insurrection has always been particular. Its appearance as a component of radical discourse connects it to the wider legitimising culture of petitioning, remonstrance and resistance theory, but not so easily to the revolutionary table-turning of Jacobin France.

Notes

1 Aspinall, *Later Correspondence*, vol. 3, p. 349: Thomas Keate to George III, 15 May 1800.

2 *True Briton*, 16 and 23 May 1800; *Morning Chronicle*, 16 and 24 May 1800; *The Times*, 23 May 1800.

3 *Morning Chronicle*, 20 May 1800.

4 *Ibid.*, 16 and 19 May 1800; *The Times*, 17 and 22 May 1800; PRO, HO 42/50: 'Depositions taken in the matter of James Hadfield', 15 May 1800; TS 11/223/11678: Examinations of John Holroyd, Thomas Harding, William Harrison, and John Le Mesurier, various dates, May 1800; Examination of James Hadfield, 15 May 1800; BL, Dropmore Papers, Add. MS 58908: Pitt to Grenville, 16 May 1800; Add. MS 58934: Portland to Grenville, 16 May 1800; Marquis of Buckingham to Grenville, 18 May 1800.

5 PRO, TS 11/223/11678: Examinations of Bannister Truelock, 16 May 1800, Thomas Harding, Sarah Lock, Bannister Truelock snr, John Ede and Elizabeth Hadfield; *Morning Chronicle*, 20 May 1800.

6 Ferrers attempted to 'prove' his own insanity as he conducted his defence before the House of Lords. As Joseph Heller could have told him, he had little chance of success because the presentation of his own case required reasoned argument and logical thought. Therefore, if he had managed to establish his insanity, he could not have been insane. See Porter, *Mind-Forg'd Manacles*, p. 115.

7 Howell, *State Trials*, vol. 27: 'Trial of James Hadfield', cols 1281–356.

8 *Hansard*, June–July 1800 (London, 1800), cols 389–93.

9 Walker, *Crime and Insanity*, pp. 78–80; Porter, *Mind-Forg'd Manacles*, pp. 116–18; G. D. Collinson, *A Treatise on the Law Concerning Idiots, Lunatics and other Persons non compos mentis* (London, 1812), vol. 1, pp. 492, 503–6.

10 For example, Wiener, *Reconstructing the Criminal*, pp. 84–5; R. Moran, 'The origins of insanity as a special verdict: the trial for treason of James Hadfield (1800)', *Law and Society Review*, 19 (1985), 517; Walker, *Crime and Insanity*, pp. 78–8.

11 *The Times*, 17 July 1800.

12 *Morning Chronicle*, 19 and 20 May 1800; *Nottingham Journal*, 24 May 1800; *The Times*, 17 May, 17 June and 11 July 1800; *True Briton*, 30 June 1800.

13 PRO, HO 42/50: Information of John How, 21 July 1800, and Ann Shepphерd, 25 July 1800; HO 49/3: Law officer's letter book, 1795–1801, John King to J. White, 13 November, 1800; Berkshire County Record Office, WI AC 1/1/4, Windsor Corporation minute book 1798–1828, entry dated 15 December 1800.

14 PRO, HO 48/9, Law officers' reports, Joseph White to John King, 13 August 1800.

15 *The Times*, 30 July 1802; PRO, HO 79/10: Private and secret entry book, 1798–1818, Pelham to the Governor of Bethlem, 25 September 1802; HO 48/9, Law officers' reports, Joseph White to John King, 13 August 1800.

16 Littlejohn is quoted in Aspinall, *Later Correspondence*, Portland to the King, 15 May 1800, footnote 1, p. 350; *Sketches in Bedlam*, pp. 14–18; Royal Bethlem Archive, Incurable Admissions Book, 1728–1853; *Northern Star*, 27 June 1840; PRO, HO 17/101: Petition of James Hadfield, 28 May 1838. My thanks to Roger Wells for sharing this reference with me.

17 *Sketches in Bedlam*, pp. 19–26; Royal Bethlem Hospital Archive, Incurable Admissions Book, 1728–1853; Committee Book, October 1800–November 1805.
18 *True Briton*, 23 May 1800.
19 *The Times*, 12 June, 14 July 1800.
20 *Ibid.*, 14 July and 23 September 1800; Royal Bethlem Hospital Archive, Admissions Book, 1797–1802; Incurable Admissions Book, 1728–1853.
21 *Porcupine*, 3 and 4 November 1800; *Morning Chronicle*, 3 November 1800; PRO, HO 42/61: Richard Ford to Duke of Portland, 23 January 1801; Richard Ford to E. J. Hatton, 19 March 1801; Examinations of Thomas Baker, John Sayers, and Palmer Hurst, 23 January 1801, with enclosures; Royal Bethlem Hospital Archive, Admissions Book, 1797–1802; Committee Book, October 1800–November 1805.
22 PRO, HO 42/61, Ford to Edward Hatton, with enclosures, 19 March 1801; Royal Bethlem Hospital Archive, Admissions Book 1797–1802; Incurable Admissions Book 1728–1853.
23 PRO, HO 42/62, Richard Ford to ?, 11 June 1801; HO 49/3: Law officers' letter book, incoming correspondence 1795–1801, E. J. Hatton to J. White, 4, 11 June 1801; HO 49/4: Law officers' letter book, outgoing correspondence 1800–01, J. White to E. J. Hatton, 9 June 1801; HO 49/5: Law officers' letter book, incoming correspondence 1801–8, J. King to J. White, 20 February 1802; Pelham to S. Perceval and J. M. Sutton, 14 June 1802; Royal Bethlem Hospital Archive, Incurable Admissions, 1728–1853: Admission of Catherine Kirby, 1 October 1803.
24 For Ford's removal to Weymouth, see HO 42/62: Richard Ford to John King, 1 September 1801. For Patrick Macmanus's efforts to deter two men from hiding in a bathing machine to spy on the princess, see *Morning Chronicle*, 18 and 23 July 1801; *The Times*, 18 July 1801. For Neil Maclean, see PRO, HO 42/62: Depositions of Patrick Macmanus and Henry Edwards, 25 July 1801, prosecution brief for the trial of Neil Maclean, 25 July 1801, petition of Neil Maclean; Assi 23/9: Case of Neil Maclean; HO 79/10: Pelham to Hunter, 7 March 1802, Pelham to Keeper of Tothill Fields bridewell 30 July 1802; HO 42/66: Richard Ford to John King, 5 August 1802; *The Times*, 24 July 1801; *Morning Chronicle*, 13 November 1802; HO 49/5: Law officers' letter book, 1801–8, J. King to J. White, 4, 11 October 1805 and 15 January 1806.
25 Devon County Record Office, Q/S 1/23: Quarter session order books, 1802–12, Epiphany 1807; Q/S B 1807: Session papers, John Zorn to Mr Eales, 5 April 1807; Royal Bethlem Hospital Archive, Criminal Lunatic Admission Book 1816: entry dated 11 December; PRO, HO 20/13: 'Register of criminal lunatics confined in county and licensed lunatic asylums'.
26 PRO, HO 42/62: Richard Ford to John King, 15 August 1801.
27 PRO, HO 42/62: Richard Ford to John King, 1, 5, 6 and 8 September, 1801; HO 44/49: Undated memorandum concerning Metcalf's past treatment; *The Times*, 3 September 1801; *Morning Chronicle*, 9 September 1801.
28 PRO, HO 48/10: Law officers' reports 1801, Edward Law to Lord Pelham, 16 September 1801.
29 Royal Bethlem Hospital Archive, Committee Book, October 1800–November 1805, entries dated 16 June 1804, 29 June, 6, 20 and 27 July and 10 August 1805; PRO, HO 79/10: Private and secret entry book, 1798–1818, Pelham to the Keeper of Tothill Fields Bridewell, 6 January 1802. Metcalf was released again as 'well' in 1806 but re-admitted in 1817 for a year, and for a further four months in 1822.

His offences continued to revolve around the Royal Family, for he was now convinced both of his own kinship via the Danish Royal Family and of his right to live in the English royal palaces, where he frequently appeared demanding admission. On his release in 1818, Metcalf published a pamphlet fiercely attacking the administration at Bethlem and accusing the governors of neglect and cruelty. Perhaps in an effort to prevent the Government from committing him yet again, his family arranged for his removal to the private asylum at York following his release in 1822 (Royal Bethlem Hospital Archive, Incurable Admissions 1728–1853: *Sketches in Bedlam*, pp. 164–5); U. Metcalf, 'The Interior of Bethlehem Hospital' (London, 1818), reprinted in D. Peterson (ed.), *A Mad People's History of Madness* (Pittsburgh, PA, 1982), pp. 74–91; PRO, HO 43/26: Sidmouth to Governor of Bethlem, 10 October 1817.

30 Royal Bethlem Hospital Archive, Incurable Admissions 1728–1853, Committee Book October 1800–November 1805: entries dated 13 November 1802 and 11 June 1803; *Morning Chronicle*, 10 November 1802, 15 November 1803.

31 Thompson, *The Making*, pp. 521–8; Hone, *Cause of Truth*, pp. 104–17; Wells, *Insurrection*, pp. 220–53; M. Elliott, *Partners in Revolution: The United Irishmen and France* (New Haven, CT, 1982), pp. 282–323; D. Worrall, *Radical Culture: Discourse, Resistance and Surveillance, 1790–1820* (Detroit, MI, 1992), pp. 53–67.

32 Modern historians have tended to the view that the Government had little choice if it was to be confident of securing convictions, and that the attack on the procession to Parliament was probably not agreed upon by all the conspirators, nor considered particularly important. See Hone, *Cause of Truth*, pp. 108–11.

33 PRO, HO 42/70: Petition of Edward Marcus Despard to the King, 16 February 1803; *Morning Chronicle*, 21 January 1803.

34 BL Add. MS 33115: Pelham Papers, George III to Pelham, 2 December 1802; PRO, HO79/10: Private and secret entry book, 1798–1818, Lord Ellenborough to Pelham, 10 February 1803.

35 PRO, TS 11/121/332: Ms transcript of the trial of Edward Marcus Despard.

36 *Memoirs of Henry Hunt*, vol. 2, pp. 87–99.

37 PRO, TS 11/122/332: Further examination of Thomas Windsor, 17 November 1802 and examination and deposition of Thomas Winterbottom, 18 November 1802.

38 PRO, TS 11/122/332: Ms transcript of the trial, examinations of Thomas Windsor and Thomas Blades.

39 PRO, TS11/122/333: Examination of William Bownas.

40 PRO, TS11/122/332: Ms transcript of the trial, examination of John Emblin.

41 PRO, TS11/122/333: Examination of William Connell (not called in the trial).

42 Burdett had been prominent in the radical campaign against the harsh conditions in which the state's prisoners of 1798–1801 (whose number included Despard) had been confined in Cold Bath Fields prison, and maintained links with the conspirators' defence committee after Despard's arrest. See Elliott, *Partners*, p. 286, and Wells, *Insurrection*, pp. 241–2.

43 PRO, TS11/122/333: Information of Sir Edward O'Brien Pryce, Bart., 16 November 1802, and Pryce to Pelham, n.d. (1803).

44 Elliott, *Partners*, p. 290.

7

The potatoes speak for themselves: regicide, radicalism and George IV, 1811–30

Threats to the security of the Royal Family in the period following the closure of the French wars were more overtly associated with radical republican discourse than they had been in the preceding century. The shift in emphasis was not unconnected with the coinciding Regency and accession to the throne of the Prince of Wales. For the hugely unpopular George IV, the miracle of apotheosis was still pending at the time of his father's death in 1820. 'Whenever the Prince drove out in his carriage', according to one historian, 'whenever he appeared at the theatre, the mob either kept a complete silence or booed'.[1] But if the new reign was remarkably free of court intrusions by troublesome subjects, the extreme reluctance of George IV to show himself in public or to promote any concern for the welfare of his subjects may go some way to explaining it. There is little evidence that George IV was as bothered by 'lunatics' as George III had been, but this may partly have been an effect of the wholesale adoption of mass platform politics by the post-war reform movement and the consequent politicisation of everyday life, leading to a far greater submergence of individual grievances in programmes of collective salvation. The 'maniac' arrested and put in the watch-house for persistently trying to break into Carlton House in 1820 was exceptional enough for a magistrate to have to ask Sidmouth how the Hadfield Act worked.[2]

Mounting discontent in the industrial north of England had already erupted into Luddism in 1811–12, and the radical platform, revived by a resurgence of interest in reform following the gaoling of Sir Francis Burdett in 1810, began fresh agitations for peace and retrenchment. The apparent unwillingness of the Government to bring an end to hostilities with either France or America amid harvest failure and industrial distress impacted deeply on public regard for the Prince of Wales. The worsening mental atrophy of the half-blind King had excluded the monarchy from active decision making since 1810, and by 1811 a Regency for the Prince could be put off no longer. Although he was already unpopular in the country for being a luxuriating wastrel, the Prince's Regency at least heralded the return of a functioning tripartite State, and his subjects were not slow in making demands of him.

The first manifestations occurred almost immediately. The assassination of Prime Minister Spencer Perceval on 11 May 1812 spurred an extraordinary series of physical threats against the Prince. Perceval's assassin, John Bellingham, a bankrupt with outstanding financial claims against the Government, successfully pressed home his final remonstrance with the sort of luck and determination that always eluded assailants of the Royal Family, and he suffered for it on the gallows. Yet, if the Prime Minister could be murdered so easily as he walked through the lobby of the House of Commons, then why not the Regent? This possibility fuelled the fantasies of the politically powerless almost from the moment Perceval fell. Two Eton schoolboys met an old soldier near Windsor who had been 'very much injured by the Government – that they owed him a fortune' and who would 'have redress' either from the new Prime Minister or from the King. The boys assumed his strange mutterings about supernatural hangings were a sign of madness, but Government was sufficiently concerned to file a report.[3] Samuel Saunders, a poor London dyer, was taken into custody on the evening of Perceval's death for telling a posse of Bow Street runners that it would 'serve them right' if the 'bloody Prince of Wales' was the next to go.[4] There followed a quite bewildering number of anonymous letters addressed to the Prince during May and June, many of which survive among the papers of the Home Office. 'The blow will come at a time and from a quarter least expected' promised one, 'Even in your Palace you are not safe. Your indifference to the distresses of your people has lost you both their confidence and affections.' One gave him six months to end the war; others instructed him to destroy 'Poppery' or appoint Burdett as Perceval's replacement. Another threatened vengeance if he did not 'look into the affairs of the country, reverse orders in council and dismiss ministers, grant reform etc.' The Prince suddenly found himself responsible for every grievance nursed in the nation. In Leicestershire a man claimed he would kill both the Regent and a local butcher if the price of flour was not reduced by two shillings a stone, and another letter alleged a conspiracy among Nottinghamshire Luddites to 'blow your brains out' if their distress was not soon relieved.[5]

The Prince's postbag was undoubtedly swelled by his decision to publish the first two threatening letters in the *Gazette*, with the offer of a reward of £1,000 for disclosure of the authors. One anonymous writer responded by offering a reciprocal '£5,000 for the Heads of the Prince R, Lord Castlereagh and secretary Ryder'. Another promised swift revenge for the execution of Bellingham against the whole 'infernal Royal Family' and looked forward to seeing his own letter reproduced in the *Gazette*. Loyalists thought the Prince's publication strategy unwise. Instead of broadcasting the panegyrics of the discontented he should do something to redress their grievances, thought one 'friend to good order, peace and quietness'. It was not only the labouring classes who wished him dead, he was assured, but many of the 'respectable' middling sort as well, 'and if you were to disguise yourself and mix among men in different situations in life, I am convinced that you would hear much more than you can possibly believe'. Another counselled him to 'avoid public place – better still quit London', for the conspiracies against him were genuine, while a Sheffield magistrate warned against a proposed royal visit to Yorkshire on the same grounds: 'should he come ... there will most certainly be a desperate effort to murder him'.[6]

Petitions of right were no more welcome than anonymous threats. The Prince's private secretary Colonel McMahon would lay no unsolicited correspondence before his master, but dutifully returned every petition with a polite note instructing the sender to present it to Beckett or Ryder at the Home Office. Most of them solicited assistance in customary tones of praise for his indisputable generosity, but some were not afraid to acknowledge the Prince's presumed faults as well. All of the inhabitants of the loyal town of Bristol loved the Prince dearly, he was assured by John Harrison in a petition requesting £200 for a passage to America, 'excepting of the general opinion of being too fond of the fair sex, which they conceive to be injurious to your health'.[7]

There is little evidence of trouble from alleged lunatics around the palaces at this time however. The best-known instance occurred in 1813, but it centred on Queen Charlotte rather than the Regent. Elizabeth Davenport, a domestic servant in the Queen's household, created a disturbance one morning by hammering on Charlotte's bedroom door and declaring that she 'could and should redress her wrongs'. Instead of accepting her petition, however, the Queen's footmen put Davenport in a straitjacket and delivered her to Hoxton asylum. The incident inspired no loyal and congratulatory addresses conjuring a royal escape from assassination. On the contrary, Charlotte's public image as an ageing, functionless and ineffectual foreigner provoked only ridicule. Peter Pindar imagined her cowering behind the door and expecting a 'second Sellis' or a 'Hadfield fired by lunacy', only to be confronted by 'a shrieking desperate girl'.[8] But the humour wrung from incidents like this in the respectable press quickly evaporated when the Regent himself was attacked by a crowd of Londoners as he went to open Parliament on 28 January 1817.

Resistance rehearsed

> Will not the people of England with justice exclaim, 'we sought for bread, and are requited with a stone?'[9]

Although it bore some resemblance to the famous attack on George III in 1795, this incident provoked rather less outrage in the radical and opposition press, and there were few exhibitions of sympathy for the Regent. 'The comparison will never do', insisted Leigh Hunt in the *Examiner*. The Prince was 'no more to be compared with his father in popularity than nothing is to be compared with something.'[10] If the political context for the 1795 event had been a popular demand for the King to end the war, in 1817 it was for the Regent to pursue reform. The crowd in Palace Yard was there to lobby the parliamentary procession and to signal support for the presentation of reform petitions. All but a handful of these would be rejected by the House as either incorrectly drafted or insultingly worded. The Regent's outward journey was met with nothing more serious than 'murmurs of dissent', but when he left the Lords the crowd closed in around his coach and obstructed its progress back through the Mall. Missiles were thrown and two circular holes made in one of the side windows. A group of about twelve demonstrators, who 'were known to each other and acted in concert', according to Lord James Murray, ran beside the procession on both sides, jeering and hissing all the way. But although the coach's protective copper panels were dented and some wooden ornaments broken off, neither the coach nor the Regent were badly damaged. Murray, a passenger in the coach who was cut above the eye by flying glass, reported to Parliament that shots had been fired; but, as in 1795, no witnesses to gunfire could be found. As soon as the Prince was back inside the palace, lines of cavalry were deployed to drive the crowds out of the park. Palace guards were doubled and troops put on standby to quell any further outbreaks.[11]

Several men were arrested and committed on charges of assault and larceny, but only one was selected for a capital charge of treason. Thomas Scott, who had been shouting loudly in the crowd, was seized by an off-duty soldier who saw him throw gravel and strike one of the Life Guards with his umbrella. Scott, a man of some property, cut an unconvincing figure as a treason suspect, and he vigorously denied the charge, but his examination was useful to the authorities because it provided them with a pretext for tarnishing the reform movement with regicide. This initiative was much to the taste of Queen Charlotte who told the Prince that she hoped 'this time the law may for once prove more than insanity against the perpetrators for this is the third attempt against a Sovereign life since I am in England, and unless some example is made, I fear that with the present disposition of the mobility much mischief may arise'. Princess Elizabeth agreed: 'I trust that if the wretches are taken up they will be hung, for this new manner of letting every one off that commits these crimes is a great deal too bad.'[12] But government's best efforts to connect Scott with the radical clubs progressed no further than the allegation that he had once been apprenticed to the same jeweller as one of the Pop Gun Plot defendants, and since no witness could be found who actually saw him throw anything, the treason charge was reluctantly dropped in favour of assault on a guardsman.[13] Testimony was nevertheless produced at Scott's examination alleging treasonable intentions by persons unknown. Members of the crowd had struck at the Life Guards with sticks and run beside the coach shouting 'Seize him!' and 'Pull the bugger out!' It was suggested to Scott that he had encouraged them, but he admitted only to shouting 'Shame, shame!', as the soldiers pressed their mounts into the crowd, for 'they struck women as well as men'.[14]

Hicks and Gifford, the examining Bow Street magistrates, repeatedly prevented Scott's counsel from offering evidence on behalf of his client because the hearing was 'not a trial'. The proceedings, which lasted several days, were given a high profile by the press however, especially when Lord James Murray was called to repeat his earlier allegation that bullets had been fired at the Prince. The holes in the coach's window 'were of that size I have seen made by shot fired out of an air gun made in the shape of a stick, about the size of a pea', he explained, and fired at an angle, as though from a tree. The evidence had been destroyed moments later by a large stone, purposively thrown to shatter the entire pane. He had since revisited the scene to investigate the matter and had found 'a great many stones there', both on the ground and 'in every other tree'. Since Murray could not identify Scott as a member of the crowd, Hicks and Gifford refused to allow the defence to question any of his evidence, and it went unchallenged. The magistrates then addressed the large crowd that had been gathering outside the Bow Street office since the start of the hearing and asked whether any of them had seen Scott taking part in the riot. One man said that he had. When Scott asked Hicks and Gifford to hear contradictory evidence from another man in the crowd, Hicks refused on the grounds that the man in question had a criminal record. Rather surprisingly, the magistrate also decided that there was sufficient evidence to charge Scott with high treason after all, for it was clear that treason 'had been committed on that day. Then the only question is, by whom was it committed? That is for a jury to decide.'[15] When defence counsel made a further request to call witnesses who would prove Scott's innocence, Gifford explained that if they heard contradictory evidence he and Hicks would have to assume the duties of a jury and evaluate the argument on both sides. This would be inappropriate, because their only concern was to establish the strength of the evidence *against* Scott and commit him for trial *if* there was a case to answer.

More witnesses were heard. John Wells, a yeoman, could not identify Scott, but offered evidence that potatoes as well as stones had been thrown. His testimony was considered very significant by Hicks. 'The potatoes speak for themselves', he declared, 'they must have been brought for the purpose of being thrown at the carriage and prove a predetermination to the commission of treasonable acts.' But Wells could not identify Scott either, and the next three witnesses all took the view that the prisoner had only used his umbrella to fend off the cavalryman because he was afraid of being trampled. Hicks said there had nevertheless been a great many 'gross violations of decency' that day, and it was not only quite proper that the arrest had been made but a great pity there had not been more. In fact, the paucity of arrests was an unfortunate symptom of Bow Street's royal security strategy. Police officers and soldiers were deployed specifically to guard the coach, prevent access to it and to ensure its safe passage. This kept them close to the Regent and effectively prevented forays into the crowd in pursuit of ringleaders. Drawing the hearing to a close, the magistrates once again changed their minds about the charge. There was not, after all, sufficient evidence to charge Scott with high treason, ruled Gifford. He might be charged with riot, but since he had already spent a week in prison, they admitted him to bail and sent him home.[16]

The other prisoners taken were dealt with more swiftly and simply. John Slaine, a tailor, was charged with assaulting General Burton of the Life Guards by throwing sticks at him, but was bailed and then discharged after apologising to Burton. George Jones, identified as a member of the crowd but against whom there was no evidence of stone throwing, was charged with stealing stockings from a hosier's shop in the Strand. Another man, charged with being in the park with a dagger several hours after the attack, was discharged.[17]

Since the otherwise fruitless examination of Scott had at least established the occurrence of treason in the park, swift and decisive legislative action against radical organisations could be justified by Government. A desire to push ahead with this had been high on ministers' agendas since the Spa Fields' 'insurrection' in December, and Sidmouth could now use royal security as a pretext for 'emergency' measures. *Habeas corpus* was suspended, the right of public meeting restricted and the election of national 'delegates' to radical assemblies forbidden. The provisions of the 1796 Treason Act, currently due to expire on the death of George III, were at the same time made perpetual and the Regent explicitly named in them. The first sign of a radical response came from the north where it was proposed to send a body of marchers to London carrying new petitions addressed to the Prince. The so-called 'March of the Blanketeers' was conceived as a constitutional response to the emergency measures, couched in the language of remonstrance. The division of the marchers into small groups, bearing multiple petitions with just twenty signatures on each, was a measure designed to protect them from prosecution under the old Stuart statutes against 'tumultuous petitioning', and William Benbow did his best to persuade moderates like Samuel Bamford of its legality. Their petitions would be 'graciously if not with some awe, received by the Prince Regent in person', he thought; but Bamford was concerned with the insurgent rhetoric of the marchers' more militant backers, who seemed anxious to associate themselves with Wat Tyler. John Bagulay of Manchester, for example, told a meeting 'they would petition the Prince and that in case the petition was not granted by parliament the next step was to petition the King – in case they had no answer, that at the expiration of forty days the people had a right by Magna Carta to imprison the King and all his family'. Other speakers thought imprisonment too good for a Prince who ignored petitions. 'We will punish him by taking his head off as was done formerly to Charles I', promised one. The execution of Charles Stuart was said to have been 'an event to which the party constantly refer'.[18] As Bamford had predicted, the marchers were dispersed by the military, and a number arrested. Many expressed some confusion about the legal status of the enterprise. 'I did not know it was wrong', said John Cheatham, 'they said it was lawful.' William Painter had 'not a good understanding but they said we must go and show ourselves before the Prince and ask him to grant us a better trade'. Richard Leigh thought they were to 'beg to him as a father to give us bread'.[19]

To clear up any ambiguities, the magistrate W. D. Evans treated fifty-three defendants to a lengthy discourse on the proper interpretation of the Constitution. Given that treasonable expressions alluding to the Peasants' Revolt had been made at the outset, any one of the marchers could have been indicted for treason. That their actions could have precipitated revolution could be shown from the historical fact that Charles I had lost his life in a civil war brought about by very similar circumstances, for,

> It is a known matter of history that the earliest proceedings of that rebellion consisted of addressing the sovereign with petitions, affecting a humility of language, but manifesting in their substance a spirit of hostility and of dictation respecting the measures of government, and one of the earliest measures taken after the restoration of legitimate authority was to provide against persons repairing to the sovereign in excessive numbers, under the pretence of presenting petitions and remonstrances.

The marchers' attempts to circumvent the law by restricting signatories was nothing but a 'ridiculous … contrivance' showing a profound disrespect for constitutional law. Their true purpose was to impose themselves on the Prince in a 'large body', a measure 'calculated to excite terror'.[20] Evans was careful not to proscribe petitioning itself as treasonable, only the blanketeers' method of presentation. The evaluation of their form and language, on the other hand, was a matter for the Regent and, as their recent experience of parliamentary petitioning had told them, 'disrespectful' phrasing would also be met by rejection. Ministers occasionally considered prosecuting petitioners for seditious language but Crown solicitors invariably advised against it for fear it would be seen as a denial of the legal protection guaranteed by the Bill of Rights.[21]

Most radical papers accused the Government of engineering over-reaction to the attack on the Regent for its own ends and played the incident down as a regrettable and unplanned outburst of expressive discontent.[22] Murray's implausible 'bullet plot' and Hicks's partial examination of Scott were treated to liberal helpings of contemptuous satire. The stones discovered by Murray during his investigations in the park should be 'committed and examined', suggested T. J. Wooler in the *Black Dwarf*, and the potatoes which '*speak for themselves*', tried for treason. In a more scurrilous satire, Wooler imagined the ceremonial mortar installed in the park and known as the 'Regent's Bomb' (but pronounced 'bum') full of rotten eggs and other conspiratorial vegetable matter, all equally ripe for arraignment.[23] 'What!', declared Leigh Hunt, 'In these times of little meat, when we will be bound to say that the PRINCE REGENT rode in his royal plenitude through multitudes of hollow cheeks, are even vegetables so scarce a commodity that nobody can be carrying them along?'[24] William Hone contributed an ecclesiastical satire, the *Bullet Te Deum*, with its exhortation to 'praise thee O stone' and 'acknowledge thee to be a Bullet ... the everlasting prop of the ministry', and the *Canticle of the Stone*; 'O all ye workers of Corruption, bless ye the Stone: praise it and magnify it as a Bullet forever.'[25]

More serious responses labelled the outrage a direct result of those 'new maxims of state' by which the 'well-founded complaints' of the lower orders had been lately overlooked. The Regent was culpable, for he had shown no concern for his people. 'No nation pays a more devoted and dutiful reverence to a monarch who entitles himself to their confidence .... In England, a Prince must identify himself with the people or be content to be treated with suspicion', argued the *Champion*. But the Prince, misinformed by his ministers until he was unable to distinguish popular faith in the Crown from contempt for the Government, had withdrawn from the people and earned their displeasure. 'The eagerness of the ministers to attach upon the multitude the crime of deliberately aiming at the life of his Royal Highness betrays their system most completely. They want a further plea for entirely secluding him from the public.'[26]

These were perhaps the real roots of the Prince's unpopularity. Even in his more derided moments, George III had rarely been accused of withdrawing from his subjects and appearing indifferent to their suffering. The press found significance even in the Prince's demeanour while under siege in his carriage. So lacking in those positive qualities of fortitude and engagement characteristic of his father, he was accused of delivering the speech from the throne as though 'his spirits were somewhat depressed', and 'sitting stiffly with his head thrown backwards' in the coach. Ministerial papers insisted that his 'upright' and unflinching posture in the coach showed that he had scarcely noticed the 'murmuring' of the crowd, provoking the incredulous Leigh Hunt to comment: 'Princes at any time, we know, do not lend a willing ear to the voice of the people, but here the attention was compelled.' He thought it likely that the Regent's 'exceeding uprightness' was actually an unfortunate 'specimen of his notions of grandeur'.[27]

Resistance reconsidered

As previously suggested, the attack on the Prince is best understood in the context of collective remonstrance over the failure of petitioning. In adopting the language of retrenchment as forcefully as it had always championed the cause of democratic liberty, the radical mass platform appealed directly to the personal – economic as well as the collective – political concerns of the unenfranchised. Respectable radicals like Bamford welcomed the arrival of a more orderly and inclusive popular polity through the influence of such leaders as Cobbett, whose *Register* 'directed his readers to the true cause of their sufferings – misgovernment; and to its proper corrective – parliamentary reform'. Rioting and individualism had lost their 'ancient vogue', thought Bamford, as protest had become more 'systematic'. As I suggested earlier, this enlargement of popular faith in the collective presentation of grievances by petition and remonstrance, together with the Prince's personal unapproachability, may have led to a reduction in the more personal attempts to gain his ear.[28] The centrality of the Regent to the radical petitioning movement was directly connected to the evaporation of any belief in Parliament as a source of amelioration. The physical remonstrance of 1817 had its roots in his refusal to acknowledge a reform petition presented to him in November 1816. This had urged him to grant universal suffrage and annual parliaments, divert some money from the civil list towards the relief of poverty and 'above all, listen, before it is too late'. It was the intention of the organisers of the ill-fated Spa Fields' meeting on 2 December to relay the Prince's response to the crowd. Hunt had over-ruled a Spencean proposal that they march to Carlton House in a body 'to demand and enforce an audience' if the response was unfavourable, and had insisted on watering down the forthright language favoured by Watson and Thistlewood in the petition itself. Part of the petition's prayer was, in fact, attended to, for the Prince ordered the establishment of soup kitchens in Spitalfields, an initiative which led to some approving remarks in the press about the empirical effectiveness of petitioning. Watson was unmoved, and he told the crowd at Spa Fields that their petition had been ignored. Any hopes they may have had that the Prince would listen had proved groundless: 'Are we going to go on from time to time, from month to month, from year to year, crying to the Father of his People, as he is called, for redress?' asked Watson. The Regent was a 'sham father', wallowing in luxury, and if they wanted relief they would have to seize it. The subsequent abortive rising in the Minories, or the 'Spa Fields' insurrection', was the fruit of Watson's rhetoric.[29]

The mass presentation to Parliament of the Hampden Club petitions on the day of the State Opening involved a theatrical counter-procession to the Prince's, the largest petition unrolled and displayed 'on the heads of the crowd', behind a man carrying a bundle of oak sticks, 'emblematic of union and strength'. This popular parade was staged almost simultaneously with the Regent's and it even shared an identical route between Horse Guards and Palace Yard. Cobbett believed the Regent's coach was attacked on its way back through the park at precisely the same time that the reform procession was making its way down Whitehall before at least 20,000 spectators. Whatever the timing, the two processions, one seeming to represent Old Corruption, and the other popular reform, established an atmosphere of physical opposition that can only have accentuated the remoteness of the Regent. While he sat unflinchingly upright in his enclosed carriage, Lord Cochrane, the MP who had agreed to present the petitions, was hoisted onto an armchair and vigorously cheered into the Commons. Cobbett and Hunt tried to dissociate these events from the attack on the Regent's coach as he made his way home, but the connection was an easy one to make and the ministerial press made it at once. The attack on the Regent was 'a great incident', reflected Cobbett, 'and though it was clear that the Acts would have been passed without its assistance, it is nevertheless true that it formed the grand feature in all the future harangues against the "Demagogues" as we were called, and the almost sole topic in the declarations of the Tax-eaters and in the diatribes against the Reformers from the pulpit'.[30]

Government's emergency measures provoked plenty of radical rhetoric about the right of resistance. In Cobbett's view, any legislation obstructive of petitioning justified physical resistance, for that was 'a right inherent in every people' – the right for which the 'gallant and learned Sidney' had been martyred. Resistance was patriotic; whereas the French had restored the hated Bourbons and rekindled the maxim '*Vive le Roi, quand meme!*' ('God save the King, though even', meaning 'whatever he may do'). But Cobbett stopped short of recommending immediate action. First they should petition the Regent again, this time for 'a restoration of those rights which we have proved to be our due. If that petition be rejected, it will then remain for us to consider what path our just rights and our duty to our King and country call upon us to pursue'.[31] Hunt, too, was reluctant to give up on petitioning. Although most of the reform petitions laid before Parliament in January had been rejected, he nevertheless attributed the voluntary resignation of Lord Camden from a sinecure worth £35,000 a year as a direct consequence of the embarrassment caused him by one of them.

Nevertheless, Hunt cheerfully delivered a 'strong declaration and remonstrance' to Sidmouth for presentation to the Regent, in September 1817, following resolutions passed in Palace Yard 'against petitioning the House of Commons any more for reform, as being proved to be useless by the total disregard which that body had manifested to the prayers and the petitions of the people during the previous session of parliament'.[32]

Not all the radicals were as sanguine about petitioning as Cobbett and Hunt. Wooler thought it a weapon of the establishment, 'thrust forward to stop the current of popular dissatisfaction'. While King and Parliament still had the 'right of neglecting your petitions', the right of petition was no more powerful than the right to complain. But 'like all other delusions it will be found out at last, and then goodbye to petitioning'. He recognised the mythical role petitioning had played in the struggle for Magna Carta and the Bill of Rights, but these were victories achieved at knifepoint. If petitioning alone had not won English freedoms, neither would it preserve them. 'The right of petitioning with our ancestors meant the right of laying their grievances before the highest authority and demanding or ENFORCING an attention to their wrongs.' Since Parliament was corrupt and the Crown was the higher authority, the Regent was the proper person to receive their complaints. Parliament's wilful interference with the popular right of approaching the throne by demanding all communications be made through the Secretary of State was the direct cause of the blanketeers' march. Those men 'thought *justly* that the Prince must have been deceived or he would never have turned a deaf ear to the complaints of his people. They therefore proposed marching to London to present their grievances to himself'.[33] In May Wooler was arrested and prosecuted for libels against the King's ministers and, in ridiculing the act of petitioning, against the whole institution of parliament, 'of and concerning King John ... Charles the First [and] ... William the Third'. The theatrical complexity of his defence and subsequent acquittal have been brilliantly analysed by James Epstein.[34]

Wooler's cynicism was shared by the republican William Sherwin. Like

Paine and Wooler, Sherwin regarded the very idea of 'one man praying to another' as 'very humiliating and degrading' to the rights of citizenship; and he thought most English kings had been 'much galled' at the inconvenience of receiving them. At the beginning of June, his tactical advice was, however, to keep on petitioning, because to cease doing so would be to accept the Government's right to interfere with it. The right to petition the throne was a condition of the Act of Settlement, argued Sherwin, and 'the method in which the right was to be exercised was not laid down, because if the new King [William III] or his courtiers had presumed to prescribe the manner in which the people should pray for redress, the probability is that they would not have received him'. Furthermore, the right of petition should never be seen merely as a right to complain but as an inalienable expression of the popular will. 'If the People have a right to petition, they have likewise a right to have what they petition for.'[35] He addressed the Prince unequivocally. The people were 'now turning to you as their last resource; and if you disappoint them, it is no difficult matter to discover the nature of the scenes that will follow'. Charles I, he reminded him, had 'lost his head by refusing to listen to the petitions of the people'.[36]

The Home Office remained understandably jumpy over possible threats against the Regent's life. In June 1818, Sidmouth ordered the arrest of an ex-seamen's strike leader, A. W. Armstrong, on the evidence of an unnamed informer that he intended shooting the Prince as he went to prorogue Parliament. Armstrong was charged with high treason, then released with the gift of a sovereign when no further evidence could be produced. His subsequent letters to Sidmouth and the Regent demanding an apology and the name of his accuser were unanswered.[37] It is worth noting, however, that radical physicality and anger was not directed as forcefully at the monarch at this point as at his ministers. Spencean insurrectionary conspiracies had turned by the summer of 1817 from Despardian plots to seize the King and invade Parliament to plans for the assassination of the Cabinet.[38] These would begin with an attempted rising during Bartholomew Fair in 1817 and culminate in the treason trials of Thistlewood and his circle after the Cato Street arrests in 1820. Remarks expressing hatred for the Regent and wishing his death were certainly reported by Sidmouth's informers at this time, but they do not seem to have been connected with any of the discussed and planned conspiracies. The Regent's role in radical discourse was developed more as that of a figure of ridicule than of hatred. As a pampered and overweight wastrel, the Prince played a leading role in the bawdy culture of the Spencean 'free and easy' as, for example, the 'Sweet Pig of fine Pall Mall (He's the one I wish to kill)'. As an absurd and ineffectual figure of authority, the Regent was roundly mocked in democratic circles, but rarely regarded as a tyrant before Peterloo.[39]

Peterloo and beyond

The Prince Regent's public exoneration of the Manchester magistrates and yeomanry for the massacre of Peterloo revitalised popular anger at his apparent indifference to distress. 'The Prince is a fool with his Wonderful letters of thanks', announced Robert Wedderburn during a debate at Hopkins Street, 'What is the Prince Regent or the King to us, we want no King – he is no use to us – and I say openly I am a Republican.'[40] Wedderburn was not the only republican to hail the Prince's words as a monarchic death-rattle. As Carlile rhetorically asked in an open 'Letter to the Prince Regent',

> How shall the future impartial historian record, with the necessary effect, that a Prince of the House of Brunswick, whose ancestors ascended the throne on the condition of keeping it only by their good behaviour ... that the Regent of Great Britain has publicly sanctioned the slaughter of several hundred of his unoffending subjects, and has not taken one step to satisfy himself of the facts of the case ... Will he not enclose the page with a black border, which records the sanction of an English Prince to such a bloody deed?

Unless the Prince called his ministers to account and relieved his people, he would surely be deposed and 'make them all REPUBLICANS', despite all 'adherence to ancient and established institutions'.[41] Although the radical critique of monarchy adopted a more overtly republican tone after Peterloo, much rhetoric remained steeped in the constitutional tradition. However much he might follow Paine in rejecting precedent, Carlile still argued the demise of monarchy in terms of its failure to observe the duties imposed upon it by Magna Carta and the Bill of Rights. The Regent's rejection of every public call for an inquiry into the massacre was a violation of his father's coronation oath to uphold constitutional liberties, and that meant he had 'forfeited his title to the Crown'. It was a 'declaration of war' akin to the crimes of Charles I and a clear signal of his preference for the army over the people. As ever, the people should send him one final remonstrance, and if it produced no change of heart, the 'rising spirit of freedom and emancipation' would guide their arm.[42]

William Sherwin, who had tried and then rejected the title 'Republican' for his journal in 1817, handed editorship to Carlile after Peterloo and the original title was suddenly restored with more confidence. As James Epstein has noted, 'such an explicit commitment to Paineite republicanism was no longer a barrier to huge sales', and Carlile's *Republican* continued for the next seven years.[43] Epstein is undoubtedly right in his assessment of growing republican fortunes after Peterloo, but we must keep them in perspective. Carlile's preference for reasoned essay writing over the emotional theatre of the mass platform has left us with an abundance of republican literature, but the depth of its political and cultural purchase is far from certain. Platform radicalism largely retained its faith in constitutional precedent, and the rational republican rejection of Christianity as a superstition no less illogical than monarchy, was almost a guarantee of marginalism.

As we saw in the 1790s, however, sympathy for Paineite rationalism did not always presuppose fully fledged enthusiasm for republican deism. While *Rights of Man* and *The Age of Reason* remained among the most influential and widely disseminated radical texts of the post-war revival, radical readers were sophisticated enough to draw without obligation from their pages general encouragement for a polity based on reason and objectivity. In this way, Paine's lasting legacy to British radicalism lay in his rational approach to political debate and inquiry, for this served in turn to legitimise the radical critique of privilege and monarchy without always necessitating wholesale denial. Such flexibility resulted, for example, in the alignment of Carlile's *Republican* with the cause of Queen Caroline in 1820, signalling a triumph of opportunism over rational disinterest. Ultra-radical hostility to the Regent would continue to plumb the depths of personal insult in preference to rational republican argument, and leading figures in the movement continued their rhetorical ambivalence. Thistlewood, for example, found it necessary to remind a crowd of physical-force men in September that it was because 'nothing would do with the P[rince] R[egent]' that 'we must fight for it'. Thomas Preston thought the whole Royal Family had been 'as much insulted as the people' by Sidmouth's administration, and the elder Watson even suggested having a banner embroidered with the slogan 'The Prince and the People against the Borough Mongers'.[44]

The Government was certainly more concerned than usual about the Regent's personal safety. The reassembling of Parliament in November prompted Lord Kenyon to press Sidmouth for a security review, since it was clear that the popular movement was once again keenly anticipating the speech from the throne, and the signalling of more repressive legislation might provoke fresh outrages. There must be 'no magpies in the trees, nor mischievous folks at the Gateways nor in the park to molest HRH', warned Kenyon, and 'no notification should be given to anyone but Cabinet of the contents of the Speech till it has been delivered'. But the procession was remarkably trouble-free.[45] The 'discovery' of the Cato Street conspiracy and the consequential break up of the Thistlewood circle early in 1820 coincided with the death of George III and the elevation of Prince to King. Security concerns were therefore now directed at the coronation and ministers seemed reluctant to publish a timetable. Some provincial authorities remained uncertain of the programme until late spring, and became correspondingly anxious about the public reception of their own civic celebrations. The borough reeve of Manchester was pleasantly surprised by the 'loyal enthusiasm' displayed at the procession by most of the town's lower orders, although the yeomanry were booed and hissed. Local magistrates were relieved to witness 'scarcely a single expression of disapprobation' at Wolverhampton, while at Halifax the mayor 'certainly did see some sulky countenances. A few infamous sentences chalked on the walls had led me to apprehend some insolence but this did not occur. I believe the disaffected were mostly absent.'[46]

Large crowds flocked around the gates of Carlton House to watch dignitaries arriving for the new King's first levee in May, but 'constables and military were on the spot and arrayed so as effectually to preserve good order, and no accident occurred'.[47] By the summer Sidmouth had become concerned about the new King's fondness for spending time at the poorly guarded 'cottage' in Windsor Forest, and temporarily persuaded him to stop using it. When the King wanted to move back in September, Sidmouth had to persuade his chief equerry Sir Benjamin Bloomfield to prevent it as his reasons for fearing an attack on the building were 'in full and augmented force'. He had lately received information from two independent sources of a radical plot to assassinate the King, but details were not disclosed. Bloomfield successfully kept the King away from the cottage, but so alarmed his monarch in doing so that Sidmouth was obliged to send him almost daily reports on the disposition of the masses. He did his best to allay the King's fears, but none of the reports was particularly encouraging.[48]

As the desperation of George and his ministers to prevent Caroline of Brunswick from attending the coronation as 'queen' reached its climax over the winter of 1820–21, the monarchy's public profile continued to decline. Sidmouth was apprehensive of disturbances at the coronation ceremony in the summer of 1821. If it was not enough that George's estranged wife threatened to demand entry to Westminster Abbey, he had received a sequence of anonymous threats and warnings of a projected outrage during the ceremony. Some mentioned suspects by name, and at least four contained specific information that the platform and canopy were to be incendiarised as the King sat on his throne, whether by a conventional fire, a gunpowder explosion or an 'infernal machine'. Interestingly, a small fire was indeed discovered among the rafters of Westminster Abbey on the morning of the coronation and extinguished just five minutes before the King made his entrance, but fire officers insisted it had been accidental. During the ceremony, an unknown man was briefly apprehended for levelling a pistol at the King from one of the spectators' boxes; but he was released by attendants when the gun was found to be empty.[49] With 1,000 regular and special constables on duty along the processional route, no further serious incident occurred during the day, but crowds gathered outside the houses of loyal illuminators that night and a number of windows were broken.[50]

Noting the near-death of the constitutional idiom beneath the hooves of the Peterloo yeomanry, Dror Wahrman has drawn attention to its reinvigoration by both sides in the war of words over Queen Caroline.[51] However, while it may be true that the Caroline affair played an important role in stemming the tide of violent insurrectionary rhetoric among frustrated and disillusioned radicals, it should also be understood that in confirming the subservience of royalty to 'public opinion' the affair damaged irrevocably the link between a monarchical Constitution and the concept of national sovereignty. The constitutionalism that emerged in the decade culminating in the 1832 Reform Act was a good deal less credulous in its appraisal of (and symbolic dependence upon) monarchy. George IV remained deeply unpopular and distant from his subjects for the entirety of his reign, 'hermetically sealed [from] all but the favoured few'.

Nineteenth-century historians were unforgiving, particularly during the liberal republican 1870s. In his *Private Life of a King* (1875), John Banvard pictured George 'enshrined within the precincts of his palatial cottage', taking 'little or no interest in the public or political affairs of the nation', and hiding from his people. He could not take a ride without 'casting his eyes into every brake or thicket to ascertain if some prying, inquisitive intruder, some peeping Tom, had not there concealed himself'. It was as though he 'expected to see an assassin in every bush, or some seventh bullet, winged with death, shot from some deep recess in revenge for his misdoings'. The King's seclusion, argued Banvard, was 'decidedly anti-national, so openly at variance with what the English people have a right to expect from their sovereign'. His embittered subjects would learn of every excursion he took to the park or Virginia Water through announcements in the *Court Journal*, and lie in wait to salute him with 'hissings, shoutings, groans and missiles'. Why? Because they 'knew nothing of their sovereign with the exception that he was still in existence'.[52]

It was not entirely a matter of George's paranoia about assassination, however, for he was also acutely embarrassed by his unprepossessing and un-kingly appearance. He plastered his face in grease-paint to hide the blemishes, but was almost crippled with gout by 1824 and had difficulty speaking clearly through his uncomfortable false teeth. It pained him to be seen even by servants of the Royal Household, and they were forbidden to stare at him on pain of dismissal. In November 1826 he announced his intention to open Parliament in person and to read the speech from the throne for the first time in two years, but his performance was thought lacklustre and reluctant. Public access and contractual interaction were not invited. Nevertheless, the event drew the largest London crowd since the coronation, according to the Tory press, 'nor was more loyal ardour ever manifested'. *The Times* was less impressed. The heavily guarded processional route may have been lined with the enthusiastic wavings of women's handkerchiefs, but the man himself looked a poor example of kingship. 'If in the face there was an increase of size anywhere, it was not, we regret to say, that sort of growth which denotes firm health', and he seemed to have great difficulty reading the speech. 'Twice he hesitated; as often he repeated the opening phrase of a sentence; and one or two words he hurried over, as if some transient pain or uneasiness were affecting him.'[53]

Public expectations of George IV, either collective or private, were therefore severely limited and not even the closing years of the popular campaign for the Reform Act involved the sort of demands made during his Regency in 1817. One of the consequences of George IV's withdrawal from the public sphere in London, where his public appearances throughout the 1820s were restricted to the occasional opening and closing of Parliament, was a marked decline in any evidence of popular bids for proximity. Peterloo was certainly something of a watershed in the narrative of popular constitutionalism, but the damage it did to the reinvention of 'open' and accessible monarchy under George III was not entirely repaired by the 'triumph' of public opinion in 1821. The constitutionalism that survived Peterloo was more republican and rational than it had ever been – an environment in which neither Margaret Nicholson nor Neil Maclean would have felt at home.

Notes

1 E. Halevy, *England in 1815* (London, 1924), p. 8.
2 PRO, HO 44/3: W. Mainwaring to Sidmouth, 9 November 1820.
3 PRO, HO 42/123: J. Keate to John Beckett, 13 May 1812; John Beckett to J. Keate, 14 May 1812.
4 PRO, HO 42/123: Arthur Graham to John Beckett, with enclosures, 12 May 1812.
5 PRO, HO 42/123: Anonymous correspondence dated 16, 17, 28 and 30 May 1812; Peter Augustus Lefargue to R. Ryder, 11 June 1812; Thomas Jones to the Prince Regent, 7 June 1812.
6 PRO, HO 42/123: Anonymous note, n.d. (May 1812); Note signed 'An Enemy to all Usurpers', n.d. (May 1812); Major General Turner to John Beckett, with enclosures, 13 May 1812; Anon. to Colonel McMahon, 22 May 1812; Anon. to Prince of Wales (n.d.); Devon County Record Office, Addington Papers, 152M/c1812/OH13: Lt Col. Laney to Lord Rolle, 25 August 1812.
7 PRO, HO 42/123: John Harrison MD to the Prince Regent, 21 and 25 May 1812.
8 *The Times*, 4 May 1813; P. Pindar, *Royal Disaster, or Dangers of a Queen; A Tale for the Quidnuncs* (London, 1813).

9 Lord Grey, punning on Matthew 7:9, and cited in *Hone's Reformists' Register*, 1 February 1817.
10 *Examiner*, 2 February 1817.
11 *The Times*, 29 and 30 January, 3 February 1817; *Examiner*, 2 February 1817.
12 Charlotte appears to have been aware only of the Nicholson and Hadfield episodes. She was, of course, never informed about Metcalf's penknife. Queen Charlotte to the Prince Regent, 29 January 1817, reprinted in A. Aspinall (ed.), *Letters of King George IV*. vol. 2: *1815–1823* (Cambridge, 1938), p. 185; Royal Archive, Windsor Castle, RA GEO Add 11/276: Princess Elizabeth to the Prince Regent, 30 January 1817. See also RA GEO Add 9/190: Queen Charlotte to Augustus, Duke of Sussex, 29 January 1817.
13 PRO, HO 42/159: Captain Fairman to Sir Henry Toren, 3 February 1817.
14 *The Times*, 30 January 1817.
15 *Ibid., 3 February 1817.*
16 *Ibid.*, 6 February 1817; Devon County Record Office, Addington Papers, 152M/c1817/OH23–5: Rodney Chambers to Lord Sidmouth, 8 and 14 February 1817, and reply, 18 March 1817.
17 *The Times*, 30 January 1817; *Examiner*, 2 February 1817.
18 Samuel Bamford, *Passages in the Life of a Radical* ([1884] Oxford, 1984), pp. 30–2; PRO, HO 42/158: Information of Peter Campbell and Samuel Fleming, 28 January 1817; E. Ethelston to Sidmouth, 1 February 1817.
19 PRO, HO 44/3: Depositions of John Cheatham, William Painter and Richard Leigh (n.d.).
20 *Address of W. D. Evans, Esquire, at the New Bayley Court House, Salford, on Discharging the Prisoners who were Apprehended on Account of an Illegal Assembly at Manchester on the 10th of March, 1817* (Manchester, 1817).
21 See, for example, the proposed case against the Spencean James Watson for disrespectfully petitioning the Regent in 1819: Devon County Record Office, Addington Papers, 152M/c1819/OH120: Robert Gifford to Lord Sidmouth, November 1819.
22 *Examiner*, 9 and 16 February 1817; *Black Dwarf*, 5 February 1817. For a thorough examination of Hunt's constitutional language and attitude to monarchy, see P. Harling, 'Leigh Hunt's *Examiner* and the language of patriotism', *English Historical Review*, 444 (1996), 1159–81.
23 *Black Dwarf*, 5, 19 and 26 February 1817.
24 *Examiner*, 9 February 1817.
25 W. Hone, *The Bullet Te Deum; with the Canticle of the Stone* (London, 1817).
26 *Champion*, 2 February 1817.
27 *Examiner*, 2 February 1817.
28 Bamford, *Passages*, p. 13; J. Fulcher, 'The English people and their Constitution after Waterloo: parliamentary reform, 1815–1817', in J. Vernon (ed.), *Re-Reading the Constitution: New Narratives in the Political History of England's Long Nineteenth Century* (Cambridge, 1996), pp. 54–9.
29 Worrall, *Radical Culture*, pp. 98–103; *Memoirs of Henry Hunt*, vol. 3, pp. 332–42.
30 *Political Register*, 16 August 1817; Bamford, *Passages*, p. 22. See also *Memoirs of Henry Hunt*, vol. 3, pp. 411–29, and Belchem, *'Orator' Hunt*, pp. 67–8.
31 *Political Register*, 12 July 1817.
32 *Memoirs of Henry Hunt*, vol. 3, pp. 431–4.

33 *Black Dwarf*, 12 February and 17 March 1817.

34 Epstein, *Radical Expression*, ch. 2: 'Narrating liberty's defence: T. J. Wooler and the law' (pp. 29–69).

35 *Sherwin's Political Register*, 7 June 1817.

36 *Ibid.*, 7 and 28 June, 12 July, 2 and 23 August 1817.

37 A. W. Armstrong, *The Particulars of the Arrest and Examination of A. W. Armstrong on a charge of High Treason on June 13 1818 for Threatening the Life of the Prince Regent* (London, 1818).

38 Physical plots against the cabinet rather than the king had been uncovered before 1820, however, at least in the imagination of government strategists and the loyalist press. The United Irish emissary Thomas Doyle was connected with an alleged conspiracy to assassinate Prime Minister Pitt and key members of his Cabinet in February 1800. According to William Wickham's information, the plotters' intention was to divert the Government from sending a force to Ireland for the repulse of a French invasion. See correspondence between Wickham and Pitt, Hampshire Record Office, Wickham Papers 38M49/1/38, especially folio 7, an undated note in Wickham's hand.

39 See for example the apparently off-the-cuff remarks against the Regent by both Thistlewood and his wife during the autumn of 1817, quoted in Worrall, *Radical Culture* (p. 124). For attitudes in free and easies see McCalman, *Radical Underworld* (pp. 116–27).

40 Worrall, *Radical Culture*, p. 138.

41 *Republican*, 3 September 1819.

42 *Ibid.*, 24 September 1819.

43 Epstein, *Radical Expression*, pp. 102–5.

44 *Ibid.*, pp. 110–20; Worrall, *Radical Culture*, pp. 143, 170. Thomas Brunt, who was anxious to establish that he had never been a traitor to his King, addressed the jury in a very similar vein after he had been sentenced to death for his part in the Cato Street conspiracy (*Ibid.*, p. 198).

45 Devon County Record Office, 152M/c1819/OH118: Addington Papers, Lord Kenyon to Lord Sidmouth, 17 November 1819. The centrality of intelligence about the Regent's speech to Spencean plans for an armed rising in a number of provincial centres is confirmed in I. Protheroe, *Artisans and Politics in Early Nineteenth-century London: John Gast and his Times* (London, 1979), p. 125.

46 PRO, HO 52/1: Rev. R. H. Whitlock to Francis Feeling, 5 February 1820; Mayor of Halifax to Henry Hobhouse, 6 February 1820; Thomas Sharp to Lord Sidmouth, 7 February 1820; J. Haden to Lord Sidmouth, 10 February 1820.

47 *Sunday Monitor*, 21 May 1820.

48 Devon County Record Office, Addington Papers, 152M/c1820/OH80–8, Marquis of Salisbury to Lord Sidmouth, 12 September 1820, and reply of 16 September 1820; Lord Sidmouth to Sir Benjamin Bloomfield, 19 September 1820; Lord Sidmouth to George IV, 21, 22, 25, 26 and 28 September 1820. At about this time Sidmouth received at least two anonymous notes threatening the life of the new King and disruption to the coronation. See 152M/c1820/76: Undated letter from 'the Ghost of Arthur Thistlewood'; and 152M/c1820/77: Undated letter offering 'to cut off the head of the King and to carry the same array as my fee on the approaching coronation', and 'signed' with a gallows and an axe. An earlier threat against the Regent's life had arrived with a Liverpool postmark in March.

See PRO, HO 52/1: Mayor of Liverpool to Lord Sidmouth, 2 March 1820. See also a letter of 6 June threatening the assassination of Sidmouth, Castlereagh and the King, reproduced in Worrall, *Radical Culture* (p. 200). A further spate of anonymous death threats received over the summer of 1820 is to be found in PRO, HO 44/2 and 44/3.

49 PRO, HO 44/8: for information about incendiarism see J. Showering to Sidmouth, 13 July 1821; A lady to Lord Gwydir, 14 July 1821; A true Englishman to Sidmouth, 16 July 1821, and Veritas to Sidmouth 16 July 1821. For the detected fire, see S. E. Lewis to Sidmouth, 31 July 1821, and for the incident with the pistol, see Robert Baker to Sidmouth, 23 July 1821.

50 PRO, HO 44/8: 'Stations of officers for the 19th' (undated memorandum). For window breaking, see J. Smith to Sidmouth, 20 July 1821.

51 D. Wahrman, 'Public opinion, violence and the limits of constitutional politics', in Vernon, *Re-Reading the Constitution*, pp. 83–123.

52 J. Banvard, *The Private Life of a King, embodying the Suppressed Memoirs of the Prince of Wales, afterwards George IV of England* (New York, 1875), pp. 610, 638–45. The King's modern apologists never forget to remind us of his 'exquisite taste and connoirsseurship in the arts': see e.g. D. Williamson, 'Why the monarchy will survive', in Smith and Moore, *The Monarchy*, p. 276.

53 C. Hibbert, *George IV, Regent and King, 1811–1830* (London, 1973), vol. 2, pp. 261; 279–81; *John Bull*, 26 November 1826; *Morning Post*, 22 November 1826; *The Times*, 22 November 1826.

8

Collins in context: William IV, affability and the reform crisis, 1830–37

At Royal Ascot, in the summer of 1832, a one-legged old sailor named Dennis Collins made one of the most dramatic assaults ever recorded on a British monarch. Flinging a stone with such force and accuracy at the head of William IV that the King was knocked from his chair by the impact, Collins inflicted more personal injury on a British monarch than any troublesome subject before or since. However, little public fuss was made of the outrage then and it is barely remembered today. Collins's grievance was a personal one, but two important contextual factors deserve consideration if we are to understand public indifference: William's 'citizenship' and his 'patriotism'. Both were regarded as deeply flawed.

Affability and the citizen King

The coincidence of the French Revolution of 1830 with the death of George IV was a happy one for the public image of the British monarchy. Just as Louis Phillipe assumed the role of France's first 'bourgeois' monarch, trailing promises of meritocracy, stability and reform, middle-class public opinion in Britain was entertaining great expectations of William IV. The unlamented George IV died while a renewed agitation for a reform of Parliament was building to a climax. Grey's Whig opposition was not slow to attach itself to the new King's coat-tails, and William soon found himself represented as the new broom of reform, the patriot King, independent of government, who would revive the Constitution, rehabilitate the Whigs and sweep away every last vestige of Old Corruption. Modern European monarchies, it was often said, should be marked by their rejection of aristocratic pomposity, grace and 'courtliness'. In liberal European states, monarchs were increasingly prone to social mixing in plain clothes to 'learn what people thought of them and how they should act'. Even the King of Denmark, remarked the *Court Journal*, forced by the institutional nature of his country to be a 'despot', was able to expose his true nature as 'the mildest and most benevolent of men'.[1] William IV's own patriotism was evident from his naval associations as the Duke of Clarence, and his matter-of-fact air persuaded many that he was both serious and approachable. The right of petitioning a solicitous throne, which had declined under George IV, could now be reasserted. In fact, William's personal support for reform was ambiguous to say the least, but his public standing benefited enormously from the belief that he was determined to push it through.[2] While the reform question dominated the summer election of 1830, and as a radical initiative to send mass reform petitions to the throne gathered strength, the political role of monarchy once again occupied the imagination of the press.

Although many radical papers expressed guarded approval for the concept of a citizen King, signs of enthusiasm for William IV are difficult to find in their pages. George IV had done such violence to the public appetite for monarchism that popular displays of unbridled joy at the prospect of his brother's succession were unlikely. The coronation ceremony in the summer of 1831 was regarded by some as a pompous waste of public money 'while one man in the country – or in the whole world – needs a pennyworth of bread'. As the *Poor Man's Guardian* reminded the nation, 'Mr William Guelph' was a mere man, yet crowds were prepared to attend the irrational and costly spectacle of the coronation 'as if the mere knowledge of a King's vicinity was a blessing'.[3] In fact the King himself seemed scarcely more comfortable with the extravagant ceremonial, and he was at some pains to express his own impatience with the 'idle and unnecessary' extravagance of the occasion. He even pledged his first Privy Council to 'devise every means of curtailing useless expense and unnecessary parade', though the radical critique was not sustained by questions of cost alone. John Wade's *Black Book* found the ceremonial form of the coronation irrational and antiquated, redolent with superstition and priestcraft, and without constitutional meaning. The ease with which recent Kings had dishonoured the coronation oath had stripped it of its former usefulness as a 'solemn compact between the King and his lieges' and made it a 'mere mockery of sacred things'.[4]

William's efforts to make himself acceptable to the cost-conscious populace were not dictated by French fashion alone. In Philip Ziegler's view, his casual air and studied informality were as much products of his brusque nautical upbringing and awkwardness in robes as they were dictated by political expedience. And they made an immediate impact. The King's relaxed and informal handshake at the levee led Hobhouse to observe that members of the Royal Family were 'like wealthy bourgeois', and William did his best to live up to this estimate, even suggesting that if his subjects wished to see him they should politely call on him in his house. He seemed to take no interest in security at all. Public access to the East Terrace at Windsor, strictly forbidden in the reign of George IV, was re-established and he advertised his intention to walk the streets in public and unguarded.[5] The radical press was not to be hoodwinked by the veneer of affability, however, and continued its assault on royal expenditure. The more ordinary that William IV appeared, the less justification there seemed to be for his lifestyle. The principal 'use' of a king, it was argued, was 'to use the money of his subjects' to build new 'King-hutches', but never to spend it on anything so useful as 'a Hospital, Refuge for the Destitute or an Institution for Free Discussion'. Kings were supposed to be the fathers of their people; 'they are so called, but they are very unlike fathers since, instead of feeding and protecting their children, their children feed and protect them'.[6]

Even loyalists had their doubts, for the cult of 'ordinariness' threatened the institution of monarchy with the taint of vulgarity. Royal policeman John Townsend thought the King's easy style undignified and inappropriate. It made him nostalgic for the personal distance of George IV. 'God rest him, he *was* a King; only two or three people could get at him; but this new King isn't half a King; he makes himself too cheap. Anybody may get at him.'[7] The satirical *Figaro* thought it ludicrous for kings to express affability by 'walking about in the public streets, shaking hands with the first man they meet, or sporting a cotton umbrella', and was gratified when William stopped doing it. Some of his subjects had apparently taken 'unpleasant advantages of his easy habits'. Mrs Arbuthnot, who thought the King showed himself too often in public, saw him cuddled and kissed by 'one of the common women' in St James's Street. She hoped he might 'soon go out of town and be quiet'.[8] It was not the over-enthusiasm of the people that forced William to abandon his high public profile by the summer of 1832, however, but their discontent. His weak command of the Government during the Reform Bill crisis made him anything but popular, and neither he nor the Queen went anywhere without guards after that.

Politics and the patriot King

Radical reformers busied themselves with petitions and addresses to the King throughout the summer of 1830. Henry Hunt declared that if reform was not granted this time and resistance therefore was 'made a duty', he would be joining the republicans. As chair of the Metropolitan Political Union, he called on Londoners to put pressure on the King to back reform in his first speech to Parliament and to prepare an appropriate response if Parliament rebuffed their overtures. Hunt took petitions to the throne from all over the country to the King's levee on 3 November. Carlile and John Gale Jones were meanwhile urging their supporters to attend the King's next scheduled public appearance, on Lord Mayor's Day, 9 November, and demand that he dismiss his obstructive Tory ministers. Fearing disorder, Wellington cancelled the procession. Unable, in the words of Francis Place, to 'pay their respects to the King', large crowds of radicals filled the streets of the city on 8 and 9 November, fought with police, paused ominously for ironic cheers around the statue of Charles I at Charing Cross and shattered Wellington's windows. A week later, the Duke's Tory administration fell and tension was temporarily dissipated by the formation of Grey's reform-minded Cabinet.[9]

Radical papers urged the King to take care of his new ministers. In 'frank, firm and decisive' language, the *Voice of the People* drafted a series of editorials 'To the King', instructing him in the duties of true patriotism and reminding him that Perceval's assassination had come about through the 'contemptuous negligence' and 'corruption of the State'.[10] But Grey's ministry was defeated by Tory obstructions to the Bill in April and another election called. The King was loudly cheered as he went to close what many now believed was the last ever unreformed Parliament. Since it was now expected that the election would favourably settle the passage of the Bill, radical emphasis turned upon the forcing of a universal suffragist amendment. Delegates were to be sent from every region to present 'loyal' addresses to the King and petitions to Parliament. If either Parliament or the King refused to listen, warned the *Voice*, 'the fault and the folly of their indifference will be upon themselves'. The mass presentation of addresses and petitions would 'show the powerful once and for all that the people are no longer to be trifled with and that they must submit themselves to their fate without risking the horrors of a sanguinary conflict'.[11]

As expected, the Whigs won a resounding victory in the summer election, but the ease with which ministers secured a majority for the re-introduced Bill in September found them in no mood to make concessions to universal suffragists; indeed they were confident enough to counter-attack the 'physical resistance' rhetoric of the more radical Unions by persuading the King to issue a royal proclamation against quasi-military arming and drilling. The temptation to do so had become more pressing in the wake of rioting in Nottingham, Derby and Bristol after the Lords' rejection of the Bill in October. Ministerial confidence was not improved by Carlile's simultaneous publication of Colonel Macerone's *Defensive Instructions For the People*, a detailed and comprehensive guide to effective street-fighting techniques, the Preface of which was most uncomplimentary about the behaviour of the 'Citizen King'.[12] Three hundred thousand Londoners had walked in procession to St James' Palace on 12 October to present addresses to the throne urging the King to prevent resistance in the Lords. 'Take away the wicked from before the King and the Throne shall be established in righteousness' pronounced a banner from the St Pancras Union. Hume told the crowd how 'graciously pleased' the King had been to accept their addresses and assured them William was 'on their side'.[13] Yet, by the end of the month, radicals were cajoling the King for spinelessly abandoning his duty to the people and letting his ministers, or his court or his ultra-Tory wife dictate his every move. If the constitutional impasse created by the stubbornness of the Lords was to be overcome, patriotic action would be required of the King. Few radicals considered him up to it. Hunt proposed testing the King's 'patriotism' by waiting on him with petitions for clemency for the condemned Bristol rioters, but no pardons were forthcoming.[14] Then, when the King processed in state to re-open Parliament in December, there were 'very few cheers besides those of a few of his own trades folk and of his own dirty troop of policemen, who formed at least three parts of the crowd'. He looked ridiculous, thought the *Poor Man's Guardian*, absurdly dressed and unintelligent.[15]

The King's wavering over Cabinet demands for the creation of sufficient new peers to force a new Reform Bill through the Lords drew plenty of criticism. He had given Grey his word on the measure in January 1832, but when prevarications in the Lords once more threatened the Bill in May, he suddenly refused to comply, ironically quoting Bolingbroke's *Patriot King* at Grey and forcing the ministry's resignation. In so doing, he plunged the whole country into crisis and did his own public standing irreparable harm. As the extra-parliamentary reform movement swiftly mobilised 'ulterior measures' to prevent Wellington's return to power, radicals accused William of 'forsaking' his own ministers and submitting to the Germanic 'petticoat government' of Queen Adelaide. Their suspicion that Adelaide was behind William's change of heart had been considerably enforced in February when the Queen publicly encouraged the Anglican Lords Spiritual to persevere in their efforts to defend Church and State – a thinly veiled announcement of solidarity with the *ancien régime*. The King's stout defence of his wife's innocence did nothing to improve his public image.[16] Lord Egremont actually thought the King's selfless devotion to his protesting Queen, as well as having to listen to the objections of other members of the Royal family, would ultimately earn him a mental breakdown. 'They are killing him', warned Egremont, 'they will worry him to death in less than two years.'[17] There was little sympathy elsewhere. Fully expecting armed clashes in the streets, the *Cosmopolite* believed 'the King has evidently joined the Lords against the People ... He has made his choice and the People have now to make theirs.' Reformers would surely win the day, however, because 'the People are stronger than the Court'; a point frequently reinforced in radical journals by reference to the exiled Charles X of France who had fled with his own court to Holyrood House. Queen Adelaide even suggested it might be better for William to join him there than to sanction the Reform Bill.[18]

When Wellington advised William IV to recall Grey rather than risk serious civil disorder in the capital, the King was not cheered as the saviour of reform, but was hissed and hooted for entertaining Wellington at all. Twenty lancers protected the royal carriage as William and Adelaide made their way from Windsor to St James's Palace to meet the Duke. They went by back roads, rather than the usual processional route, to minimise crowd interference. At Brentford 'the people who had assembled in great numbers began to groan, hiss and make the most tremendous noises that can be imagined'. Insults and mud were hurled at the windows throughout the journey into London, and when the coach finally swung into St James's Park 'the mob saluted their majesties with yells and execrations of every description'. William's only comfort was that when Wellington arrived, 'if possible, the people treated him worse'. The more the monarchy took refuge in theatricality, the less reason there seemed to be for outrage at its adverse reception. 'We believe that a person has as much right to hoot royalty as to applaud it', reasoned the *Figaro*, 'and as their majesties were wont to court the huzzas of the people as a luxury, a good stout yell may now be prescribed by way of an antidote'. The King was not yet ready to give way, however. He tried without success to persuade Grey to dilute the Bill in exchange for his support in packing the House of Lords and, if Francis Place is to be believed, even considered the Queen's suggestion that he flee to Hanover, gather an ultra-army about him and return to fight for the old order.[19]

Physical demonstrations against the Duke of Wellington continued sporadically for the next four weeks. In fact, on the day before William IV was assaulted by Dennis Collins, Wellington was ambushed by a hostile crowd, first on Tower Hill and then again at Holborn. He was pelted with dirt and stones, and almost unsaddled, before police moved in to break up the crowd.[20] By 18 May Grey's ministry had been recalled by the King and the creation of 50 or 60 new peers agreed. On 4 June the Bill finally passed through the Lords and three days later received the Royal Assent, but the King continued under fire throughout. The *Satirist* thought his recalling of Grey and reluctant acceptance of the demand for new peers the clearest indications of a weak-minded and indecisive monarch. Meanwhile, *The Times* and the *Morning Chronicle* criticised the King for allowing the Assent to be granted by commission rather than make a popular and symbolic gesture in person. In fact, William was simply not prepared to pander any longer to the wishes of a public who had become so insulting to both himself and his Queen. 'Was he to cringe and bow?' asked Sir Herbert Taylor; 'was he to kiss the rod held out *in terrorem* by the mob?'[21]

In many respects, the King's performance throughout the Reform Bill saga had been a public relations disaster and an object lesson in bad kingship. Thanks to the actions of the King, wrote Place, 'absurd loyalty has now been destroyed and can never again exist. The demonstrations made by the King ... [have] compelled the people to progress towards entertaining republican opinions to an extent which no one had anticipated'.[22] Yet, despite the jeering and sullen silences he was repaid with by his unadmiring subjects, the most extreme expressions of public vitriol were reserved for Wellington and the Tory Party. William's failure should still therefore be seen within the customary context of a well-intentioned king, undone by the venality of Parliament and an autocratic foreign wife. As Annabel Patterson has recently emphasised, the publication in the midst of the critical days of May of 'Lady Anne Hamilton's *Secret History of the Court of England* was aimed entirely at marketing this idea. The book detailed Tory machinations in the Court since 1760 and promoted the Bill as the only antidote.[23] Kings were never a lost cause but their symbolic 'deafness' and erring judgement were perpetual irritations. This is also the context, then, in which we must try to understand events at Ascot races on 19 June. Dennis Collins was no conscious advocate of reform; indeed he is usually dismissed almost humorously as an eccentric one-legged sailor with no genuine grounds for complaint. His case might equally be read, however, as a demonstration of the stubborn continuation of popular contract theory in the nineteenth century, marked by a direct line of descent through Hadfield and Frith to Margaret Nicholson nearly half a century earlier.

The case of Dennis Collins, 1832

When Mrs. Margaret Nicholson
Assaulted George the Third,
That Monarch had a very near escape, upon my word.
Again, by one John Hadfield,
He perished very nearly,
Who criticised both plays and Kings,
Acutely, but severely,
He shot at George and missed him
From the middle of the pit;
But Dennis, he made King William
Sing out 'Oh! Lord, I'm hit!'
St. Dennis is for England now that us'd to be for France,
Sing, 'Honi soit qui mal y pense'.[24]

After a long naval career during which he lost a leg in action against the French, Dennis Collins retired from service in 1830 and was admitted to Greenwich Hospital on an invalidity pension worth £14 per year. For alleged insolence to four superior officers in December 1831, however, he was locked up for a week, stripped of his pension and expelled. With no other means of supporting himself, Collins soon fell into extreme poverty, hobbling about the streets of London on a wooden leg 'of the most rude construction', a 'wretched' and 'tattered mendicant' in his battered sailor's uniform.[25]

Convinced that the Lords of the Admiralty had acted illegally in depriving him of his livelihood for such a minor offence, he petitioned them unsuccessfully for restoration and was then jailed for a fortnight under the vagrancy laws for persistent begging. On his release, in April 1832, he petitioned the King for justice but, instead of the reply from William IV he had expected, received only another refusal of help from the Admiralty and a dismissive letter from the Secretary of State. In June he appealed personally to Admiral Rowley, but 'he swore at me and kicked me'. Finally, after going three days without food, he confronted the King in person at the Ascot races. As a former sailor himself, the King would surely intercede on his behalf. If the King was offended by the imposition, Collins later explained, it scarcely mattered because '[I] might as well be shot or hanged as remain in such a state'. Arriving at Ascot with all his case papers, Collins appeared 'perfectly collected and rational', in the *Morning Chronicle*'s opinion. He had stopped for some beer before entering the raceground, but was not drunk.[26]

Given the state of popular feeling over the King's role in the reform crisis, the royal party did not attend Ascot unprotected. Besides the usual complement of county magistrates and constables, Bow Street's chief magistrate lodged Townsend, Sayers and several others along with a detachment from the Horse patrol in the royal stand. It was a larger force than was customary, and Cobbett thought it a telling indication of William's unpopularity. By the time Collins arrived at Ascot, William IV had already spent a day there under siege from petitioners. He had behaved very properly to them according to the *Court Journal*, receiving their petitions with good grace and earning applause for it from spectators. 'The shouts of the populace were renewed on the departure of their majesties and, indeed, many times in the course of the day in consequence of various acts of beneficence performed by the King towards the petitioners by whom he was assailed.' His accessibility to petitioners was the 'connecting lustre between the people of Great Britain and its Prince', boasted the paper, for it promoted contact 'without any chance of public degradation' and permitted the King to 'judge the true temper of the nation with regard to his government and its measures'.[27]

If this were true, then Dennis Collins must have given the King pause for thought. Walking out onto the ground directly in front of the Royal Stand, he faced his monarch and at once threw a large flint at him. The stone hit William squarely on the front of his head and knocked him backwards, but he was saved from serious injury by the thick brim of his hat. 'My God! I am hit!' he exclaimed before recovering his self-composure and declaring himself unhurt. Before he could be restrained by the police, Collins threw a second stone which thudded into the window frame but missed its target. He was 'passive' as he was manhandled away. A crowd quickly gathered in front of the royal stand to peer at the King and cheered when they saw he was unharmed, leading Lord Holland to believe the outrage would do for William's popularity what Nicholson and Hadfield had done for George III's, however much people had been 'estranged from the King by his late conduct'.

Such optimism was blunted somewhat by reports of the sullen crowds who attended the heavily guarded King at a military review in Hyde Park a few days later. The King and Queen were received with a'profound silence' as they arrived and with 'the most discordant yells' as they left. In August, the respectable radicals of the National Political Union rejected Joseph Hume's call for a toast to the King's health at a reform banquet and substituted 'the sovereignty of the people' instead. *God Save the King* was supplanted by *Rule Britannia*. While the radicals of the 1790s had often retained their respect for George III despite the obstructive behaviour of his ministers, William was never fully forgiven for the May Days.[28]

The law officers, meanwhile, were deliberating the best course of action to take against Collins. 'It is difficult to avoid trying him for High Treason', mused Holland, but 'equally difficult to convict him thereof.' The first question to be settled was Collins's mental condition. At his examination and in the press, the familiar doubts were aired. Like Hadfield before him, a scar from a war-wound was found on Collins's head, and hopes were entertained that Collins was mad. The *Court Journal*, convinced that Collins had been driven insane through 'habits of intemperance and vice', was pleased to disassociate him from political affairs. But Cobbett disagreed. 'Never was an act more deliberate in the whole world', he wrote. 'Here was premeditation, predetermination, everything proving that the malice was *prepense*; and all this proves to demonstration the absence of insanity.' The crime could therefore only be construed as high treason, wrote Cobbett, however uncomfortable ministers found it, but Collins's ill-treatment by the Admiralty would provide the King with a golden opportunity to exercise the mercy prerogative and restore his own public support. The same view was taken by the *Examiner*, which suggested that 'addresses of condolence' ought to be sent to poor Collins rather than the usual loyal addresses to the throne, for the King had suffered nothing more than a 'slight annoyance' from the episode. Collins 'threw a stone at the King because his Majesty had not answered his letter'. His petition for redress had been sent to 'one whom, he has rudely conceived, as a sailor and as a chief magistrate, he has a right to expect it from'. Given that he was ignored, 'can we be surprised at any misconduct subsequently committed by the miserable wretch?' The *Satirist* did not think Collins was mad either. Compared to Admiral Rowley, in fact, Collins was 'a hero', and although his action was 'most ill-judged' it was 'not wholly unaccountable'.[29]

In Parliament Peel did his best to connect Collins's outrageous behaviour with the prevailing 'excitement' for reform, and blamed Hume for speaking out in favour of physical resistance to tyranny. Although Whig MPs strove to deny Collins any political legitimacy, Peel's close friend the ultra-Tory John Croker accused reformers of fomenting the earlier attack on Wellington and the hissing of the King and Queen, and of creating an atmosphere in which unstable maniacs like Collins were almost bound to commit outrages. He 'believed the wretch was mad. At least, if it be mania to be one falsely reasoning from false premises, he was as mad as if he had just escaped from Bedlam.' Moreover, it was in the nature of maniacs 'to be excited by public excitement. There was no instance in which such persons were not excited and urged forward by some great degree of public commotion produced by agitation, by the press and by violent and gross attacks upon the King and Queen and other high personages of the realm.'[30] Public sympathy for the King was unlikely to be enhanced by bullish declarations of this sort from anti-reforming conservatives, and there is little evidence of public horror over the behaviour of Dennis Collins. When his trial for high treason opened on 22 August at the Berkshire assize, 'the interest ... was not great and appeared to be confined to the upper classes ... There was no crowd outside the court, or any appearance whatever, save that of a few javelin men, which indicated that an individual was on trial for his life, charged with the highest offence known to our law.'[31]

The Attorney General opened the prosecution case with assurances that the throwing of stones at the King was an overt act within the meaning of both the ancient treason laws and the newer 1795 and 1800 Acts. An accurate blow to the head might have killed the King if it had not been cushioned by his hat, but even if Collins had not intended to murder the King, his intention to wound was undeniable; and it was probable the King would have been maimed if the stone had struck him in the eye. There was no reason to believe Collins insane. The defence tried to draw comparisons between Collins and Hadfield. Collins did not appear to be mad; but he had 'laboured under an aberration of the mind' brought on by 'hunger and despair' when he threw the stone, and had been 'unable to control his own actions'. Throwing a stone at the King in broad daylight and in front of thousands of witnesses 'was the conduct of any but a sound mind'. The gambit failed. No effort was made by the defence to produce medical witnesses to testify the defendant's insanity, either then or at the time of the offence, and the prosecution drew attention to it. It was ridiculous, insisted the Attorney General, for the defence to pronounce Collins mad simply because his actions suggested he ought to be. If such a plea were admitted, 'it would afford a complete impunity to all highly criminal and absurd acts'. Moreover, both the defence and the prosecution hinted to jurors that it was unlikely the court would order Collins's execution if they found him guilty, but would probably sentence him to life imprisonment. After ten minutes' thought, they cleared him of any intention to kill the King, but found him guilty of an intention to cause him 'some bodily harm'. Mr Justice Bosanquet immediately donned his black cap. In sentencing Collins to be hanged, drawn and quartered, Bosanquet reminded him that mercy was not within the gift of the court but of the King, and it was to the Crown that he must now appeal if his life were to be spared.[32]

Members of the jury were clearly taken aback by this because half-an-hour after Collins had been removed from the dock, they drew up a mercy petition of their own on the prisoner's behalf and requested it be laid before the King. The foreman complained they had been given to understand Collins would not be sentenced to death, and announced that had they realised the truth 'they would have acquitted him altogether'.[33] They need not have worried. In mid-September, Collins was respited by the King. 'No man can better understand than William IV, the impulsive vagaries and eccentricities of a sailor', commented the *Globe*, with some sarcasm.[34] Instead of being eulogised for his humanitarianism, however, William was mocked by the press for bringing the treason laws into disrepute, for Collins's guilt had never been in dispute, and if the King had not wanted him to suffer for it he should not have permitted a treason trial to take place. 'Poor crazy Collins, wooden legged and lone/ Whose understanding was at least half-gone' meanwhile found himself celebrated in popular doggerel. In *Quarterless Collins*, for instance, written 'to register an act of Royal grace which is imperfectly understood', the poor homeless prisoner's avoidance of 'quartering' was punned upon at some length.[35]

Neither the passage of the Reform Act nor the first election under the widened franchise enabled William to fully recover his popularity. Once he had been persuaded to stop walking the streets like a bourgeois, the King does not appear to have been regularly bothered by individual subjects. John Monkhouse, a 'fanatic' of Marlow, had been turned away by the sentries at Windsor Castle when he tried to deliver to the King a 'message from God' during March 1831, and there is no evidence that he re-offended.[36] A writer of threatening letters, Michael Larragan, was taken more seriously in February

1833. Larragan had outstanding financial claims on the Government and told the King he would kill him if he was not paid soon. Traced to his home and removed to Bow Street for questioning, Larragan remained unapologetic and insistent on his right to 'vengeance'. After a more thorough examination by the Privy Council, he was committed to prison but does not appear to have been prosecuted.[37]

Many radicals seemed to regard the King as too weak-minded a man to be worth troubling any more with addresses. In May 1833, the Sheffield Political Union proposed submitting a 'humble prayer' to the King to dismiss his ministers and call a fresh election. P. T. Bready, a Carlilite, objected to its 'utter uselessness ... beset as he is with a pack of greedy place-hunting Whigs, and confident that a humble prayer would never reach his ear'. Since the King was so deficient in 'courage', argued Bready, the wording should be changed from 'humble prayer' to 'demand'. The motion was carried and the respectable committee of the Union, including the Corn Law 'Rhymer' Ebeneezer Elliot resigned the following week. As a result, the Union was wound up.[38] Petitions and addresses praying for further reform were 'fast getting out of fashion', noted Hetherington after a whole parliamentary session went by without a single universal suffrage petition being delivered to the Commons.[39]

Richard Carlile went to see the King open Parliament in 1833, 'to see and hear what the office of King was deemed worth among the people'. He found the crowd 'upright and silent ... it was observed by men who knew me not that the reception of the King was entirely an altered circumstance and that not a man was seen to hail him'. Silence, he thought, was 'just the thing for a King', for it showed the people to be politically conscious but polite enough not to hiss him. 'This is the truth ... No one cried, the King comes. No one shouted, God bless him. No one exhibited gladness. It was a dumb pantomimic show. I rejoiced.'[40] Hetherington thought the King 'indifferently received' at the same event in 1834, the heavily marshalled crowd looking on in 'sullen apathy'.[41] The people were not always entirely silent, however. Two journeymen tailors, Thomas Garrett and James Catchpole, were jailed in February 1835 for being prominent in a crowd that hissed and booed the King as he went to open parliament. 'There goes a damned villain', shouted Catchpole as the carriage rattled through New Palace Yard.[42]

Narratives of royal inaccessibility were rehearsed once again after the sentencing of the Tolpuddle labourers in 1834. Memorials requesting a pardon for the men were forwarded to the King by trades union and reformist organisations, although few expected a positive outcome. A memorial from Manchester was adopted, according to T. W. Parkin, simply 'to make his Majesty acquainted with the feelings of Manchester men on the subject and to let him know that such tyrannical and infernal conduct would not be tolerated by Britons'. But, like many other similar addresses, the Manchester memorial was blocked by the Secretary of State as 'too disrespectfully worded' to be laid before the King. Customary radical accusations of constitutional interference by designing and unpatriotic ministers were now refined by the newer languages of class. It was not the King or the aristocracy who were to blame for preventing the voice of the people from being heard; nor simply a cabal of corrupt ministers; it was the middle class. The oppression of labouring men, maintained Hetherington, was a functional interest of their employers. He was 'sickened at hearing people abuse Louis Phillipe and William Guelph as despots ... for who does not know that if [either] were to die tomorrow, their places would instantly be filled with another brace as bad, or perhaps worse?' Hetherington's view thus accommodated traditional arguments about the obstruction of popular dialogue with the Crown by including social class in its analysis. Effectively, such language implied a growing confluence of interest between the monarchy and the bourgeoisie: an idea certainly in keeping with European inventions of a citizen king, and one which emphasised only the concept's distance from working-class interests.[43]

Notes

1 *Figaro in London*, 11 February 1832.

2 The political identity of William IV is rarely agreed upon. David Starkey calls him 'a life-long Tory Ultra ... passionately opposed to the Great Reform Bill', and this was also the more contemporary view of Prince Albert's advisor Baron Stockmar. Yet, for Frank O'Gorman he was 'without much political passion. If anything, he had Whiggish tendencies'. The King's principal modern biographer Philip Ziegler finds him constitutionally dutorious but rather uninterested in politics. As Duke of Clarence he had aligned himself with the Whig opposition, but opposed the Foxite reformers and defended the slave trade: see D. Starkey, 'The modern monarchy: rituals of privacy and their subversion', in Smith and Moore (eds), *The Monarchy*, p. 249; E. Von Stockmar, *Memoirs of Baron Stockmar by his Son* (London 1872), vol. 1, pp. 326–7; F. O'Gorman, *The Long Eighteenth Century: British Political and Social History, 1688–1832* (London, 1997), p. 360; P. Ziegler, *King William IV* (London, 1971), pp. 90, 97. He was certainly uneasy about the Reform Bill. As Sir Herbert Taylor reminded Grey amid the agitation, the Duke of Sussex excepted, 'the members of the Royal family, male and female, are hostile to it' (*Ibid.*, p. 213).

3 *Poor Man's Guardian*, 23 July, 6 August and 10 September 1831.

4 *The Holland House Diaries, 1831–1840: The diary of Henry Richard Vassall Fox, third Lord Holland, with extracts from the diary of Dr. John Allen*, ed. A. D. Kriegel (London, 1977), pp. 3–4; J. Wade, *The Extraordinary Black Book: An Exposition of Abuses in Church and State* (London, 1832), p. 384.

5 Ziegler, *William IV*, pp. 150–5.

6 *Radical Reformer*, 12 January 1832; *Voice of the People*, 23 April 1831.

7 From reminiscences published shortly after Townsend's death, *Court Journal*, 28 July 1832.
8 J. Cannon and R. Griffiths (eds), *The Oxford Illustrated History of the British Monarchy* (Oxford, 1988), p. 548.
9 Belchem, *'Orator' Hunt*, pp. 209–13, 233–4; Prothero, *Artisans and Politics*, pp. 278–9; Clark, *English Society*, p. 411; Tilly, *Popular Contention*, pp. 286–7.
10 *Voice of the People*, 8 January 1831.
11 *Ibid.*, 14 May 1831.
12 F. Macerone, *Useful Knowledge for the People! Containing The New and Improved Combination of Arms called Foot Lancers; Miscellaneous Instructions on the Subject of Small Arms and Ammunition, Street and House Fighting etc. etc.* (London, 1831–32). The pamphlet was given even wider circulation when Hetherington reprinted it in the *Poor Man's Guardian*, 11 April 1832.
13 *Morning Chronicle*, 13 October 1831.
14 Belchem, *'Orator' Hunt*, p. 253.
15 *Poor Man's Guardian*, 10 December 1831.
16 Ziegler, *William IV*, pp. 210–11.
17 Kriegel, *Holland House diaries*, p. 15.
18 *Satirist*, 13 May 1832; *Cosmopolite* 12 and 15 May 1832; Ziegler, *William IV*, p. 213.
19 *The Times*, 14 May 1832; *Figaro in London*, 2 June 1832; Ziegler, *William IV*, p. 218.
20 *The Times*, 19 June 1832.
21 *Satirist*, 27 May and 10 June 1832. Taylor is quoted in Ziegler, *William IV*, p. 220.
22 BL Add. MS 27795, fols 26–9; Francis Place Papers, 'Narrative of Events, Sunday May 20th 1832'.
23 A. Patterson, 'Secret history: liberal politics and the 1832 Reform Bill', *Literature and History*, third series, 7:1 (1989), pp. 33–53. Hamilton was not the real author; Patterson suggests it was a group production by friends of Brougham. See Lady A. Hamilton, *Secret History of the Court of England from the Accession of George III to the Death of George IV* (London, 1832), vol. 1, pp. 43, 59, vol. 2, p. 233. Queen Adelaide was suffering 'almost daily insult from the populace' by the summer of 1832. For suggestions that the King and Queen were at loggerheads over the Bill, but that it was the Queen who wore the breeches, see *Figaro in London*, 2 June and 19 May 1832.
24 From a satirical poem, 'The Ballad of St. Dennis', printed in the *Examiner*, 2 September 1832.
25 *Morning Chronicle*, 20 June 1832.
26 *Ibid.*; *Cobbett's Political Register*, 23 and 30 June 1832.
27 *Cobbett's Political Register*, 23 June 1832. *Morning Chronicle*, 20 June 1832, protested that the police presence was no more than 'customary'. *Court Journal*, 23 June 1832.
28 *Morning Chronicle*, 20 June 1832; *The Times*, 27 June 1832. The King was protected on his way to and from Hyde Park by the Royal Horse Guards, two squadrons of Life Guards and a strong force of the Metropolitan Police. Kriegel, *Holland House Diaries*, p. 193; *Cobbett's Political Register*, 18 August 1832.
29 Kriegel, *Holland House diaries*, p. 195; *Court Journal*, 23 June 1832; *Cobbett's*

Political Register, 23 and 30 June 1832; *Examiner*, 24 June and 1 July 1832; *Satirist*, 1 July 1832.

30 *Cobbett's Political Register*, 23 June 1832; *Courier*, 21 and 25 June 1832.

31 *The Times*, 23 August 1832.

32 *Ibid.*; *Satirist*, 26 August 1832; *Examiner*, 26 August 1832.

33 *Examiner*, 26 August 1832.

34 Reprinted in *Figaro in London*, 15 September 1832. Collins was transported for life to Van Diemen's Land where he died two years later. See G. T. Crook (ed.), *The Complete Newgate Calendar* (London, 1926), vol. 5.

35 *Quarterless Collins, a Comic Poem* (London, 1833), by W. R. V.

36 *Voice of the People*, 2 April 1831.

37 *The Times*, 11 and 12 February 1833.

38 *Gauntlet*, 26 May 1833, 2 June 1833.

39 *Poor Man's Guardian*, 29 March 1834.

40 *Gauntlet*, 8 September 1833.

41 *Poor Man's Guardian*, 8 February 1834.

42 *Ibid.*, 7 March 1835; *The Times*, 26 February 1835.

43 *Poor Man's Guardian*, 5, 12, 19, 26 April, 10 May 1834.

9

Monarchy goes private: Peel's Protection Act and the retreat from approachability, 1837–50

As David Cannadine has rightly said, Queen Victoria and Prince Albert are the royal pair most regularly regarded as the epitome of modern monarchy. Historians have made them the principal architects of a revitalised and successful monarchy 'based on political impartiality and a happy family life'. This is a myth Cannadine has devoted a good deal of energy to 'exploding',[1] and it is a question of some relevance here. For, between 1837 and 1842, the embracing of modernity became a curiously backward-looking process as far as the development of the royal sphere is concerned. While the ceremonial orbit of the sovereign expanded, and as she became spectacularly accessible to ever-widening circles of ordinary people, tolerance of individual intrusions into royal space was forcibly contracted; and informal or individual petitioning was severely obstructed and criminalised. In effect, the monarchy's encounter with mid-nineteenth-century modernity led to the reinterpretation of contractualism as a requirement to be seen rather than spoken to and the formal replacement of interaction with non-participation.

Cannadine's reassessment acknowledges the pioneering work undertaken by Victoria and Albert in 'profoundly adjusting the whole relationship between the crown and the nation'; particularly in identifying themselves with the new bourgeoisie, and in going 'out among the people' in industrial and working-class areas.[2] Yet these appearances in public were meticulously managed to avoid personal contact while maximising exposure. The royal couple appeared most often, not as dimly recognised waving hands and nodding heads behind the foggy bullet-proof windows of an enclosed coach, but in a low, open landau. Yet, when the Queen's subjects tried to exploit such accessibility by dropping petitions into her carriage, they were forcibly rebuffed. Accessibility, argued many radicals, was thereby reduced to a meaningless spectacle, exposing 'the utter want of connection between the People and the Queen, so long as she is surrounded by a host of myrmidons who guard every avenue of approach with all the vigilance of Cerberus'.[3] The rigid rules of etiquette surrounding the Queen's rare and experimental appearances on foot among her people are tellingly illustrated in news reports of a 'walkabout' at the Great Exhibition in 1851:

> Everybody kept their places with an admirable and praiseworthy sense of propriety. Everybody seemed to feel the novelty of the situation and to desire that justice might be done it. It was, in point of fact, the first extempore walk of the Sovereign in the presence of her people without the Guards. The occurrence seemed greatly to surprise and please the many foreigners who happened to be present.[4]

Cannadine is right to read Prince Albert's determination to raise the monarchy above the venality of party as a move designed to reinvigorate the Crown's constitutional role, and not, as some have claimed, to reduce it. What needs to be emphasised, however, is not just the intention but the effect. In referring back to George III's efforts to give the monarchy more power, purpose and independence from Parliament, Albert's endeavour can only have encouraged popular expectations of active intercession. Indeed, such expectation was further enhanced by Albert's genuine interest in the improvement of working-class housing and sanitation. When the royal couple embraced privacy, bourgeois 'correctness' and distance, conflicting messages were sent into the public sphere. The monarchy appeared to grow simultaneously closer to and further apart from the people. Contractualism was refigured, but not discussed.

David Starkey sees the engagement with privacy as a renegotiation of the concept of the monarch's 'two bodies': the one public and the other private, amounting to a 'revolution in the nature of monarchy. The most public office that an individual can hold had become private.'[5] Paradoxically, perhaps, the withdrawal of monarchy into a state of privacy did not hasten its end or, in the long term, damage its popularity. Victoria's descent into personal grief and her neglect of public life after the death of Albert certainly spurred the resurgence of republicanism, but the monarchy's re-emergence at the century's end ushered in a new age of processional competence and ritual and a fresh resolve to perform before the public. This was a far cry from the rumbustuous performance of George III, however, or the poorly choreographed street wanderings of William IV. Proximity, within the boundaries of monarch–subject relations at the close of the nineteenth century, was imaginary, spectacular and theatrical.

The accession of Victoria was important for another reason. The new monarch was female, 'young and lovely – blending the charm of beauty with a regal dignity'.[6] If reformers had welcomed the prospect of a rejuvenated contract at the accession of William IV, their expectations of the young Victoria were even more idealistic and not a little patronising of her feminine ignorance and inexperience. The fledgling London Working Men's Association, the earliest organisational force of southern Chartism, addressed the Queen in September 1837, urging her to instruct ministers to prepare a bill for universal suffrage and to ignore their attempts to 'dazzle and mislead' her from taking political initiatives with the 'pomp, gaiety and false glitter of a court'.[7] Expectation was heavily gendered. The sensibility of the young Queen would naturally promote a patriotic compassion for the poor and a concern for their improvement. But she lacked 'masculine' know-how according to Thomas Paine Carlile. If only 'common sense reigned in the place of an amiable young lady' he thought, the sufferings of the poor would 'immediately cease'. He lectured the Queen about the degraded state of the nation as though her innocence and disengagement from the real world obstructed her knowledge of it. 'To you, hunger is unknown, poverty an idle tale, destitution a mere fiction to raise sweet sorrow, read of only in novels.' She must learn to rely on the counsels of 'men of intellect' if she was to be guided towards sound policy.[8]

Radical attitudes to the new reign were never demonstrated to better effect than at Chartist meetings to address the throne after John Frost, Zephaniah Williams and William Jones were sentenced to death as leaders of the Newport rising in November 1839. These appeals for clemency were lent added resonance by their coincidence with the Queen's marriage to Prince Albert in February 1840. A platform speaker at Huddersfield had grave doubts about the dignity and propriety of pleading to 'a young woman of twenty-one (for) the life of a man old enough to be her father and who was, indeed, the father of a numerous family', but most maintained a faith in Victoria's instinctive feminine compassion. Mercy had always been the brightest gem in the crown of a king, declared another speaker at the same meeting: 'how much more bright, then, in the coronet of a virgin Queen? (*Cheers*) He had heard that her Majesty was charitable, benevolent and kind; and he sincerely trusted she would add to these qualities that of mercy.' The memorialists were encouraged by an unexpected and sudden Cabinet decision to commute the death sentences to transportation at the beginning of February. Many believed the Queen's influence was behind the decisions, although there is no evidence to support such a view. A fresh wave of memorials now entreated her to grant an absolute pardon. Although there was the usual scepticism about any of them getting past the Secretary of State, the Convention looked to Victoria rather than to Parliament 'as our hope of delivery; we cannot again demean ourselves by applying to a body that pretends to represent us without our consent'. O'Connor hoped to confront the Queen with John Frost's family at the levee.

'Our Monarch is called gracious; is a female; imbued with all the soft and kindly feelings of her sex; and could she, on the day after her marriage, refuse the application of Mrs Frost and her lovely daughters, when imploring pardon for husbands and fathers?' The idea was applauded by several female radical associations, but the interview was never sanctioned and the transports sailed for Van Diemen's Land without further interruption.[9]

If the Queen's gender and immaturity raised questions for some men about her ability to understand complex affairs of State, her determination to *try* was nevertheless admired. She had, after all, acceded to the throne only after overcoming the rival claim of a Hanoverian male relative in a way not wholly dissimilar to the celebrated struggles of 'Queen' Caroline against the same dynasty in 1820. Her conservative uncle Ernest, the already unpopular Duke of Cumberland, acceded to the throne of Hanover because women were debarred from it by the Salic Law, and remained a shadowy figure behind the young Queen at her accession. To some extent, the progressive public enjoyed equating Cumberland with George IV against Victoria's Caroline, and rumours of Hanoverian plots to destabilise her reign before she could produce an heir fell on willing ears. Victoria's triumph was therefore also Britannia's victory over the staid and corrupt forces of conservative legitimacy. Radical critiques of slothful royal extravagance were not levelled at Victoria's coronation ceremony as they had been against her predecessor's, and republican rhetoric was dampened. Victoria's good reception by the crowd as she opened Parliament for the first time, in December 1837, was extensively commented on as though it represented a new and liberal era in British polity. Wellington's fears for the safety of William IV at the same event after he had taken the throne in the dying days of the conservative *ancien régime* seemed to show only how times had changed. Prudent reform had saved the State from disaffection, concluded a satisfied Lord Holland. Here was the proof of it, and 'the Tories were twitted with it in every journal and almost in every conversation'.[10]

Male politicians and commentators appeared to find enticing the challenge of mentoring Victoria in her political duties. However, senior ministers like Melbourne, her first premier, quickly found themselves learning to inhabit an unfamiliar political world in which the impersonal masculinity of the public sphere gradually became coloured with the feminine sentiment and feeling of the private. This was a consequence largely of Victoria and Albert's championing of the homely pleasures of the domestic sphere and of the new Queen's determination to celebrate the virtues of personality rather than distance in the affairs of state.[11] However, the reconfiguration of the political sphere with elements of personableness, compassion and approachability also fed male fantasies about Victoria's vulnerability and need for protection. The Queen's susceptibility to the attentions of the troublesome was presumed to be far greater than that of any male monarch, and the early years of her reign would therefore witness unprecedented levels of surveillance against 'insane' subjects who invaded the royal space; they would also produce a new Treason Act, in 1842, and cement the process of royal withdrawal usually associated only with the death of Prince Albert in 1861.

Uneasiness over Victoria's accession was not slow to surface among the populace. The new monarchy's identification with domesticity and bourgeois family values was paradoxical in that, while kings might make excellent fathers, the role of wife–mother was ill-suited to the public sphere. This issue was made doubly controversial by the parallel growth of female radical societies, the appearance of which had split Chartist opinion and outraged the conservative press. Active female participation in politics, warned one Chartist, always resulted in 'peculation, bickering, backbiting, jealousy, scandal, and matrimonial separation ... Woman's sphere is the *home*. When she enters into the strife, contention and animosity of politics, she is out of it.'[12]

For James Stevenson, a 31-year-old Scotsman, the very idea of a female monarch was oxymoronic. Arrested and charged with seditious speech against the Queen in 1843, Stevenson believed Victoria unfit to reign for the simple reason that she was a woman. All women were subject to the superior will of their husbands, he explained, but it was impossible for a monarch to defer to anybody. Stevenson claimed that he had more right to the throne himself, but was pronounced a 'deranged lunatic' and consigned for the rest of his days to Bethlem and Broadmoor.[13] John Goode, an ex-soldier, had been discharged from custody in May 1837 after making a disturbance at Kensington Palace on the Queen's birthday, but six months later was arrested in Birdcage Walk for shouting obscenities and calling her an impostor. Goode thought himself the rightful heir, and accused the police of treachery when they arrested him. He, too, ended his life in Bethlem, confined under the Hadfield Act.[14]

Others fantasised about their own eligibility as suitors, paternal guides and protectors. Victoria's susceptibility to interference from men who believed themselves in love with her is unsurprising. She came to the throne unmarried and virginal amid much public speculation about eligible suitors, and the annoucement of her betrothal to Prince Albert drew critical comment. Even the Chartist press, which liked to imagine itself beyond caring about the identities of the 'individuals of Royalty', was disturbed by the Queen's choice of a German as husband. It was bad enough to be called upon to support a German Prince out of the public purse when workless Englishmen were being consigned to the workhouse, but worse yet 'the looseness of the marriage tie and of sexual morality in German estimation, is notorious, and remarked by every traveller'. Settling £400,000 per annum on Albert would only provide him with the 'means and the opportunities for the indulgence of ... irregularities'.[15] 'Must her majesty marry a foreigner?' demanded the *Charter*,

> Must the Virgin Victoria of necessity look abroad for a husband, when her throne is surrounded by young, generous and handsome Englishmen? Must we owe a future king or queen to a foreign country when one might be raised all British? ... We may, on a future occasion, return to this subject, running over a few names of Englishmen, justified in becoming candidates for the royal hand.[16]

The *Charter's* proposed list of patriot bachelors was never published, but it is unlikely to have included Patrick Lindon. In January 1838 Lindon, a Liverpudlian of 'wild appearance', got into a fight with the Buckingham Palace sentries after requesting an audience with Victoria. Believing himself 'deputed to tell the word of God to the inhabitants of the Palace and that he was the husband especially intended for the Queen', Lindon had come to claim his bride. He was currently out of work, he told magistrates, 'but when I am married to the Queen, I shall be differently situated'. The magistrates committed Lindon to Tothill Fields for assaulting the sentry and a policeman; but after two months, during which Lindon wrote several letters to the Queen asking her to visit him and bring 'divers little articles of provision', he was adjudged insane and removed to Bethlem. An identical fate awaited John Shockledge, 'the Queen's latest lunatic lover', who tried to gain access to Windsor Castle in November 1839.[17]

Despite popular irritation at Victoria's choice of a German for her husband, and notwithstanding the torrential rain, the royal wedding of February 1840 was celebrated in the streets with genuine enthusiasm. In a densely crowded St James's Park, battle was joined between enterprising spectators in pursuit of a clear view and the desire of the authorities to control the processional space of the Mall. Irish labourers fought with police who tried to prevent them renting out chairs and tables as unofficial grandstands whilst grenadiers used bayonets to coax scores of men and boys out of the trees. Amid so many 'acclamations of love and loyalty', noted the *Sun*, the 'faint cry of tortured envy' emanating from 'the malignant' in one corner of the park was barely noticeable. It was noticed by the *Northern Star*, nevertheless, and attributed to the unfulfilled promise of the new reign, the unacceptable cost of nuptial pageantry and the inexorable growth of the civil list.[18]

Fears over Victoria's vulnerability at times like these prompted ministers to take action against individual petitioners who tried to approach the Queen as she passed through the park in her open carriage. At least seven men and three women were apprehended by police for this offence between her accession and March 1842. Most were released with a reprimand, but Lawrence

Cochlin, who believed the Government owed him money, spent a year in Tothill Fields bridewell because his petition had hit the Queen in the face. It was a 'dreadful assault', in the eyes of the conservative press, the petition having been thrown with 'such violence'. Another exception was Henry Hayward who tried too hard to attract the Queen's attention by presenting his letter rather than just throwing it, and for this he was more thoroughly examined, found insane and committed to Bethlem.[19]

By 1840 Chartists had become impatient with Victoria. She had now been Queen for three years. Yet the 1834 Poor Law still stood, working-class living standards were deteriorating and new workhouses were still under construction; the People's Charter and National Petition had been rejected and Chartist meetings declared seditious and unlawful; and a growing number of Chartist leaders were behind bars or awaiting transportation, their 'remonstrances interpreted as levying war against the Sovereign'. As Parliament re-assembled in January 1840, the *Northern Star* assessed the state of the nation and found Victoria wanting:

> In what light has the Queen, at such an awful crisis, been presented to the contemplation of her subjects? It is the province of a Sovereign to feel for all the people's ills the anxiety and yearning of a parent; to view their wrongs and grievances, their evils, and afflictions as matters of *first rate* importance, and to think of self, of royal wants and royal conveniences, only when the people's sufferings have been allayed. Such was in olden times – in by-gone days, and among barbarous people – the wont of royalty; but we live in other and more 'liberal' times; and now, the Virgin Queen of England ... places before [her people] as a matter of *first* consequence and highest import the beggarly affairs of her own personal comfort, bedroom convenience, and pecuniary affairs.

Although Victoria remained 'a poor young girl, whom we sincerely pity and as sincerely love', she needed shaking from the lethargy and indifference of her ministers.[20] Three shakes were to follow, from Edward Oxford, John Francis and John Bean.

Oxford, Francis and Bean

On the evening of 9 June 1840 Oxford, a young man in his late teens, drew two pistols from inside his jacket and discharged them at the Queen's carriage as she and Prince Albert rode up Constitution Hill. Both balls missed their presumed target. They were never recovered, and the prosecution case proceeded on the assumption that, although he was 'not an unskilful shot', Oxford had nevertheless fired both pistols too high and over the wall. Bullets and a mould were later found in his rooms. Oxford showed no sign of remorse when questioned by police. 'I am very sorry I did not kill the pair of them', he said. The following day, after answering a series of questions from the Cabinet Council with 'flippancy and indifference', Oxford was committed for high treason. A political motive was not ruled out, but there was little evidence to support it at first beyond a rumour that 'he occasionally indulged in some expressions that would tend to prove that he had imbibed republican notions, and on one occasion he observed that he did not think it right that a country like England should be governed by a woman'.[21] Papers were found in his lodgings, however, associating him with a secret organisation called 'Young England'. One was a letter summoning Oxford to a meeting to receive 'communications of an important nature from Hanover'. Whether a Hanoverian conspiracy was credible or not, Oxford had outraged public decency by firing his guns at the Queen, who happened to be a defenceless young woman. There was no reason to suspect him to be mad, it was said, although he was known to be prone to fits of unprovoked laughter, to crying and motiveless acts of bullying and mischief, and his trial for high treason was assured. The ultra-Tory *John Bull* sincerely hoped for an exemplary hanging for once, because leniency would 'produce the worst effects'.[22]

Sydney Taylor, Oxford's attorney, opened the defence by suggesting, firstly, that the pistols were not loaded and, secondly, that Oxford was mad. 'It was impossible that any man in his senses could have imagined such a crime', he asserted, and in any case 'what motive could any sane person have for killing the Queen of England?' When Hadfield had tried to kill George III, there had at least been an ideological war against Jacobinism in progress which might have given him a motive, but even he was found to be insane. 'Young England' was, according to Taylor, a fictitious organisation; Oxford's 'membership' of it was pure fantasy and the three letters were all in his own handwriting – further evidence of his self-delusion. The defence then called a number of witnesses to establish Oxford's insanity as a condition inherited from his father and grandfather, for 'every person at all connected with lunatic asylums knew that a very large portion of the patients inherited the disease' and Oxford was 'just at an age when it would be most likely to develop itself'.

Some influential expert opinion was given by Dr Birt Davis, the physician who had attended Oxford's father. In his professional consideration, any man who shot at the Queen in public without motive, then conspicuously drew attention to himself as the culprit and talked candidly to the police about what he had done 'with the danger staring him in the face', was 'undoubtedly' insane. This provoked questions from the bench. Did Davis believe 'any crime that is plainly committed to be committed by a madman?' inquired Lord Denman. No, the doctor recanted. Two more physicians, Dr Hodgkin and

Dr Chowne, agreed. Delusions could turn eccentricity into insanity under certain conditions, causing a *lesion* of the will; 'a loss of control over the conduct. It means morbid propensity. Moral irregularity is the result of that disease.' It could be the cause of motiveless crimes far more terrible than his unencumbered eccentricity was capable of producing. Lord Denman demanded clarification. Were the doctors arguing that Oxford's eccentricities were actually a form of madness? The distinction was crucial, because although a madman was not responsible for his actions, an eccentric man was. Where was the dividing line to be drawn? Hodgkin was unhelpful. 'It is very difficult', he explained, 'to draw the line between eccentricity and insanity.'

The prosecution countered by arguing that Oxford's father and grandfather had never been confined as insane but were eccentric and violent, just as he was. The young man's invented membership of a non-existent secret society may have been a 'foolish fabrication', but it was absurd to call it a 'mental delusion'. Hadfield had experienced mental delusions, but those had been morbid, making their victim crave punishment. Oxford, on the other hand, craved nothing but notoriety and public recognition. By inference, if he was genuinely deluded, they remained immoral and more worthy of punishment than sympathy. The Hadfield Act had not been intended to give succour to a lout like Oxford. On the contrary, he must be punished, for 'criminal responsibility secured the very existence of society'.

Denman told the jury members they could not find Oxford guilty if delusion had impaired his ability to understand the consequences of his actions, or if they were not completely convinced that his pistols had been loaded with ball. If, however, the guns had been loaded and he had fully understood the likely result of firing them at the Queen, then he remained a fit subject for punishment. He warned them to treat the claims of the defence about lesions of the will with the utmost caution, for it would be dangerous for the court to adjudge Oxford insane just because it was difficult to understand how a merely eccentric individual could possibly commit such a terrible crime. Jurors should not be tempted, in other words, to understand serious yet motiveless offences like this one by attaching 'delusion' to 'eccentricity' and then suddenly to discover an ameliorating insanity. This would be to invite anyone to commit heinous offences because he or she stood a better chance of acquittal than they would had the offences been minor ones. After forty-five minutes the jury returned an unworkable verdict. They found Oxford guilty of firing his guns but not of using live ball, and they judged him 'of unsound mind at the time'.

The Attorney General accepted the verdict with good grace and called for Oxford's indefinite detention under the Hadfield Act. Taylor objected. The jury should not have returned a guilty verdict of any kind. If Oxford had not used live ball, as specified as the overt act of treason in the indictment, he must be acquitted of high treason, and if that were so, regardless of his insanity, he could not be confined by order of the court under the Hadfield Act. Denman immediately ordered the jury to reconsider the central charge that Oxford had fired live ball at the Queen. The foreman appealed to him. How could they be sure when no satisfactory evidence on the matter had been offered? The only logical course open to the jury in that case was to find Oxford not guilty, but the Attorney General reminded them that it would be 'monstrous' to let him go free to commit the outrage again. The jury accordingly considered for a further sixty minutes, then found Oxford 'Guilty, he being at the time insane'. The altered verdict allowed Denman to use the Hadfield Act to acquit on grounds of insanity but to order Oxford's confinement at Bethlem in the customary manner. Her Majesty was pleased to detain Oxford for a total of twenty-eight years at Bethlem and Broadmoor. He displayed little evidence of mental illness at any time during his detention, and bore his punishment with fortitude. Even the Home Office's own 1846 report on Bethlem's criminal lunatics found him 'healthy and sane'. In 1867 he emigrated to Australia, where he achieved a measure of fame publishing titillating observations on the low-life of Melbourne under the pseudonym John Freeman.[23]

In May 1842, Victoria was shot at once again, this time as she rode through Hyde Park. The culprit was a 19-year-old journeyman carpenter named John Francis. He fired once, and was then apprehended. Again no bullet was recovered and again the crime appeared to have been without motive. He was not known to harbour any ill-feeling towards the Queen and he was silent under examination, though one witness had heard him say: 'Damn the Queen; why should she be such an expense to the nation? It is to support her in such grand style that us poor persons have to work hard.'[24] Certainly, Francis was frustrated by debt. He had recently left home, taken lodgings and rented a shop in which to start his own business as a tobacconist, but he was already in arrears. Three days before his arrest, he had been evicted from his lodgings and had his stock repossessed by creditors. He went out that same afternoon and bought a hand-gun.[25]

The shooting was not a sudden or spontaneous act. Francis was seen by Prince Albert pointing something at the carriage on the evening prior to the Hyde Park incident. Both he and a witness, William Richards, presumed Francis was going to throw a petition into the carriage; a threatening letter of some kind had apparently been thrown at the royal couple earlier that day. 'They may take me if they like', Francis had said, 'I don't care. I was a fool that I did not shoot.' Albert tried to keep the incident from the Queen, but she had learnt about it by the next morning and the decision to take a carriage ride as usual that evening was consequently a brave one. Forty plainclothed policemen were posted in Hyde Park to reduce the risk; two equerries rode very close to the carriage and the horses spurred to a faster than usual pace. 'We looked behind every tree and I cast my eyes round in search of the rascal's face', recalled Albert.[26]

Victoria refused to be confined to her palace by fear of assassins. Her customary carriage ride on the evening after the Francis shooting was therefore a triumphant piece of monarchical theatre. Escorted this time by liverymen in eye-catching scarlet instead of the usual anonymous and sombre black, Victoria cantered out to cheering crowds. To keep pistol firers and petitioners out of the picture once and for all, Peel and Albert had jointly drawn up new orders to post twenty-four policemen 'at the points ... where danger is most to be apprehended'.[27] Interestingly, the police recorded no more arrests of petition throwers between the time of Francis's arrest and 1852 when the register was abandoned.

On 3 July, before Francis could be brought to trial, the Queen was shot at again, this time by John Bean, a diminutive 18-year-old. Bean had left home several weeks earlier to seek his fortune, telling his parents, 'it is not my intention to rob or plunder, but if I do not meet with success, I shall resort to desperate means'. He bought an old and defective flintlock pistol, stuffed it with powder, wadding and a broken piece from a clay pipe, and fired it at the Queen's carriage. It did not go off.[28] Charles Dassett, aged 16, tried to apprehend him, but was laughed at by a policeman who 'thought it a frolic'. PC Thomas Hearn and a colleague declined to make an arrest because they 'did not think it amounted to a charge', and everyone in the crowd was laughing. Several people told Dassett to let Bean go, before a third officer arrived and arrested Dassett for creating a disturbance. Hearn was subsequently suspended from duty.[29] This is not to argue, of course, that the public as a whole was indifferent about Victoria's safety. Henry Jefferson, an unemployed man, was seen on the day following Bean's attack 'wandering about outside the Palace with a knife in his hand, as he said, to protect the Queen'. He was pronounced insane by Bow Street magistrates and sent to St Martin's workhouse.[30]

Bean was arrested at home. Like Hadfield, he told his interrogators that he was 'tired of life' and, like Hadfield, he denied any intention to kill: he knew the pistol would not go off. Indeed, it could not have done. The pawnbroker who sold it to him had covered the flint in paper to stop it from falling out, and Bean had never removed it. It was therefore clear to the police as soon as they examined the weapon, that although Bean had packed the barrel with a clay-pipe fragment as though intending to fire it as a projectile, the gun could not have been fired. The difficulty, therefore, of demonstrating an intention either to kill or to wound persuaded the Privy Council that a capital charge would not stick and Bean should be tried for a misdemeanour only.[31]

Interpretation and punishment

The trials of Oxford, Francis and Bean all occurred at a time when treason was most easily equated with Chartist republicanism and the new class politics, or with Hanoverian subversiveness. However, there was no obvious outpouring of sympathy for any of the three men in the Chartist press, and few people took the Hanoverian threat seriously enough to believe in assassination attempts from that quarter.

Lord Normanby expressed an initial interest in Oxford's 'Young England' connection and was reluctant to accept its invention. Yet little importance was attached to it by the Attorney General, and few Britons shared Leopold of the Belgians' fears about the importation from Europe of a 'sort of fashion' for slaying monarchs.[32] One informant claimed Oxford regularly entertained foreigners at his house and another that he heard Oxford telling a coachman that if Victoria died, 'Old Ernest' would come to England, causing a 'real shindig in the country'. One claimed Oxford knew Richard Carlile, and another that he knew William Lovett and a large number of people whose names ended in 'owski'.[33] Albert's private secretary George Anson took Oxford's 'stern sulleness' as confirmation that he was 'the dupe of some foul conspiracy yet to be unmasked', but the Prince's mentor Baron Stockmar assured him it had nothing to do with Ernest of Hanover. He may be a 'wicked man', reasoned the Baron, but even he would balk at 'conniving at the murder of one of his own family'.[34] King Ernest was not slow to extend his sympathies to Victoria. They must not believe Oxford was simply mad, he advised her, for he must surely be connected to a club like the 'Young Germans' who wished his own death and 'who declare they will destroy all the monarchs in Europe'.[35] A Hanoverian plot to assassinate Victoria before she produced a male heir was alleged to the Government in 1841, but Home Secretary Sir James Graham dismissed it as 'improbable'.[36] One or two ridiculous rumours were circulated in the press that Francis 'was a German', and allegations that he was 'well known as a Chartist' were investigated by police but proved groundless.[37]

Conspiracy theories were inseparable from the discourse of factional politics. While Tory papers like the *Globe*, *John Bull*, the *Courier* and the *Morning Post* did their best to implicate the Chartists, or, in the case of Oxford's outrage, even the Whig Government; the Whiggish *Satirist* threw the allegations straight back. Unlike the Tories, it contended, radicals had nothing to gain from the Queen's death, and everything to lose – Chartism would be repressed, free speech muzzled and reform abandoned. Victoria would be succeeded by the detested Ernest of Hanover, a lifelong Tory. 'Who were the instigators?' asked the *Satirist*. At the very least, Oxford was 'a great friend to the Tories'.[38] The Chartist *Northern Star* asked similar questions after the arrest of Bean. The consistent inability of any of the 'Queen-shooters' to hit their target was enough to persuade the paper that a conspiracy was afoot which sought to justify new repressive legislation to put down Chartism.[39]

Despite their fondness for endorsing 'victims' of tyranny, Chartists did not see Oxford, Bean and Francis as the new Frost, Williams and Jones, and were unmoved by them. Nevertheless the *Northern Star* was determined to find greater fault with its adversaries in Parliament than with their 'witless tool, the boy Oxford'. The Whigs and the Tories had so undermined the 'virtuous, beautiful, accomplished' young Queen by preventing popular memorials from reaching her ear and by passing so much socially damaging legislation that the 'ignorant and undiscriminating' now blamed the Queen for all their ills. Lord John Russell's successful obstruction of a Chartist delegation to wait on the Queen by insisting that working men appear in 'full court dress' was resurrected and used once more to admonish him. The people had been 'ear-wigged' against their own Queen. 'How, we ask, can great devotion to her person be expected?!! She is represented as a perjurer, an infidel and a conspirator by one party; and as cruel, unrelenting, unforgiving and unapproachable by the other party.'[40] To many Chartists, the unacceptable crimes of Oxford, Francis and Bean were further proof, if any were required, of the need for both the Government and the monarch to end the distress of the poor. Provincial public meetings to adopt cross-party addresses of congratulation to the Queen on her providential escape were interrupted by Chartists. An amendment calling for the dismissal of the ministry and an amnesty for all political prisoners as 'the best means to uphold the throne' were proposed, but were lost amid enormous uproar at Norwich, and a separate address to Prince Albert was opposed because 'the people of this country can never congratulate Prince Albert whilst he is receiving £30,000 a year and they are starving'. An address to Victoria's mother, the Duchess of Kent, was similarly rejected 'so long as mother and child are separated under the new poor law in Bastilles'.[41]

The *British Statesman* regarded all 'legal executions as legal murders', but was at one with the *Times* in demanding firm punishment. Francis and Oxford were nothing more than 'vicious hobbledehoys', and the paper was not interested in speculation about their insanity. If Francis was to be looked after in an asylum, 'a general immunity should be established for the perpetrators of every crime – straightjackets should supersede the convict ship ... Oxford was no more mad than the heads of colleges at the university which is his namesake – and Francis is no more mad than Oxford.' The jury was persuaded to find Oxford insane because its members 'knew that, if convicted, death and cutting up must follow'. They did it, in other words, only 'to save him from the rope and the knife'.[42] The free-thinking *London Phalanx* took a similar line. The death of the Queen would only accomplish an unpopular regency and could not therefore have been either planned or supported by radicals. The culprits should be punished.[43]

The cases of Oxford, Francis and Bean expose one of the central difficulties of the monarchy's encounter with bourgeois ordinariness; Victoria's vulnerability. By interrupting a young woman's carriage ride with such violence, their outrages offered a stern challenge not to monarchy alone but to the domestic ideal itself. These are central themes in contemporary graphic illustration. The *Illustrated London News* for instance, depicted Victoria and Albert in their open landau in domestic dress topped with bonnet and parasol. The informality of the occasion is clear from the absence of crowds and the sparsity of the escort: two unarmed equerries in top hats. A lone gentleman waves his hat as though cheering a passing locomotive while other women and men dressed identically to the royal pair take their ease in the park. As the Queen's attention is diverted by the gentleman's gesture of loyalty, treason intrudes from the opposite side of the picture; Francis raises his gun and the nearest coach-horse rears in apprehension. Two unarmed officers are frozen in the act of restraint, unable to avert disaster. The respectably dressed Francis looks no different from anyone else in the picture; heightening the sense of treacherous duplicity.[44] Such a scene, insisted the *ILN*, ought not to be possible in an advanced and moral nation:

> We are supposed to dwell in a well-ordered country – a land wherein social virtue has been more studied, and social decorum more firmly maintained, than in any other within the pale of civilisation. A land where peace is the result of prowess – wealth the landmark of order – manliness the symbol of the people and their institutions ... Society has undergone none of the disorganizing influences that have made a wreck of the morality of France.[45]

So, just as the social mapping of the painter W. P. Frith pandered to a Victorian desire to demarcate, decode and make safe the complexities of modern life, the *ILN*'s illustration complicitously exploits contemporary fears about anonymity and ordinariness. True horror lay in the possibility that assassins looked like everybody else.

Once conspiracy had been discounted, commentators grappled for an understandable motive. Anonymity in the modern urban crowd, where insignificance was a commonplace, created anxiety for many Victorians about self-identity. But attention-seeking behaviour among the socially marginalised smacked of moral degeneration and social disintegration. These elements at least indicated a viable explanation for such motiveless and cowardly acts among frustrated

Figure 3 Royal domesticity under attack. John Francis's attempt on the life of Queen Victoria in 1842 as seen by the *Illustrated London News*.

and apparently disinterested young men. Nothing else made any sense. An uncomprehending King Leopold wrote to Victoria after Oxford's arrest:

> What a melancholy thing it is to see a young man without provocation capable of such a diabolical act! That attempts of that sort took place against George III and even George IV one can comprehend, but you have not only been extremely liberal but in no instance have you come into contact with any popular feeling or prejudice; besides, one should think that your being a Lady would alone prevent such unmanly conduct. It shows what an effect bad example and the bad press have.[46]

The respectable press adopted a three-point perspective. Firstly, the outrages of men like Francis were peculiar to the individual and stood in stark contrast to the collective loyal 'passions of the millions'. Secondly, this aberrant individualism was a form of madness, but one undeserving of any sympathy. It was rooted in 'morbid imagination' and narcissism; a 'kind of moral madness' brought on by 'vanity or discontent'. And, thirdly, the vanity of such individuals was pandered to and inflamed by the complicity of the popular media in the celebration of notoriety.[47] The most chilling confirmation of such fears was the moral laxity of the crowd who laughed at the treason of John Bean and turned his apprehension into carnival. These people, warned the *Court Journal*, were obviously part of that 'degraded class [which] has already become familiarized with the idea of the heinous crime ... It requires now but the suggestions of the dark zealots of republicanism to advance the mob within a shade of complicity.'[48] The inquisitiveness and amorality of the popular press had engendered a lamentable climate of 'liberality' and a woeful inability to distinguish between unrepresentative and factious 'clamour' and genuine public opinion.[49] Oxford, Francis and Bean were the awful offspring of those 'fashionable ideologues who bawl so lustily for cramming the People with that "knowledge" exclusively which suits their own views. [They] have sedulously stuffed vacant minds with notions that Sovereignty is a mere conduit pipe for the unsettled "will" of "The People".'[50] 'Political demoralizers' were everywhere promoting 'systems' reminiscent of the French Revolution and tending to the breakdown of social order. Liberalism and the unwelcome politics of class had produced 'hideous reptiles' inflicted with the 'poison of envy' and 'a desire to be revenged upon society'. 'Things are fast verging to an extreme', warned *John Bull*. 'The course of what is termed Liberalism lies before us, beginning in absurd theories, ending in criminal practices' and threatening both throne and altar with a 'revolutionary tide'.[51]

With the unsettling experience of Oxford's trial behind it, the Government quickly dismissed any suggestion that Francis was insane. As soon as he was safely in custody, Home Secretary Sir James Graham wrote to assure the Prince, 'He appears quite sane and rather intelligent than otherwise.' Albert was satisfied. 'He is not deranged', he declared, 'but a thorough scoundrel … a good for nothing creature. I hope his trial will be concluded with the greatest severity.' Royal relatives offered similar sentiments. Leopold and his Queen both hoped Francis would not be thought 'a mere maniac', and blamed the attack on the leniency of Oxford's judges. Leopold could not see why men like Oxford and Francis should be 'screened by some oddity from the punishment they deserve', and hoped for a hanging. Victoria agreed. After Oxford's trial she had told Leopold that if future assailants were 'treated with so much leniency, they would end by somebody being assassinated'.[52]

The trial of John Francis began on 17 June before Sir Nicholas Tyndal, barely a fortnight after his arrest. The prosecution case was primarily directed at establishing the prisoner's culpability and sanity, and appeared uninterested in witness testimony that Francis had deliberately aimed his gun at the carriage wheel, rather than at the Queen.[53] There was to be 'not the slightest plea of defence, on the ground of the prisoner's insanity', insisted the Attorney General, for Francis was 'in the full possession of his senses and of his faculties and judgement'. This assertion was not challenged by the defence for his counsel had no intention of suggesting otherwise.

Lessons had been learned from the Oxford case. Francis's indictment did not depend upon the firing of live ball but on his intention in pulling the trigger. It made no difference, explained the Attorney General, whether the gun was loaded with a marble, a bullet or a piece of gravel. 'The law of treason makes the intention the crime and not the overt act – the overt act is but the evidence of that intention.' Defence counsel Clarkson followed the prosecution's agenda and concentrated on disputing Francis's intention. Since no projectile of any kind had been recovered from the scene, the gun might have contained mere wadding. If so, an intention to kill or even wound the Queen must be considered doubtful. The jury were therefore invited to clear Francis of high treason but to convict him on the non-capital charge of common assault. On the question of motive, Clarkson fell in with the 'pure vanity' thesis prevailing in the public sphere. Francis had used no bullet because he had no real wish to harm the Queen. He sought only to better his miserable condition by being looked after at public expense in an asylum, like Edward Oxford. This interpretation was vigorously denied by the Crown because the prosecution of the treason charge depended on establishing an intention to kill the Queen. Since insanity had not been introduced as a defence, Francis must either be acquitted or sentenced to death. The prisoner was found guilty on the second count of 'firing certain destructive materials and substances', and Tyndal duly sentenced him to be hanged, drawn and quartered. It was tempting, conceded the *Times*, to persist in the belief that Francis '*must* have been insane, the pistol unloaded, the intention a mere desire for notoriety', but it was clear from the evidence that such was not the case.[54] But Tyndal and his two co-judges, Sir John Patteson and Sir John Gurney, afterwards advised Home Secretary Graham that, since no proof of any 'destructive materials' had been produced, the verdict was unsafe. Graham reported the anomaly to Cabinet and on 1 July it was decided to commute the sentence to transportation for life to Australia.[55]

Commutation was expected to appeal to the public mood. Francis had impressed a number of newspapers, since the verdict, with his dignified behaviour in prison and his insistence that there had been nothing harmful in the gun.[56] Peel, who was as loathe to let Francis become a victim of injustice as he was to allow him to wallow in notoriety, was only too pleased to abandon a high-profile hanging. He explained the Government's position in the Commons, assuring members he had not taken the decision out of 'false humanity', but avoiding any reference to Tyndal's qualms about the verdict.[57] Neither Albert nor Peel were happy with the outcome, however. The Prince sought clarification from the Chancellor Lord Lyndhurst, a man whose expertise had already been proven as the prosecutor of Thistlewood, and the Solicitor General, William Follett, who convinced him that the problem lay in the proof of intention. Unless intention could be proved, safe convictions even for wounding the Queen could not be guaranteed. The law did provide for an alternative, but only in a prosecution for common assault, a measure that took no account of the monarch's status.[58] The law must be changed, Albert insisted in a memorandum to the Cabinet. A female monarch required special protection, especially as her vulnerability was heightened 'in our times by the increase of democratical and republican notions and the licentiousness of the Press'.[59]

Albert's view was backed, it seemed, by the intervention of John Bean on 3 July: Bean was living proof that the public interest had been poorly served by the mercy shown to Francis, but the English were fanatical about the law, he considered. There was no public appetite for Francis's execution and, since 'a vindictive feeling in the mass of the people would be a thousand times more dangerous than the mad wickedness of individuals', the law had clearly become an obstacle to justice.[60]

Peel's Royal Protection Act, 1842

As V. A. C. Gatrell has pointed out, Peel's major contribution to the criminal law lay not so much in resisting Whig attempts to scale down and liberalise the bloody code of the eighteenth century, but in colouring Whig reforms with alternative physical punishments. Peel 'trusted in the punitive efficacy of bodily pain', and he had always been a more enthusiastic advocate of flogging and harsh prison discipline than of hanging.[61] By 1842, public opinion increasingly regarded execution with distaste. It could even be counter-productive, argued the *Court Journal*: 'It has been found that the more exemplary and excruciating the punishment, the more numerous the appearance of assassins of kings; ridicule, silence or the charge of lunacy being more effective than the severest retribution. It is thus with all species of crime. Capital punishment fails of effect in deterring criminals.'[62] These were the considerations underlying Peel's reform of the treason laws.

On 12 July Peel introduced his Royal Protection Bill to the Commons. In essence it sought to create a new category of offence under the common law of assault, specifically to cover non-fatal attacks on the monarch. An assault, he explained, should encompass any action 'calculated to excite the alarm and apprehension of the Sovereign, and to disturb the public mind by natural and just apprehensions' for their safety. The contents of a gun levelled at the Queen, or the precise direction of its aim, would cease to have any bearing on the offender's guilt. The Act might be invoked even in cases where a weapon had been held but not fired or thrown. The intention was to protect the monarch from any situation 'in which she might be frightened or alarmed by the wilful acts of any person or persons'. He was not out to create any 'new treasons', Peel assured the House. On the contrary, he was convinced that the 'needless forms and solemnities' of English treason trials tended to encourage rather than deter those attention-seeking individuals disposed to publicly threaten the Queen. His concern was to make a clear distinction in law between constructive treason as a collective and political act of insurrection and the individual and intimidatory intrusions of troublesome subjects. Behind the broad assumption that such individuals simply sought notoriety lay an important denial that they also sought to draw the attention of the monarch to a personal grievance. Their punishment would be deliberately unspectacular, demeaning and discrete. Here Peel showed himself to be a considerably more canny politician than Albert, who had pressurised him without success to make the punishment as severe as possible. Transportation or imprisonment should be for life, thought the Consort, to prevent second attempts after release. But Peel was anxious 'not to run counter to the public feeling and temper of the times', and rebuffed him.[63]

The Hadfield Act had usefully amended the treason statutes of Edward III, Peel argued, but not those of Pitt in 1796. In other words, the use of an insanity defence to effectively reduce the crime to the status of the common law, and to thereby deny the accused any of the special privileges granted to treason defendants, was limited to assaults in which the monarch's life was endangered. It could not be used if the indictment followed the terms of the 1796 Act and referred only to wounding. The Hadfield Act could not be used without a full indictment for compassing and imagining the death of the monarch. This may have been Peel's pretext for altering the law, but it was not his primary concern. He had no wish to simply extend the provisions of the Hadfield Act, for he did not believe men like Oxford, Francis or Bean to be mad. What he wanted very much, however, was to withdraw from them the privileges of treason defendants, especially the right to retain the most eminent counsel in the land at public expense. Under the new proposals, culprits would be treated as common felons, eligible for transportation for seven years or imprisonment for three with an optional flogging in each year of the sentence. Peel was particularly keen on the latter part of the proposed penalty, for it was:

> a punishment more suitable to the offence and more calculated to repress it ... Instead of dignifying those miscreants with the solemnities of a trial for their life and inciting them to those offences by making them the objects of that most misplaced and stupid sympathy with which some persons are apt to view such offenders, let us make known to the world ... that for these contemptible acts they shall receive the degrading punishment of personal chastisement.[64]

'Hearty floggings in public', agreed *The Times*, were just 'the kind of medicine which this disgraceful vanity best deserves'. Transportation alone was wasted on people like Bean and Francis, because it 'requires some degree of intellect and sobriety to appreciate', whereas they were too 'inane' to feel terror at anything less than physical pain. 'Let us be allowed to flog or pillory them into sobriety. Let them return to their friends after the short absence which the law requires, after having been made recipients at Charing Cross of all the rotten eggs of Westminster, or having had their backs most unheroically scored before the gates of Newgate.' A correspondent calling himself 'Flagellator' wrote to congratulate the editor, and concluded that flogging could prevent all crime if only its use were resorted to more frequently. But until 'this is agreed on, hanging must be continued. Had Oxford been hanged, there would have been no Francis; and because Francis has been reprieved, there will be a host of Beans.'[65] There was approval from the *Satirist*. Boys like Bean deserved a good flogging, 'less to reform them than to deter others. It is of less consequence that they should be transformed into loyal subjects than that their example should not be imitated.'[66] In the parliamentary debate that followed, no MP expressed any sympathy for the possibility that perpetrators might be insane or that they could have any motive beyond a desire for notoriety. Developments in print culture had assuredly made national publicity a greater certainty than it had been in the time of Nicholson, Frith and Hadfield. Despite its stated disapproval for his presumed vanity, the *Illustrated London News* not only carried a dramatic artistic reconstruction of Francis's attack on Victoria but followed it with a picture of his examination and a half-length portrait.[67] Immediate recognition and notoriety were assured in the Victorian public sphere. Peel's Bill became the Act for the Safety of Her Majesty's Person within four days of its introduction.[68]

Peel personally informed Albert of the success of his measure, assuring him that under the broad terms of reference of the new law 'the explosion of Lucifer matches for instance, under the carriage of the Queen, if intended to create alarm, will be punishable with transportation – or imprisonment with corporal punishment'.[69] He hoped too that the Act would deter hostile political crowds from demonstrating grievances in front of the Queen. The royal couple had just announced an intention to visit Scotland during the summer, and Peel was afraid their coach would be surrounded by hostile working-class demonstrations as they made their way north through England's strike-torn industrial districts. He prevailed upon them to make the journey by sea instead, but they were still forced to endure the shouts of Chartists running beside the coach as they rode through Edinburgh and Leith. He even expressed fears to James Graham of a Chartist-inspired assassination attempt at Windsor, where she remained 'a good deal exposed'.[70] A few days later, an unemployed and scruffy man named Quested was discovered in the footmen's waiting hall at the castle and assumed to be a Chartist, 'armed to the teeth'. In fact he had walked thirty miles to beg the Queen for a pension. Graham sent him to Bethlem.[71]

John Bean could not be tried under the Royal Protection Act because his crime pre-dated it. He was arraigned on 25 August before Lord Abinger. Like Francis, he was not presumed to be insane, but unlike Francis he was not tried for treason. Bean was prosecuted for a common assault since it was clear the gun could not have been fired and that it held no ball. The indictment charged him severally with possessing a gun with intent to commit an assault, aiming it at the Queen and aiming it at her carriage. There was little obvious public interest.

The Attorney General argued that Bean had intended to fire, and that had he done so he would have created an alarm. The prisoner had committed the act, not to injure the Queen, but 'with a view to some strange unenviable notoriety … in furtherance of his declaration to do something desperate'. Defence counsel asked witnesses to recall the levity with which the 'crime' had been greeted in the park, and argued that there had been no alarm whatsoever. One such witness, Henry Vosper, said Bean had been standing with the pistol in his hand, and in full view of anyone who cared to look, for twenty minutes before the Queen went past. He had not drawn the attention of the police to Bean because he was more moved to 'watch the result' than prevent it. A shocked Lord Abinger told Vosper that if what he said was true, he was himself guilty of misprision (concealment) of treason. Certainly Vosper had compassed and imagined the death of the Queen. The jury found Bean guilty of attempting to fire his pistol at the wheel of the coach, and Abinger found a clear intention to cause Victoria distress. In sentencing him to eighteen months in prison, the judge told Bean that in future anyone convicted of such a crime under Peel's Act would be 'publicly whipped at a cart's tail through any street in the metropolis'.[72]

The idea that either Francis or Bean intended to harm the Queen can be discounted. Both men seem to have deliberately aimed away from her, and there is no evidence that their pistols were loaded with shot. These circumstances of intention, which bear some resemblance to those of Nicholson and Hadfield, either support Franklin Ford's 'incompetence' thesis, or invite some other explanation. The 'vanity' argument is dubious, at least in Francis's case. His overheard (and undenied) remarks criticising the Queen's pampered and idle lifestyle do not prove political motivation, but they do suggest dissatisfaction with unearned privilege and assume Victoria's indifference to the suffering of her poorer subjects. If, as his defence counsel claimed, he had simply wanted to be, like Oxford, looked after in an asylum, the perfectly sane Francis could hardly have inflicted more damage to his own case. His language was more likely to be taken as evidence of political motivation than of derangement; more likely to send him to the gallows than to Bethlem. In fact, Francis made no attempt to fake madness after his arrest; he refused to answer any questions put to him at his examination, and there was never any question of an insanity defence.

Bean had also been prone to the making of seditious remarks in the days before committing his offence. The police examined witnesses who claimed Bean was 'repeatedly heard to say that he admired the conduct of Francis, and regretted that he had not succeeded in his diabolical attempt; that Francis was a brave fellow, and he wished he had been in Francis's place, for he would do for the Queen; that he had a prime air-gun and pistol, and he would use them in the same cause'. Despite Bean's anti-monarchical opinions being enough to make him 'well-known to nearly all the constables in the Somerstown division', he had never been arrested for them because the police did not want to pander to his vanity by doing so.[73] Once again we are reminded of the distance between eighteenth- and nineteenth-century *mentalités* concerning the punishment and prevention of sedition. This information about Bean's political character was not made use of at his trial because neither the prosecution nor the defence had any interest in establishing a political or treasonous motive. On the contrary, the defence called a number of witnesses to affirm Bean's quiet, passive and loyal character.

Both of these young men were poor and were frustrated by their inability to earn an independent living. Both had left home and had lost direct contact with their families. Both harboured resentments against a Queen who, rather than offer them assistance, enjoyed unearned luxury at their expense. There is no evidence that they were frustrated petitioners of the Queen before they committed their crimes, but their circumstances and behaviour are not dissimilar to the better-documented physical petitioning of Margaret Nicholson, James Hadfield and Dennis Collins.

The Crown and Government Security Act, 1848

The unruffled survival of the Victorian monarchy amid the European revolutions of 1848 may be seen as some testament to the institution's continuing popularity. It was not achieved without some further tinkering with the treason laws, however.

Energised by the overthrow of Louis Phillipe and the declaration of the second French Republic in the spring of 1848, British radicals rallied in London under the slogan 'The Republic for France and the Charter for England'. If the third National Petition were to be rejected, declared William Cuffay, 'we should then begin to think about a republic'. But most Chartists remained content to honour the throne as a potential source of salvation. Even Ernest Jones, whose republicanism would later be unquestionable, adopted the time-honoured line. Petitioning the 'middle class parliament' was undoubtedly worthless, but it could be overcome if they assembled in millions to 'petition the throne direct'. Delegates from all over the country, escorted to the palace by 200,000 Londoners, should wait upon the Queen 'with the same words upon their lips ... should leave be refused for the deputation to approach the Queen, no matter. The millions meet again to consider the next step.'[74] Importantly, Jones did not suggest that the Queen herself would refuse to see them, but that ministers would prevent it. The 'next step' was not necessarily revolution, therefore, but the forcible circumvention of the Government in pursuit of access to the throne.

Four days later, several days of disorder and street-fighting with police began in and around Trafalgar Square. Led by a man shouting 'to the palace!', a crowd armed with staves processed past St James's and Buckingham Palace, breaking street-lamps and looting shops. There was no attempt to break in, only to be seen and heard. Sentries outside both palaces were invited to come over but they 'politely declined', and one man prevented the lamps outside Buckingham Palace from being destroyed for fear of 'getting the poor sentries into trouble'. The crowd then left, pursued by the police, but later that evening an 'evidently insane' man was heard delivering an impromptu address at Charing Cross. The people must 'go to Buckingham Palace and insist upon the Charter being given; if it was refused, to do to the palace the same as the people in France did. He should like to see, provided they did not hurt the Queen, the throne burnt in the middle of Trafalgar Square.' For these remarks, he was 'loudly applauded', and we could hardly wish for a clearer demonstration of popular nineteenth-century attitudes to the Crown.[75] The gaudy and expensive trappings of monarchy; its palaces and its thrones, insulted the predicament of the poor and the unrepresented, and fully deserved destruction, but the Queen herself was not to be hurt. The *idea*, at least, of a popular and patriotic monarchy still prevailed in London, even as thrones tottered and fell across Europe.

The point is further illustrated by Chartist responses to attempts to repress the movement after the famous Kennington Common meeting on 10 April. The State disempowered Chartism's potentially greatest moment by constructing it as a far greater danger to the realm than any Chartist had ever imagined it could be. The Queen was sent to the Isle of Wight, ostensibly for her own safety; Westminster was garrisoned with troops to prevent the collective delivery of the Chartist petition to Parliament, and an emergency amendment to the Treason laws suddenly introduced.[76]

The Crown and Government Security Bill was effectively a further attempt to separate and redefine treasonable offences in the spirit of the 1842 Royal Protection Act. The primary concern was to increase the potential punishment for 'seditious' speech without dignifying 'rabble orators' with the notoriety of a trial for high treason; and to tidy up a loophole in the law which made the 1817 Treason Act of doubtful legality in Ireland. Political miscreants, it was argued, should be treated in much the same way as attention-seeking mavericks like Francis and Bean. 'As personal notoriety is one of the strongest motives for treasonable exhibitions', asserted the Solicitor General, 'this Bill will put a stop to them, for the man who might reckon upon sympathy as a traitor was not sure of meeting it as a felon'. Offences in which treason might be committed through 'open and avowed speaking' of a treasonable nature, as distinct from a direct attempt to hurt or kill the person of the sovereign, was therefore to be classed as a felony and punishable by transportation for life. This would include any speech-making or publishing that might result in either Parliament or the Queen being 'overawed' into changing policies. Under the laws of 1796 and 1817, it will be remembered, conviction on a charge of making treasonable expressions could, at least in theory, result in hanging, drawing and quartering. There was some opposition in the Commons. George Thompson objected to the punitive nature of a gagging law that criminalised any man who 'expressed his preference in the abstract for a republic as compared with the monarchy', but the measure nevertheless became law on 22 April.[77]

Chartists argued forcefully that the Bill would push radicals into the arms of insurrectionists and alienate the people from their Queen at a time when 'there does not exist in any factory, workshop or mine, a feeling of hostility towards your Majesty, but against the present system of government'. The Bill was also seen as a flagrant attack on the protection to petitioning offered by the Bill of Rights, for, as a correspondent in the *Northern Star* saw it, transportation now awaited any man who 'had the audacity to stand before a public meeting and advocate the propriety of her Majesty to change her measures or her counsels'.[78] This was currently a moot point because Jones's suggestion of a monster memorial to the Queen, delivered in person by a large procession, had been approved by the Convention and plans for its presentation were well under way. Now conceived as a confrontational response to the Security Act as much as a remonstrance over the rejection of the National Petition, the Chartist memorial required the Queen to dismiss her ministers and call a general election under the terms and conditions of the Charter. It was, said one delegate, 'their last resource; a last appeal'.

Predictably enough, the Home Office would countenance no personal presentation, however, and the Convention spent several weeks arguing about what to do. Some delegates were for the customary compromise of submitting the memorial to the Secretary of State's office, but others, including Jones and W. E. Adams, insisted they had a right to present their prayers to the Queen in person and that there was no statute to prevent them doing so. Adams wanted the forthcoming public meeting on Clerkenwell Green on 29 May to 'form itself into a procession and proceed with the memorial to Buckingham Palace and demand an immediate audience with the Queen and that the Executive Committee march at the head'. But agreement could not be reached, and the memorial was finally submitted, without consequence, via the Home Office.[79]

The Chartist revival of 1848 nevertheless unnerved Prince Albert and prompted a series of royal initiatives aimed at promoting the happiness and welfare of the working classes. Albert made a number of public appearances in the ensuing months, actively associating himself with charitable projects for the improvement of health and sanitation; encouraging the civilising benefits of the arts and preaching the virtues of social unity.[80] The British monarchy was reflective and proactive in 1848; keen under Albert's tutelage to be seen to be playing its contractual role. Despite the language of the Security Act, the very title of which appeared to confirm the indistinguishability of Crown and Government, popular *mentalités* continued to imagine the Queen in a rarefied, patriotic and separate sphere of contractual beneficence, fouled only by ensnarement in the stupefying web of government.

An English queen's castle is her home: privacy, intrusion and the early Victorian monarchy

Reviewing the state of the public sphere after John Francis's attack on the Queen, the *Times* was regretful about the ease with which increasing levels of public inquisitiveness and vulgar imposition had achieved normalisation. These were, it supposed, the price monarchy had to pay for its own popularity.

> The ill-mannered curiosity of the public, where propriety should teach them to abstain – the absurd, but not therefore less provoking, intrusions to which the palace itself has been subject – these are evils to which royalty must submit as a necessary consequence of the very interest which it attracts to itself, galling as they must often be to one who feels acutely the pleasures of a more easy privacy.[81]

Public intrusions within the walls of the royal palaces were, of course, an 'evil' to which royalty had long been exposed. There was something new, however, in the idea that the levels of intrusion and the growth in public taste for inside information on royal lifestyles and the habits of the court were connected.

The increased efficiency of the royal police after the creation of the Metropolitan force in 1829 might have been expected to cause a reduction in palace intrusion rather than an increase, but this is not what happened. Something about the Victorian monarchy drew people inexorably towards its centre. In the eight years between January 1838 and 1846, at least thirty 'lunatics' were discovered either attempting to gain entry to or else actually being on the premises of one of the royal palaces; and another six were taken into custody for breaking the palace windows, using threatening language or simply 'annoying' Victoria and Albert.[82] One man 'annoyed' Prince Albert by running alongside the royal carriage carrying a baton like a policeman. Not all were harmless or merely insulting. An 'unquestionably insane' woman calling herself the Countess Amelia of Resterlitz armed herself with a sword and tried to run into Buckingham Palace in 1840 with the apparent intention of murdering Prince Albert.[83] A small number of these individuals were turned over to the care of their friends or families, but the majority were committed at Government expense to either Bethlem or the new Middlesex pauper asylum at Hanwell; given three-month sentences for vagrancy at Tothill Fields, or sent to the workhouse. The temerity of men like Charles Mann, who arrived at the Palace in a raging fury, claiming to be the Prince of Wales and desperate to present a Bible in a locked writing desk to Victoria, caused outrage in the press and brought demands for tougher action to protect her from such 'crying evil'. Mann was straitjacketed and despatched to Bethlem.[84]

The number of people apprehended as 'troublesome lunatics' might have been higher, but a degree of discretion was maintained over arrests at least until after the passage of the Royal Protection Act. Those deemed 'harmless' were generally allowed to remain at liberty, but were closely watched. At least two frequent 'visitors' to the palace, and five persistent letter-writers, were traced to their homes and placed under surveillance between 1841 and 1842. Their names and home addresses were noted and enquiries made about their mental health, but they were not detained or obstructed. One, William Grant of Margate, was known to have 'once shot a man', but as long as he remained in Kent, the police were not concerned. An exception was made for Charles Stuber, a German-immigrant baker whose letters threatened the lives of 'the whole of the reigning dynasty' in 1837, but his removal to the Hanwell asylum may have been prompted as much by his nationality and concern about the approaching coronation ceremony as by his presumed insanity.[85] The high number of individuals caught after actually gaining entry to royal premises, however, did expose serious flaws in security. The low garden walls with overhanging branches were easily climbed by homeless men like Arthur Scott in search of a quiet place to sleep, and by prostitutes like Sarah Jones in search of a groom for the night. Twice in 1846 Alexander Reid, a deserting sailor seeking Victoria's protection, was found 'snoring in a tent' on the lawn.[86]

But one case of trespass captured the public imagination sufficiently to make the culprit a minor celebrity. In December 1838, Edward 'The Boy' Jones was discovered inside Buckingham Palace at night, stealing clothing. The police took him at first for an enterprising burglar and committed him to the Westminster sessions, but he was acquitted when defence counsel persuaded the jury that his motivation was 'not felony but curiosity'. Two years later he was found in the palace again, hiding under a sofa in an audience chamber close to the Princess Royal's bedroom. Jones told magistrates he was gathering material for a book about Royal secrets. 'I wanted to know how they lived at the Palace ... an account of the Palace, and of the disposition and arrangement of the chambers, and particularly of the dressing room of Her Majesty, would be very interesting'. Jones's father tried without success to persuade a Privy Council inquisition that the boy was mad, and Jones told them he would not mind being as 'well off' as Oxford at Bethlem. A magistrate sent him to hard labour at Tothill Fields for three months instead. Within days of his release, Jones was discovered for a third time inside the palace, carrying food upstairs from the kitchens. Again, he insisted he was only researching his book, but magistrates sent him back to the bridewell for another three months. His father's protests that the boy was being committed arbitrarily by an 'unenglish secret court' were only quietened when Jones agreed to enlist as cabin boy on a warship when next released. Once at sea, he could not reoffend.

The Boy Jones became an overnight public sensation after his second discovery, in 1840. 'The subject engrosses public attention at the west end of the town', reported the *Times*. 'Nothing else is talked of.' James Fennimore Cooper allegedly tried to entice him to America to 'make his fortune', and the author of a play based upon his exploits, *Intrusion, or A Guest Uninvited*, wanted to parade him to an opening-night audience. Jones's fame lasted for at least twenty years. In 1860, the author of a penny dreadful account of a royal visit to America adopted his name as a pseudonym: 'The Boy Jones! That's *me!* and as I suppose everybody has heard of me, I shall make no apology for my appearance.' His celebrity status was rooted in public enjoyment of his negotiation of the most secret recesses of the palace or, as one journal put it, his 'stealthy and suspicious progress to the very *penetralia* of the Royal privacy'. Over an unspecified number of days and nights during which he lived unobserved in the passages and shadows of the Palace, Jones claimed he had 'sat upon the throne, that he saw the Queen, and heard the Princess Royal cry'. This was a most delicious, clandestine and audacious voyeurism; subversive, taboo and soon to be revealed to the world in a publicised account. Although old enough at 17 to have been called a young *man*, it was his immaturity that the public press preferred to emphasise, quickly coining his sobriquet 'The Boy Jones'. A youthful impression offered a cloak of respectability for popular titillation, publicly negating the dangerous innuendo of his intrusions and rendering him no worse than an artful and awe-struck young rogue, 'mischievous and *espiègle*'. An invented account of his examination made light of sexual contexts:

Lord Melbourne:	What did you first do after you got in?
Jones:	I tried if I could see anything of Her Majesty.
Melbourne:	And what were your intentions, sirrah?
Jones:	Strictly honourable, in course.

Some papers mulled over the effects of the imposition as though the Queen had been physically violated. 'We are happy to state that Her Majesty and the Princess Royal suffered no ill effects from the extraordinary occurrence', assured the *Standard*, 'the answers to inquiries this morning being that the Queen and infant Princesses were going on well'.

But Jones was also the most consummate proof of poor royal security. The fact that his second discovery occurred so soon after the Oxford shooting outrage was acutely embarrassing for the police, and a reminder that however harmless Jones might seem he *could* have been a gunman. He claimed he had been in the palace on several occasions without being caught, and often stayed overnight when it was quieter and he could explore without interruptions. Entrance by the french-windows was easy. Many had weak or broken fastenings; others had never been securely closed. They would now be barricaded with iron bars, but the Home Secretary would not consider either raising the height of the garden wall or crowning it with iron spikes for fear of making the Queen appear endangered. Instead, three extra sentries would be posted in the garden by day and two additional constables by night, and two sergeants were posted inside each night to patrol the stairwells.[87]

After the Jones fiasco and with the advent of Peel's Act the attitude of the Metropolitan Police towards the protection of Buckingham Palace from lunatic intruders underwent a marked change during 1842. From that point onwards, suspected lunatics were regularly taken into custody and then removed, usually to a nearby workhouse, merely for being in the vicinity of the palace. It was no longer necessary for someone to appear at the palace door, or to make any overt attempts to gain access or cause injury to the Queen. These pre-emptive strikes, apparently designed to sweep the neighbouring streets and the royal parks clean of *potentially* troublesome visitors, removed at least forty-nine men and women in the next ten years. Various reasons were cited. Mary Sexton and Lawrence Fuller were taken away for 'wandering in front of Buckingham House and causing a crowd to gather', and Caroline Wetherall for lying down in the road outside the palace gates, but a homeless man named George Welsh was arrested merely for being 'apparently insane' in Birdcage

Walk. John Cousins, William Lardner and Bethesda Clarke were removed for the same reason from St James's Park and the Mall, and others were taken up at a greater distance. Henry Watson and John Russell were considered a threat to royal security because of something they said or did in Whitehall, but committals were also instigated for 'mad' behaviour in Scotland Yard, Charing Cross, Trafalgar Square, Hyde Park and New Palace Yard. Mary Steele was taken away for 'sitting down in Cockspur Street'.[88] The police file on troublesome subjects is a remarkable enough document in itself, but it is not comprehensive. Although it lists nearly 100 people, others whom the police certainly dealt with are not included. Henry Maporth and Alexander Reid are noted only in the newspaper press; and the sole source for Margaret Dunn is her entry in the Hanwell Asylum admissions' book.[89] One can be certain, therefore, that in the decade following the three shooting incidents involving Queen Victoria determined measures were taken to protect the Royal Family from attacks and intrusions, and that these were contemplated on a scale never previously seen, but what one cannot do is quantify the real scale of the operation.

While the police concentrated on sweeping away potential intruders from the outside of the palace, Albert simultaneously forced an extensive review of security arrangements on the inside. Between the second discovery of Boy Jones in 1840, and 1844, he and Stockmar, drew up new plans for the management of the Royal Household. The sheer number of domestic servants, each with his or her own idiosyncratic, traditional and jealously guarded roles and duties, constituted a security risk in itself in Albert's view, yet forcing change upon unwilling servants was difficult. It was not until 1844 that Albert was able finally to confer the entire economy and organisation of the palace on the Master of the Royal Household.[90]

To what extent had the popular press contributed to the upsurge of palace intruders, and how had it done so? Some journals certainly took an unprecedented degree of interest in the domestic rituals of the Victorian monarchy and the life of the Royal Court. For the *Court Journal* (a paper whose very existence depended on an insatiable appetite for royal 'news'), the inquisition began at the outset of the new Queen's reign. Its front page 'Peep into the Interior of the Palace', in January 1838, began with the proposition that many people nursed anxieties about the effect of Victoria's youth and gender on the masculine order of the court. In some detail, the *Journal* then set about allaying all such fears with a minute description of the Queen's daily habits, and her unique ability to balance feminine sensuality (manifested in activities like drawing, reading and riding) with the masculine rigour of State affairs. She approached the 'demands of the toilet' with proper attention but without wasting a single second, readers were assured, and when the day's 'grave devotion to duties' was over, there was still 'the opera or the theatre ... or the fascinations of the drawing room' to be enjoyed.[91] It is not easy to imagine a male monarch being written about in such language.

In April of the same year, readers were taken on an imaginary excursion into the private chambers of St James's Palace, firstly as members of the more privileged, or *entrée*, company attending the Queen's levee, then as members of the more inferior 'general' company. The description was sufficiently detailed as to give a virtual experience to readers who were

> ushered by the Yeomen and Gentleman Porters to the staircase, which is angular and perfectly plain, with very slight hand-railing, and giving no indication whatever of the splendour to which it leads. Two turns of this staircase lead to a small room, wainscoted and matted all over at right angles, from which immediately opens a long narrow gallery.

The order in which the successive rooms should be penetrated, and corridors negotiated by visitors of each class before the climactic arrival in the Throne Room was slowly and teasingly revealed. Finally, readers were led before the throne, 'elevated on a platform which is reached by three low steps, the platform and steps covered by a Persian carpet', and left to imagine the arrival of the monarch.[92] In a similar piece, but this time with pictures, the *Illustrated London News* took its readers into Victoria's first 'Drawing Room' of the summer season in 1843. Most of the those likely to have read this account would have been restricted in real life to watching arrivals from the surrounding streets, as very few were fortunate enough to be admitted to an inside corridor 'to gaze at the royal family'; but in the fantasy world of the *ILN* they became virtual visitors: 'Thither let our illustrations take our readers until such of them as are aspirant after the presence of royalty can mingle in the throng themselves.'[93]

Less than a month after Edward Oxford fired his pistols the *Court Journal* published another 'Peep into the Interior'. This time readers were invited to imagine themselves walking inside St James's Palace:

> Forward! Proceed, we of the rougher sex, two and two; Ladies *seule, à distance*, into the presence of royalty. Most imposing are the objects around ... but the most striking object – that on which all eyes are riveted – is immediately before you, standing before the steps that conduct to that regal canopy. It is the Queen! What easy, graceful, dignified affability!

After enjoying the 'manly form', of Prince Albert at her side, the virtual intruder found himself suddenly and magically whisked away to the yellow drawing room at Buckingham Palace where a series of doors were thrown open in turn to afford access first to a royal ball, and then to the supper room where 800 distinguished guests could be seen dining on 'fowls, soups, *entrées, pièces montées*, and confections numberless'. The Queen's black satin and diamond dress was minutely described and her 'unaffected affability' once more emphasised.[94] Lest anyone should think the affable Victoria was accessible to anyone at any time however, the *Journal* provided some helpful information about the security of the Queen's bedroom. One of the lesser-known duties of her lady-in-waiting was to lock her majesty into her sleeping quarters every night by securing the door to the ante-room, 'and retain the key under the custody of her pillow till the morning'. However, this information was merely a vehicle for the telling of another lurid and voyeuristic tale. A footman named John Perkins had one night chanced to see the lady-in-waiting, 'her zone unbound, her tresses floating in the breeze, and her night gear scantily concealing the graces of her form' as she hurried through the darkened palace with her key. In order to 'spare her blushes', Perkins generously concealed himself beneath a table in the Queen's ante-room, only to find himself locked in for the night when he re-emerged. 'Who would not envy the position of that footman, prisoner though he was ...?' queried the paper.[95]

The sexual themes of voyeurism and transgression which underlie so much of this writing are the same themes that underlie the Boy Jones narrative and the public's somewhat hypocritical enjoyment of it. The identification by 'respectable' papers of salacious and inquisitorial reporting as one of the motivators of Oxford, Francis and Bean's quest for notoriety did not prevent those same papers indulging in it under a loose cover of innocent celebration. Neither did public and judicial 'outrage' over the intrusions of Boy Jones prevent his rise to celebrity status. Public interest in the interior life of monarchy was an inevitable consequence of Victoria and Albert's engagement with domestic values. By making themselves a more 'ordinary' family than had previous monarchs the royal couple inhabited a more imaginable private world; their daily experience richer and more colourful, but ultimately still accessible to public knowledge. The contradictory urges to envy and shatter or to watch and protect Victoria's privacy were each fed by the greater urge to explore, map and know its intimacies. The layout, routine and organisation of the palaces and their vicinities therefore became a focus of previously unencountered levels of public fascination.

Notes

1 D. Cannadine, 'The last Hanoverian sovereign? The Victorian monarchy in historical perspective, 1688–1988', in A. L. Beier, D. Cannadine and J. M. Rosenheim (eds), *The First Modern Society: Essays in English History in Honour of Lawrence Stone* (Cambridge, 1989), pp. 127–30. Cannadine's contention is essentially that

Victoria and Albert thought and behaved far more as George III had done with respect to constitutionalism, temperament and domesticity than as George V ever would.

2 *Ibid.*, p. 133.

3 *Northern Star*, 30 June 1838.

4 *The Times*, 25 June 1851. My thanks to Flora Fraser for sharing this reference with me.

5 Starkey, 'Modern monarchy', pp. 250–6.

6 *Illustrated London News*, 8 July 1843.

7 Birmingham Public Library, Lovett Papers, 'The Queen and her ministers', and a comment from Leigh Hunt, 'The Queen and the working classes', fols 110–19.

8 *Regenerator and Chartist Circular*, 3 November 1839: an open letter 'To her Royal Highness Victoria the first'. T. P. Carlile was the son of Richard.

9 *Northern Star*, 25 January, 1 and 8 February, 7 March 1840; D. J. V. Jones, *The Last Rising: The Newport Insurrection of 1839* (Oxford, 1985), p. 197. Jones acknowledges the Government's change of heart over the hangings as 'still something of a mystery', but cites Victoria's journal as evidence that she supported execution for Frost, Williams and Jones.

10 This view of Victoria's importance has been forcefully put in Thompson, *Queen Victoria*, pp. 15–30, 87–97, but see also Homans, *Royal Representations*. Kriegel, *Holland House Diaries*, pp. 376–7.

11 For an interesting exploration of paternalism and feeling in Victoria's early relations with her ministers, see K. Chase and M. Levenson, 'I never saw a man so frightened: the young Queen and the parliamentary bedchamber', in Homans and Munich, *Remaking Queen Victoria*, pp. 200–19.

12 *Regenerator and Chartist Circular*, 2 November 1839.

13 *Court Journal*, 11 March 1843; Royal Bethlem Hospital Archive, Criminal Lunatic Case Book, 1816–50: entry dated 21 March 1843.

14 Royal Bethlem Hospital Archive, Criminal Lunatics Case Book, 1816–50: entry dated 27 November 1837; *The Times* 7, 13 and 20 November 1837. Goode's precise grievance is not recorded, but as an ex-soldier his background is familiar enough.

15 *Northern Star*, 18 January 1840.

16 *Charter*, 3 February 1839.

17 *The Times*, 9 January, 1 March 1838 and 7 December 1839.

18 *Sun*, 11 February 1840; *Northern Star*, 15 February 1840.

19 PRO, MEPO 2/44, 'Return of all persons who have come under the cognizance of the police force for offences against her majesty Queen Victoria since her accession, and his Royal highness Prince Albert, viz. from 1837'. For Cochlin, see *Court Journal*, 25 August 1838.

20 *Northern Star*, 25 January 1840.

21 *Court Journal*, 13 June 1840.

22 See the Attorney General's opening remarks at Oxford's trial in Howell, *State Trials*, p. 110; *John Bull*, 21 June 1840.

23 Howell, *State Trials*, pp. 118–50; *The Times*, 11 July 1840. For analysis and for an attempt to contextualise Freeman's *Lights and Shadows of Melbourne Life* (1888) with the true identity and history of its author, see F. B. Smith, 'Lights and shadows in the life of John Freeman', *Victorian Studies*, 30 (1987), 459–73. See

also PRO, HO 44/39: Quarterly Report of the Criminal Lunatics at Bethlem Hospital, December 1846.

24 *Illustrated London News*, 4 June 1842.

25 PRO, TS 11/80/253: Crown brief for the case against John Francis.

26 PRO, TS 11/80/253: Crown brief for the case against John Francis, and evidence of William Richards; RA VIC/M67/17: Robert Peel to Prince Albert, 31 May 1842, RA M67/2: Memo of Robert Peel, 29 May 1842. Albert related the incident in almost identical language to the Duke of Saxe-Coburg-Gotha: RA VIC/Y/185/15, 31 May 1842; *Illustrated London News*, 4 June 1842.

27 RA VIC/M67/17: Robert Peel to Prince Albert, 31 May 1842.

28 *The Times*, 5 July 1842.

29 RA VIC/M67/46, 48, 49, 51, 52: Undated depositions of William Jones, Charles Dassett, P. C. Partridge and Thomas Hearn.

30 PRO, MEPO 2/44: 'Return of all persons ...', entry dated 4 July 1842.

31 *The Times*, 7 July 1842.

32 RA VIC/Y66/61: Leopold King of the Belgians to Queen Victoria, 13 June 1840; RA VIC/B2/62, B2/64, B2/65, B2/66: Lord Normanby to Victoria, 13, 14 (two letters) and 15 June 1840.

33 PRO, HO 44/36: J. P. Rhoades to Marquis of Normanby, 13 June 1840, G. Heywood to Normanby, 19 June 1840, R. Price to Normanby, 16 June 1840; Anon. to Normanby, 18 June 1840.

34 RA VIC/Y54/5: Memorandum of George Anson, 11 June 1840.

35 RA VIC/Z480/204: Ernest King of Hanover to Queen Victoria, 18 June 1840.

36 RA VIC/M67/29: Sir James Graham to Prince Albert, 7 June 1842, RA VIC/M67/34: Information of Mrs Blow (undated). Blow reported conversations to have claimed she overheard between a Frenchman, another man and a woman she believed to be a maid in the Royal Household. Information about the Queen's movements was to be provided by the maid, and a sum of £30,000 was promised to pay an unidentified assassin to kill the Queen on May 26 1842.

37 *The Times*, 31 May 1842; PRO MEPO 3/18: Report of Inspector Hughes, 9 June 1842.

38 *Satirist*, 14 and 21 June 184.

39 *Northern Star*, 9 July 1842.

40 *Ibid.*, 20 June 1840.

41 *Ibid.*, 27 June 1840. There were similar scenes at Carlisle.

42 *British Statesman*, 5 June 1842.

43 *London Phalanx*, 29 July 184.

44 The illustration appeared on the front cover of the *Illustrated London News*, 4 June 1842.

45 *Illustrated London News*, 4 June 1842.

46 RA VIC/Y66/61: Leopold King of the Belgians to Queen Victoria, 13 June 1840.

47 *Illustrated London News*, 4 June 1842; *The Times*, 31 May 1842.

48 *The Times*, 5 July 1842; *Court Journal*, 9 July 1842.

49 On the essential difference between 'popular clamour' and 'public opinion', see W. A. MacKinnon, *On the Rise, Progress and Present State of Public Opinion in Great Britain and Other Parts of the* ([1828] Shannon, 1971), pp. 15–23; and for a modern assessment of 'public opinion' as a vehicle for the language of the 'middle

class', see D. Wahrman, *Imagining the Middle Class: The Political Representation of Class in Britain, c. 1780–1840* (Cambridge, 1995).

50 *Felix Farley's Bristol Journal*, 4 June 1842.

51 *Court Journal*, 13 June 1840 and 20 November 1841; *John Bull*, 14 June 1840.

52 RA VIC/M67/2: Memo of Robert Peel, 29 May 1842; RA VIC/M67/8: Sir James Graham to Prince Albert, 30 May 1842; RA VIC/Y. 185/15: Prince Albert to the Duke of Saxe-Coburg-Gotha, 31 May 1842; RA VIC/Y. 68/12: King Leopold of the Belgians to Queen Victoria, 3 June 1842; RA VIC/Y. 9/82 & 83: Louise Queen of Belgium to Queen Victoria, 2 AND 6 June 1842; RA VIC/Y. 69/33: King Leopold of Belgium to Queen Victoria, 3 February 1843.

53 PRO, TS11/80/253: Case papers for the prosecution of John Francis; RA VIC/M67/12: Information of George Gower. Conflicting evidence was, however, provided by a soldier who was sure Francis had fired 'at Her Majesty's head' (RA VIC/M67/13: Information of Pte Henry Allen), and by a shoemaker who judged the gun to have been aimed well *above* her head (RA VIC/M67/31: Information of William Richards).

54 *The Times*, 18 June 1842.

55 RA VIC/M67/39: Sir Nicholas Tindal's notes on the trial, 17 June 1842; RA VIC/M67/42: Judges' opinion on the trial, 30 June 1842.

56 *Illustrated London News*, 25 June 1842.

57 *Hansard*, vol. 65, 12 July–12 August 1842 (London, 1842), cols 24 and 84.

58 RA VIC/M67/72: Lord Lyndhurst's memo on the law; RA VIC/M67/71: 'Memo on the state of the law of treason', by W. F. Pollock and William Follett, 6 July 1842.

59 RA VIC/M67/44: Prince Albert to the Cabinet, undated memorandum.

60 RA VIC/Y.185/5: Prince Albert to the Duke of Saxe-Coburg-Gotha, 4 July 1842.

61 Gatrell, *Hanging Tree*, pp. 566–85.

62 *Court Journal*, 4 June 1842.

63 RA VIC/M67/76 and 77: Prince Albert to Robert Peel, 10 July 1842; Robert Peel to Prince Albert, 12 July 1842.

64 *Hansard*, vol. 65, 12 July–12 August 1842, cols 24–5.

65 *The Times*, 5, 7 and 12 July 1842.

66 *Satirist*, 17 July 1842.

67 *Illustrated London News*, 4 and25 June 1842. Francis's outrage occurred within a month of the paper's first issue and so became the paper's first significant story.

68 *Hansard*, vol. 65, 12 July–12 August 1842, col. 81.

69 RA VIC/M67/79: Robert Peel to Prince Albert, 12 July 1842.

70 C. S. Parker (ed.), *Sir Robert Peel from his Private Papers*.

71 *Morning Chronicle*, 17 August 1842.

72 *The Times*, 26 August 1842. In fact it was not so simple. As the Criminal Law Commissioners noted in their Fourth Report, a previous Act of George I made the whipping of women unlawful. 'It is to be hoped that no female will attempt, by shooting at the Queen, to solve in her own person the present perplexity' (Howell, *State Trials*, p. 150).

73 *The Times*, 4 July 1842.

74 *Northern Star*, 11 March 1848. Similar sentiments were voiced at mass meetings on Kennington Common and at Southwark on March 13. Reynolds attacked the profligacy of the civil list and unacceptable levels of spending on palatial improve-

ments, while Thomas Clark made jokes at the expense of the 'ornamental' but costly Prince Albert; *Northern Star*, 18 March 1848.

75 *Sun*, 7 March 1848; *The Times*, 7 March 1848; *Northern Star*, 11 March 1848; *Observer*, 12 March 1848. However, it was alleged in the *Sun* that crowds which took to the streets of Glasgow on the same night had shouted 'Down with the Queen' as well as 'Vive la République' and 'Bread or Revolution'. The Trafalgar Square riots are discussed without explicit reference to the monarchy in D. Goodway, *London Chartism 1838–1848* (Cambridge, 1982), pp. 111–14, and in J. Saville, *1848: The British State and the Chartist Movement* (Cambridge, 1987), pp. 88–90.

76 The story of the ill-fated Kennington Common meeting and the rejection of the petition is well known. For the best accounts see Goodway, *London Chartism*, pp. 72–9, 129–42; Saville, *1848*, pp. 102–29; Thompson, *The Chartists*, pp. 307–30.

77 *Northern Star*, 15 April 1848.

78 *Ibid.*, 13 May 1848.

79 *Ibid.*, 22 April, 13 and 20 May, 3 June 1848.

80 Prochaska, *Royal Bounty*, pp. 84–91.

81 *The Times*, 31 May 1842.

82 Except where otherwise noted, the following information is all taken from PRO, MEPO 2/44: 'Return of all persons ...'.

83 *Court Journal*, 19 December 1840. She was sent to Bethlem.

84 *The Times*, 16, 18 and 20 November 1841; *Court Journal*, 20 November 1841. Mann was still in Bethlem in 1846: PRO HO 44/39: Quarterly Report of the Criminal Lunatics at Bethlem Hospital, December 1846.

85 PRO MEPO 2/44: 'Return of all persons ...', with the exception of Maporth, who is recorded in the *Court Journal*, 19 September 1840, and Stuber, whose details are in *The Times*, 5 June 1838.

86 *The Times*, June 10, 16 1846.

87 All details of the Boy Jones case are taken from PRO, MEPO 2/44: 'Return of all persons ...', *The Times*, 5 and 7 December 1840, and 17, 18, 23 and 26 March 1841, *Satirist*, 13 December 1840; *John Bull*, 7 December 1840; and *Court Journal*, 5 December 1840; *Extraordinary Narrative of the Prince of Wales' Trip Across the Atlantic by the Boy Jones* (London, 1860). For security improvements, see *Court Journal*, 27 March 1841.

88 The above cases are all taken from PRO, MEPO 2/44: 'Return of all persons ...'.

89 London Metropolitan Archive Centre, H11/HLL/B1/1: Middlesex Lunatic Asylum Female Admissions, 1831–41, Margaret Dunn, entry no. 714.

90 T. Martin, *The Life of His Royal Highness the Prince Consort* (London, 1875–80), vol. 1, pp. 155–60.

91 *Court Journal*, 6 January 1838.

92 *Court Journal*, 7 April 1838. To have *entrée* was to be entitled to enter the park via Constitution Hill, and was for the higher nobility only.

93 *Illustrated London News*, 8 July 1843. A similar series of verbal and visual texts was offered when the Queen held a State Ball at Buckingham Palace in August: *Illustrated London News*, 5 August 1843.

94 *Court Journal*, 27 June 1840.

95 *Ibid.*, 9 June 1838

10

Conclusion

By contextualising the behaviour and beliefs of such insane assailants as Nicholson, Frith and Collins within the rubric of contractualism and the parallel discourses of radical politics, the preceding chapters have endeavoured to understand constitutional madness as something more than irrationality. Deranged petitioners like Neil Maclean, John Dunlop and Elizabeth Davenport are not marginal figures in the popular historical narrative of constitutionalism, but men and women who, on the contrary, help to delineate and amplify its boundaries. Mad their assertive and physical engagement with monarchy may have been, but there was undoubtedly a method in their madness. Moreover, while it is the common denominator of ascribed insanity that unites them most readily, and which has presided over their collective descent into historical obscurity, it is not their broadly conceived madness but their broadly conceived constitutionalism that offers the greater insights. By casting these troublesome subjects as frustrated petitioners in pursuit of contractual dues, I have also challenged their traditional representation as incompetent assassins. Not one of Nicholson, Frith, Sutherland, Hadfield, Collins, Oxford, Francis or Bean appears to have been trying to kill her or his sovereign. Their actions and their utterances point more often to physical remonstrance after experiences of extreme frustration with an ineffectual petitioning process.

Similarly, it has been suggested, treasonous radical plotters against George III do not seem to have relished the prospect of his death so much as his detention, re-education and reconfiguration as the monarch of a revolutionary democracy. This is the gist of the evidence in the cases of both Despard and Sayre, and it broadly fits Greg Claeys's assertion that in eighteenth-century Britain, 'most republicans in principle did not seek so much to abolish the monarchy as to reinforce the popular component in government'.[1] Richard Carlile found it far easier to argue the case for republicanism in response to George IV's disregard for his coronation oath and the Bill of Rights than by presenting it as the more rational system of government. Consequently, the very radicals who danced on the grave of George IV were re-intoxicated with royalism at the accessions of William IV and Victoria.

In some ways, the Reform Act was a watershed. On the one hand, it rendered

Parliament considerably more accountable and in so doing reduced the urgency of the compact between monarchy and people. On the other hand, it made the politics and language of social class absolutely central to subsequent debates about privilege, wealth and representation. The working-class movement that grew into Chartism needed to believe in the intercessionary impartiality of the Crown, embattled as it was by the bourgeois legislative agenda of the reformed electorate. Hetherington, for example, understood both the sentencing of the Tolpuddle martyrs and the imposition of the new Poor Law by the 'reforming' Whigs as classic expressions of class interest. But the meritocratic discourses of 'middle class' also coloured popular radical intolerance of unearned royal expenditure and produced suspicion and cynicism around the Crown.

While the theoretical undercurrents of contractualism are constant and unmodified in the period here discussed, the inexorable manoeuvring of the State renegotiated the boundaries of royal space from a position of apparent openness to one of effectual closure. The accessibility and secular domestic manliness of George III offered petitioners encouragement and hope of redress, however misplaced and unrealistic. George IV closed down these channels: William IV opened them briefly through the promotion of affability, but closed them when his political popularity declined. While cartoonists such as Rowlandson and Gillray celebrated the ordinariness of George III by emphasising his bluff, unruffled juxtaposition with the brawling, plain-speaking and physical culture of John Bull, Victoria's ordinariness was constructed quite differently. Victoria's accession offered her subjects a quieter, more respectable and withdrawn ordinariness: a believable monarchy that was paradable, and yet private. The trouble with royal privacy, even where subjects are tossed crumbs of comfort in the form of processional pageantry, is that it brooks no intrusion while positively inviting speculative voyeurism. Privacy may *seem* counter-contractual. At any rate, the reduction of contract to spectacle was not achieved without the legislative superstructure of the 1842 and 1848 Protection Acts and a policy of zero-tolerance towards the troublesome, whether mad or not.

The language of madness through which the discourses of royal assault were mediated in the eighteenth century was infused with pathos, sentiment and sensibility on the one hand and an entrenched opposition to French politics and jurisprudence on the other. But nineteenth-century attitudes became increasingly intolerant of dysfunctional behaviour, especially where the monarch was female, and regimes of punishment and distance slowly took precedence over sympathy. This transformation of an empathetic 'Age of Reason' into a demarcatory age of disciplined self-control and regulation was commented on by the barrister Walter Townsend in 1850. It was 'the painful lot of George III to be the mark at which poor maniacs, silly women, discharged soldiers with gun-shot wounds in their heads, mad lieutenants ... tried the knife or pistol', he observed. Most remarkably, '[the] humanity of the age and kind-heartedness of the Sovereign would not permit a hair of their heads to be touched'. While it was right for Britons to take pride in the contrast between their own nation's humanitarianism and the brutality of the execution of Damiens 'in what the French deem the centre of civilisation', Townsend understood the modern world in completely different terms. The 'half-witted miscreants' and 'imbecile monomaniacs' who fired pistols at Queen Victoria committed their crimes out of pure vanity and love of infamy, he insisted, and rejoiced that Peel's Act had made it possible to subject modern regicides not to outmoded care and compassion but to a sound flogging. 'This very useful measure saved the royal person from further insult', he concluded, 'and reads a salutary lesson to those reformers of our criminal jurisprudence who would push their merciful theories to excess'.[2]

Contractualism is not dead.[3] Provided even the most obsessive petitioners practise their art with becoming detachment, they are accommodated. Some are even celebrated; and none more so than Robert Andrews, who died in 1997 after spending thirty-five years of his life quietly petitioning the Queen and Parliament for personal redress on a number of issues. Politicians attended his funeral, if not to his case.[4] But Elizabeth II is as prone to the unreasonable attentions of troublesome subjects as any of her historical forebears. Moreover, languages of insanity are still deployed in the public sphere to situate the troublesome outside of the boundaries of rational constitutional acceptability. This is true of reportage in the case of a 'crazed' and 'hysterically shrieking' woman, dragged out of Crathie Church, Balmoral, after running down the aisle and 'trying to give the Queen a present' in 1995,[5] and of the five principle 'weirdoes ... known to police for harassing the Royals' whose identities were revealed by the *Sun* in 1996. One was an obsessive letter-writer seeking help in finding employment, and another thought he ought to be king. This was a man who, after he attempted to break into Kensington Palace,'should never have been released', according to a 'senior police source'.[6] In 1999, an inspectorate of constabulary report concluded that more than 6,000 'mentally disturbed persons' had visited the royal palaces as paying tourists over the previous six years. The police, it was suggested, were in need of proper training to help them distinguish 'eccentric behaviour' from other more dangerous displays of insanity.[7]

The best-known recent intruder, Michael Fagan, twice broke into Buckingham Palace at night in 1982. On the first occasion, he walked around, drank some wine and then left. On the second, he found his way into the Queen's bedroom, sat down on her bed and asked his monarch for a cigarette. Rumours were circulated in the press that he had intended to commit suicide in front of her. Fagan's successful evasion of a security network involving sophisticated electrical alarm systems, twenty policemen and forty soldiers, created a public outcry, calls for the resignation of Home Secretary William Whitelaw, a complete security review and demands for changes to the law of trespass. After studying a medical dossier on Fagan, the Crown Prosecution Service was convinced he posed a very real danger to the public, and so chose to 'throw the book at him' with a jury trial at the Old Bailey, despite proferring charges that could more easily have been dealt with summarily. Fagan was not charged with any offence for his nocturnal visit to the Queen because there was no evidence he had intended to commit a crime. Instead, he was committed for 'stealing' wine on his earlier visit and for assaulting his stepson on a different occasion altogether. When the jury acquitted him on these charges, regret was expressed that a magistrates' court had not been permitted to try the case instead. Rather like James Hadfield, however, Fagan was detained as a schizophrenic under the Mental Health Act after prosecuting counsel and a consultant psychiatrist successfully argued that he was 'a great danger to whoever becomes the subject of his delusions'.[8]

Apart from inviting as yet unexplored historical comparisons with the cases of James Sutherland, 'The Boy' Jones and James Hadfield, the Fagan case also raised a number of questions about the wisdom of the 'demystifying' of monarchy. In an essay entitled, 'Getting too close to the Queen', Nicholas Wapshott claimed that the present Queen's greatest achievement had been to 'soften the pomp and ceremony around the Royal family, making it more accessible and more understandable while attempting not to dilute its majesty'. By making use of the universalising medium of television, by which the Queen had become better known as a person, and so more ordinary, than any previous monarch, the House of Windsor had become fully integrated with modern life. 'This universal integration of public Royal lives with private family behaviour is the most effective defence for the constitutional monarchy and one which republicans will find hard to dismantle. But it has its drawbacks, as shown in the past two weeks.' But these drawbacks, by which Wapshott means the attentions of troublesome subjects like Michael Fagan, are not simply the product of a televisual dumbing-down exercise. They have been present in very similar form since the reign of George III, and the constitutional problem that gives them life is contractualism itself. Michael Fagan may well have been diagnosed a schizophrenic, just as men and women who believe themselves in love with a member of the Royal Family are now rationalised as victims of de Clerambault's Syndrome. But the cultural or constitutional 'madness' of Michael Fagan was far better expressed during the trial by his defence counsel Richard Slowe. Entreating the jury not to regard Fagan as a common criminal, Slowe recounted Fagan's words as he was dragged from the Queen's bedroom by security men: 'I want to talk to the Queen, my Queen, it's urgent.' Slowe's next question was a rhetorical one. 'Is this the behaviour of a normal person?' he asked.[9]

Notes

1 G. Claeys, 'The origins of the rights of labour: republicanism, commerce, and the construction of modern social theory in Britain, 1796–1805', *Journal of Modern History*, 66 (1994), 253.

2 W. C. Townsend, *Modern State Trials*, vol. I (London 1850), pp. 103–5.

3 In 1998 an electronic BBC 'Talking Point' poll on the question 'Should the Queen be accountable?' elicited a large number of responses from puzzled subjects who were convinced she already was: *http://news1.thls.bbc.co.uk/hi/english/talking%5Fpoint/newsid%5F45000/45013.asp*

4 BBC Radio 4 News, 14 January 1998.

5 *Sun*, 11 September 1995: 'Berserk woman charges at Queen'.

6 *Ibid.*, 25 November 1996: 'Royalty plagued by nuts'.

7 *The Times*, 10 June 1999: 'Mentally ill pose main palace risk.

8 *Ibid.*, 13, 16 and 20 July, 24 September and 5 October 1982.

9 *Ibid.*, 21 July 1982: 'Getting too close to the Queen'; 24 September 1982

Select bibliography

Manuscript primary sources

Berkshire County Record Office, Reading
Windsor Corporation Minute Book 1798–1828, WI AC 1/1/4.

British Library, Department of Manuscripts, London
Pelham Papers, Add. MSS 33122, 33115.
Place Papers, Add. MSS 27795, 27808, 27820.
Dropmore Papers, Add. MSS 58908, 58934.

Devon County Record Office, Exeter
Quarter Session Papers, Q/S 1/23, Q/S B 1807, John Zorn, 1807.
Addington (Sidmouth) Papers, 152M.

Hampshire County Record Office, Winchester
William Wickham Papers, 38M49.

London Metropolitan Archive Centre
Hoxton Asylum, Registers of Male and Female Admissions, 1831–50, H11/HLL/B1/1 and B4/1.
Cold Bath Fields Prison Papers, MA/G/GEN.

Public Record Office, London
Assizes, Assi 23/9: Neil Maclean, 1801.
Chatham Papers: PRO 30/8.
Court of Kings Bench:
KB 33/6/4: Pop Gun Plot.
KB 33/8/3: James Hadfield, John Frith.
Home Office:
Petitions, 1819–54: HO 17, 18.
Criminal lunatics: HO 20.
Domestic correspondence: HO 40, 42, 44 and 52.
Domestic entry books: HO 43.
Law officers' reports and entry books: HO 48, 49.
Police entry books: HO 65.
Private and secret entry books: HO 79.
Metropolitan Police:
MEPO 2 and 3.

Privy Council Papers and Minutes:
PC 1/18/A21: Examination of John Frith, 1791.
PC 2/131: Examination of Margaret Nicholson, 1786.
PC2/134: Examination of John Frith, 1791.
State Papers:
Domestic: SP 37.
Treasury Solicitor's Prosecution Papers:
TS 11/209/884: *Crisis*, 1775.
TS 11/542/1758: Stephen Sayre, 1775.
TS 11/1026: John Frith, 1791.
TS 11/1119/5766: Richard Smith, 1794.
TS 11/837/2832: Richard Lee, 1795.
TS 11/1045/4504: George Elliot and William Unwin, 1795.
TS 11/927/3272: Kidd Wake, 1795.
TS 11/223/11678: James Hadfield, and Bannister Truelock, 1800.
TS 11/121/332 and 333: Col. Edward Marcus Despard, 1802.
TS 11/80/249: Nathaniel Highmore, 1821.
TS 11/180/253: John Francis, 1842.

Royal Archive, Windsor Castle

Correspondence of Princess Elizabeth, 1786: RA Add. 9/12, 15/8168, 11/276.
Correspondence of Queen Charlotte: RA Add. 9/190.
Correspondence of Prince Albert: RA Add. Y/185.
Correspondence of Queen Victoria: RA Add. Y/66, 68 and 69, B2/62–6.
Attempts on the Life of Victoria: RA M67.

Royal Bethlem Hospital Archive, London

Admissions Book, 1797–1802.
Committee Book, October 1783-February 1791; February 1795-September 1800, October 1800–November 1805.
Criminal Lunatics Case Book, 1816–50.
Incurable Admissions Book, 1728–1853.

Contemporary newspapers and periodicals

Annual Register
Black Dwarf
Champion
Charter
Cobbett's Political Register
Cosmopolite
Courier
Court Journal
Examiner
Figaro in London
Gauntlet
Gentleman's Magazine
Hansard's Parliamentary Debates
Hone's Reformists' Register

Illustrated London News
John Bull
London Chronicle
Morning Chronicle
Morning Herald
Morning Post
Northern Star
Oracle
Politics for the People
Poor Man's Guardian
Public Advertiser
Radical Reformer
Regenerator and Chartist Circular
Republican
St James's Chronicle
Satirist
Star
Statesman
Sun
The Times
True Briton
Voice of the People

Parliamentary papers

Minutes of the Evidence of the Witnesses Examined by the House of Lords upon the 29th Day of October, 1795 (London, 1795).

Report from the Committee on the State of the Police of the Metropolis (London, 1816).

Printed primary sources

Address of W. D. Evans, Esquire, at the New Bayley Court House, Salford, on Discharging the Prisoners who were Apprehended on Account of an Illegal Assembly at Manchester on the 10th of March, 1817 (Manchester, 1817).

'Amicus Patriae', *British Liberty; of Sketches Critical and Demonstrative of the State of English Subjects* (London, 1803).

Armstrong, A. W., *The Particulars of the Arrest and Examination of A. W. Armstrong on a charge of High Treason on June 13 1818 for Threatening the Life of the Prince Regent* (London, 1818).

Authentic memoirs of Margaret Nicholson who attempted to stab his most Gracious Majesty with a Knife as he was alighting from his carriage (London, 1786).

Banvard, J., *The Private Life of a King embodying the Suppressed Memoirs of the Prince of Wales, afterwards George IV of England* (New York, 1875).

Baxter, J., *Resistance to Oppression: The Constitutional Right of Britons asserted in a lecture delivered before Section Two of the Friends of Liberty on Monday November 9, 1795* (London, 1795).

Baxter, J., *A New and Impartial History of England from the most Early Period of Genuine Historical Evidence to the Present and Alarming Crisis* (London, 1795).

Binns, J., *Recollections of the Life of John Binns, Twenty-nine Years in Europe and Fifty-three in the United States* (Philadelphia, 1854).
Britain, J., *History of the Life of Jonathan Britain* (London, 1771).
Burrows, G. M., *Commentaries on the Causes, Forms, Symptoms and Treatment, Moral and Medical, of Insanity* (London, 1828).
Carlile, R., *A New View of Insanity* (London, 1831).
Collinson, G. D., *A Treatise on the Law Concerning Idiots, Lunatics and other Persons Non Compos Mentis* (London, 1812).
'Eunohoo', *Elegy on the Death of James Sutherland Esq.* (London, 1791).
Extraordinary Narrative of the Prince of Wales' Trip Across the Atlantic by the Boy Jones (London, 1860).
Gifford, J., *An Account of the Attack made upon the King* (London, 1809).
Hamilton, Lady A., *Secret History of the Court of England from the Accession of George III to the Death of George IV*, 2 vols (London, 1832).
Highmore, N., *A Letter etc. etc. to his Most Gracious Majesty the King* (London, 1819).
Highmore, N., *A Petition Humbly Praying His Majesty (then Prince Regent) to Dismiss from his Ministry the Earl of Liverpool; Presented at the Levee* (London, 1820).
High Treason Committed by Margaret Nicholson (London 1786).
Hone, W., *The Bullet Te Deum; with the Canticle of the Stone* (London, 1817).
Howell, T. B., and Howell, T. J. (eds), *A Complete Collection of State Trials* (London 1817).
Hunt, H., *Memoirs of Henry Hunt Esq., Written by Himself, in His Majesty's Jail at Ilchester in the County of Somerset*, 3 vols (London, 1820–22).
Jephson, H., *The Platform: Its Rise and Progress*, 2 vols (London, 1892).
Jesse, J. H., *Memoirs of the Life and Reign of King George III*, 2 vols (London, 1866).
Lee, R., *The Rights of Kings: Number One of a Political Dictionary* (London, 1795).
Lee, R., *Account of the Proceedings of a Meeting of the London Corresponding Society, held in a Field near Copenhagen House, Monday, October 26, 1795* (London, 1795).
Lee, R., *King Killing* (London, 1795).
Lee, R., *The Happy Reign of George the Last: An Address to the Little Tradesmen and the Labouring Poor of England* (London, 1795).
Lee, R., *A Summary of the Duties of Citizenship; Written expressly for the Members of the London Corresponding Society; Including Observations on the Late Contemptuous Neglect of the Secretary of State with regard to their Late Address to the King!* (London, 1795).
Lemaitre, P. T., *High Treason!! Narrative of the Arrest, Examination Before the Privy Council and Imprisonment of Paul Thomas Lemaitre* (London, 1795).
Macerone, F., *Useful Knowledge for the People! Containing the New and Improved Combination of Arms called Foot Lancers; Miscellaneous Instructions on the Subject of Small Arms and Ammunition, Street and House Fighting etc etc.* (London, 1831–32).
Martin, T., *The Life of His Royal Highness the Prince Consort*, 5 vols (London, 1875–80).
Memoirs of the Life of Col. E. M. Despard with his Trial at Large (Manchester, 1803).
Metcalf, U., 'The interior of Bethlehem Hospital' in Peterson, D. (ed.), *A Mad People's History of Madness* (Pittsburgh, PA [1818], 1982).
Murray, Rev. J., *Sermons to Asses* (London, 1817).
Murray, Rev. J., *New Sermons to Asses* (London, 1818).

Moore, J. E., 'On Margaret Nicholson', in *Miscellaneous Poems on Various Subjects* (Dublin, 1796).

Perfect, W., *Select Cases in the Different Species of Insanity, Lunacy or Madness, with the Modes of Practice as Adopted in the Treatment of Each* (Rochester, 1787).

Pindar, P., *Royal Disaster or Dangers of a Queen; A Tale for the Quidnuncs* (London, 1813).

Prince, J. H., *A Vindication of Mr Jefferys and his pamphlet against the Prince of Wales* (London, 1807).

Rose, J., *A Constitutional Catechism* (Bristol, 1795).

Sketches in Bedlam, or Characteristic Traits of Insanity as Displayed in the Cases of 140 Patients of Both Sexes ... By a Constant Observer (London, 1823).

Smith, J., *Assassination of the King! The Conspirators Exposed, or An Account of the Apprehension, Treatment in prison and Repeated Examination before the Privy Council of John Smith and George Higgins on a Charge of High Treason* (London, 1795).

Some Particulars of the Life and Death of Jonathan Britain who was Executed at Bristol for Forgery, by a Gentleman who Attended him (Bristol, 1772).

St John, H., Viscount Bolingbroke, *The Idea of a Patriot King*, ed. Jackman, S. W. (Indianapolis, IN, [1749] 1965).

Stockmar, E. Von, *Memoirs of Baron Stockmar by his Son*, 5 vols (London, 1872).

Sutherland, J., *A Letter to the Electors of Great Britain by James Sutherland Esq., Late Judge of the Admiralty at Minorca* (London, 1791).

Titus, S. and Sexby, E., *Killing No Murder* (London, [1657] 1792).

Townsend, W. C. (ed.), *Modern State Trials* (London, 1850).

The Trial of David Tyrie for High Treason at the Assize at Winchester, August 10, 1782 (London, 1782).

The Trial of Josiah Phillips for a Libel on the Duke of Cumberland and the Proceedings Previous thereto (London, 1833).

The Trial of the cause on an Action brought by Stephen Sayre Esq. against the Right Honourable William Henry, Earl of Rochford ... For False Imprisonment (London, 1776).

A True and Particular Account of the Behaviour of Charlotte Georgina Mary Ann Guelph (London, 1796).

Truth and Treason! or a Narrative of the Royal Procession to the House of Peers, October 29th, 1795. To which is Added, an Account of the Martial Procession to Covent Garden Theatre, on the Evening of the 30th (London, 1795).

Wade, J., *Treatise on the Police and Crimes of the Metropolis* (London, 1829).

Walpole, H., *Journal of the Reign of King George III, 1771–1783*, ed. D. Doran (London, 1858).

W. R. V., *Quarterless Collins, a Comic Poem* (London, 1833).

Selected secondary sources

Arnstein, W. L., 'Queen Victoria opens Parliament: the disinvention of tradition', *Historical Research*, 63 (1990), 178–94.

Aspinall, A. (ed.), *Letters of King George IV* (Cambridge, 1938).

Aspinall, A. (ed.), *The Later Correspondence of George III*, 5 vols (Cambridge, 1962–70).

Barrell, J., 'Imaginary treason, imaginary law: the State trials of 1794', in *The Birth of Pandora and the Division of Knowledge* (Basingstoke, 1992).

Barrell, J., 'Imagining the King's death: the arrest of Richard Brothers', *History Workshop Journal*, 37 (1994), 1–33.

Barrell, J., 'Sad stories: Louis XVI, George III and the language of sentiment' in Sharpe, K. and Zwicker, S. N. (eds), *Refiguring Revolutions: Aesthetics and Politics from the English Revolution to the Romantic Revolution* (Berkeley, CA, 1998).

Belchem, J., 'Republicanism, popular constitutionalism and the radical platform in early nineteenth-century England', *Social History*, 6 (1981), 1–32.

Belchem, J., *'Orator' Hunt: Henry Hunt and Working Class Radicalism* (Oxford, 1985).

Belchem, J., *Popular Radicalism in Nineteenth-Century Britain* (London, 1996).

Bloch, M., *The Royal Touch: Sacred Monarchy and Scrofula in England and France* (London, 1973).

Bradley, J. E., *Popular Politics and the American Revolution in England: Petitions, the Crown and Public Opinion* (Macon, 1986).

Cannadine, D., 'The context, performance and meaning of ritual: the British monarchy and the invention of tradition, c. 1820–1977', in Hobsbawm, E. and Ranger, T. (eds) *The Invention of Tradition* (Cambridge, 1983), pp. 101–65.

Cannadine, D., 'The last Hanoverian sovereign? The Victorian monarchy in historical perspective, 1688–1988', in Beier, A. L., Cannadine, D. and Rosenheim, J. M. (eds) *The First Modern Society: Essays in English History in Honour of Lawrence Stone* (Cambridge, 1989).

Cannon, J., 'The survival of the British monarchy', *Transactions of the Royal Historical Society*, fifth series, 36, (1986).

Carretta, V., *George III and the Satirists from Hogarth to Byron* (Athens, GA, 1990).

Black, J., *Robert Walpole and the Nature of Politics in Early Eighteenth-Century Britain* (London, 1990).

Brewer, J., *Party Ideology and Popular Politics at the Accession of George III* (Cambridge, 1976).

Claeys, G., 'The origins of the rights of labour: republicanism, commerce and the construction of modern social theory in Britain, 1796–1805', *Journal of Modern History*, 66 (1994), 249–90.

Claeys, G. (ed.), *The Politics of English Jacobinism: Writings of John Thelwall* (Pennsylvania, 1995).

Clark, J. C. D., *English Society, 1688–1832: Ideology, Social Structure and Political Practice during the Ancien Régime* (Cambridge, 1985).

Colley, L., 'The apotheosis of George III: loyalty, royalty and the British nation, 1760–1821', *Past and Present*, 102 (1984), 94–129.

Colley, L., *Britons: Forging the Nation, 1707–1837* (New Haven, CT, 1992).

Condren, C., *The Language of Politics in Seventeenth-Century England* (London, 1994).

Dickinson, H. T., 'The eighteenth-century debate on the Glorious Revolution', *History*, 61 (1976), 28–45.

Dickinson, H. T., *Liberty and Property: Political Ideology in Eighteenth-Century Britain* (London, 1977).

Eastwood, D., 'Patriotism and the English State in the 1790s', in Philp, M. (ed.), *The French Revolution and British Popular Politics* (Cambridge, 1991).

Eastwood, D., 'John Reeves and the contested idea of the Constitution', *British Journal of Eighteenth Century Studies*, 16:2 (1993), 197–212.

Elliott, M., *Partners in Revolution: The United Irishmen and France* (New Haven, CT, 1982).
Epstein, J., *Radical Expression: Political Language, Ritual and Symbol in England, 1790–1850* (Oxford, 1994).
Fargé, A., *Subversive Words: Public Opinion in Eighteenth-Century France* (Oxford, 1994).
Ford, F. L., *Political Murder: From Tyrannicide to Terrorism* (Cambridge, MA, 1985).
Fortescue, J. (ed.), *Correspondence of George III, 1760–1783*, 5 vols (London, 1928).
Fraser, P., 'Public petitioning and Parliament before 1832', *History*, 46 (1961), 195–211.
Gatrell, V. A. C., *The Hanging Tree: Execution and the English People, 1770–1868* (Oxford, 1994).
Gossman, N. J., 'Republicanism in nineteenth-century England', *International Review of Social History*, 7 (1962), 47–60.
Harling, P., 'The Duke of York affair (1809) and the complexities of war-time patriotism', *Historical Journal*, 39:4 (1996), 963–84.
Harling, P., 'Leigh Hunt's *Examiner* and the language of patriotism', *English Historical Review*, 444 (1996), 1159–81.
Hellmuth, E. (ed.), *The Transformation of Political Culture: England and Germany in the Late Eighteenth Century* (Oxford, 1990).
Hobsbawm, E., and Ranger, T. (eds), *The Invention of Tradition* (Cambridge, 1983).
Homans, M., *Royal Representations: Queen Victoria and British Culture, 1837–1876* (Chicago, IL, 1998).
Homans, M., and Munich, A. (eds), *Remaking Queen Victoria* (Cambridge, 1997).
Hone, J. A., *For the Cause of Truth: Radicalism in London, 1796–1821* (Oxford, 1982).
Hunt, T., 'Morality and monarchy in the Queen Caroline affair', *Albion*, 23 (1991), 697–722.
Jacobson, D. L. (ed.), *The English Libertarian Heritage* (San Francisco, CA, 1965).
Kelly, G., 'From lèse-majesté to lèse-nation: treason in eighteenth-century France', *Journal of the History of Ideas*, 42:3 (1981), 270–86.
Kley, D. K. Van, *The Damiens' Affair and the Unravelling of the Ancien Régime, 1750–1770* (Princeton, NJ, 1984).
Knights, M., 'Petitioning and the political theorists: John Locke, Algernon Sidney and London's monster petition of 1680', *Past and Present*, 138 (1993), 94–111.
Kriegel, A. D. (ed.), *The Holland House Diaries, 1831–1840: The diary of Henry Richard Vassall Fox, third Lord Holland, with extracts from the diary of Dr. John Allen*, London, 1977.
Kromm, J. E., 'The feminisation of madness in visual representation', *Feminist Studies*, 20:3 (1994), 507–35.
Kuhn, W. M., *Democratic Royalism: The Transformation of the British Monarchy, 1861–1914* (London, 1996).
Laqueur, 'The Queen Caroline affair: politics as art in the reign of George IV', *Journal of Modern History*, 54 (1982), 417–66.
Leys, C., 'Petitioning in the nineteenth and twentieth centuries', *Political Studies*, 3:1 (1955), 45–64.
Loriga, S., 'A secret to kill the King: magic and protection in Piedmont in the eighteenth century', in Muir, E. and Ruggiero, G. (eds), *History from Crime* (Baltimore, MD, 1994).
Macalpine, I. and Hunter, R., *George III and the Mad Business* (London, 1969).

McCalman, I., *Radical Under: Prophets, Revolutionaries and Pornographers in London, 1795–1840* (Oxford, 1993).

McWilliam, R., *Popular Politics in Nineteenth-Century England* (London, 1998).

Malcolm, J. L., 'Doing no wrong: law, liberty and the constraint of kings', *Journal of British Studies*, 38 (1999), 161–86.

Mee, J., 'Apocalypse and ambivalence: the politics of millenarianism in the 1790s', *South Atlantic Quarterly*, 95:3 (1996), 672–97.

Monod, P. K., *Jacobitism and the English People, 1688–1788* (Cambridge, 1989).

Morris, M., *The British Monarchy and the French Revolution* (New Haven, CT, 1998).

Munich, A., *Queen Victoria's Secrets* (New York, 1996).

Newman, G., *The Rise of English Nationalism: A Cultural History, 1740–1830* (London, 1987).

Palmer, S. H., *Police and Protest in England and Ireland, 1780–1850* (Cambridge, 1988).

Patterson, A., 'Secret history: liberal politics and the 1832 Reform Bill', *Literature and History*, third series, 7:1 (1989), 33–53.

Porter, R., *Mind-Forg'd Manacles: A History of Madness in England from the Restoration to the Regency* (London, 1987).

Porter, R., *A Social History of Madness: Stories of the Insane* (London, 1987).

Prochaska, F., *Royal Bounty: The Making of a Welfare Monarchy* (New Haven, CT, 1995).

Prothero, I. J., *Artisans and Politics in Early Nineteenth-Century London: John Gast and his Times* (London, 1979).

Rempel, L., 'Cartnal satire and the constitutional king: George III in James Gillray's *Monstrous Craws at a New Coalition Feast*', *Art History*, 18:1 (1995), 4–23.

Rogers, N., *Crowds, Culture and Politics in Georgian Britain* (Oxford, 1998).

Rudé, G., *Wilkes and Liberty* (London, 1962).

Sack, J., *From Jacobite to Conservative: Reaction and Orthodoxy in Britain, c. 1760–1832* (Cambridge, 1993).

Sainsbury, J., *Disaffected Patriots: London Supporters of Revolutionary America, 1769–1782* (Gloucester, 1987).

Saville, J., *1848: The British State and the Chartist Movement* (Cambridge, 1987).

Schama, S., 'The domestication of majesty: royal family portraiture, 1500–1850', *Journal of Interdisciplinary History*, 17:1 (1986), 155–83.

Scull, A., *The Most Solitary of Afflictions: Madness and Society in Britain, 1700–1900* (New Haven, CT, 1993).

Sheppard, E., *Memorials of St. James's Palace*, 2 vols (London, 1894).

Small, H., *Love's Madness: Medicine, the Novel and Female Insanity, 1800–1865* (Oxford, 1996).

Smith, F. B., 'Lights and shadows in the life of John Freeman', *Victorian Studies*, 30 (1987), 459–73.

Smith, R. and Moore, J. S. (eds), *The Monarchy: Fifteen Hundred Years of British Tradition* (London, 1998).

Strachey, L. and Fulford, R. (eds), *The Greville Memoirs*, vol. 5: *1814–60* (London, 1938).

Taylor, A., 'Reynolds's Newspaper, opposition to monarchy and the radical anti-Jubilee: Britain's anti-monarchist tradition reconsidered', *Historical Research*, 68:167 (1995), 319–35.

Thale, M. (ed.), *The Autobiography of Francis Place* (Cambridge, 1972).

Thale, M. (ed.), *Selections from the Papers of the London Corresponding Society, 1792–1799* (Cambridge, 1983).
Thompson, D., *The Chartists* (London, 1984).
Thompson, D., *Queen Victoria: The Woman, the Monarchy and the People* (New York, 1990).
Thompson, D., 'Queen Victoria, the monarchy and gender', in *Outsiders: Class, Gender and Nation* (London, 1993).
Thompson, E. P., *The Making of the English Working Class* (London, 1963).
Tilly, C., *Popular Contention in Great Britain, 1758–1834* (Cambridge, MA, 1995).
Vernon, J. (ed.), *Re-Reading the Constitution: New narratives in the Political History of England's Long Nineteenth Century* (Cambridge, 1996).
Wahrman, D., *Imagining the Middle Class: The Political Representation of Class in Britain, c. 1780–1840* (Cambridge, 1995).
Walker, A. M. and Dickerman, E. H., 'Mind of an assassin: Ravaillac and the murder of Henry IV of France', *Canadian Journal of History*, 30 (1995), 201–29.
Walker, N., *Crime and Insanity in England*, vol. 1: *The Historical Perspective* (Edinburgh, 1968).
Walzer, M., *Regicide and Revolution: Speeches at the Trial of Louis XVI* (Cambridge, 1974).
Wells, R., *Insurrection: The British Experience, 1795–1803* (Gloucester, 1986).
Wharam, A., *The Treason Trials, 1794* (Leicester, 1992).
Wharam, A., *Treason: Famous English Treason Trials* (Stroud, 1995).
Wilson, K., 'Inventing revolution: 1688 and eighteenth-century popular politics', *Journal of British Studies*, 28 (1989), 349–86.
Wilson, K., *The Sense of the People: Politics, Culture and Imperialism in England, 1715–1785* (Cambridge, 1995).
Worrall, D., *Radical Culture: Discourse, Resistance and Surveillance, 1790–1820* (Detroit, MI, 1992).
Zaller, R., 'The figure of the tyrant in English revolutionary thought', *Journal of the History of Ideas*, 54:4 (1993), 585–610.
Ziegler, P., *King William IV* (London, 1971).

Index

Lightning Source UK Ltd.
Milton Keynes UK
UKOW030615170712

196099UK00003B/17/P